THE SIGNET CLASSIC POETRY SERIES is under the general editorship of poet, lecturer, and teacher JOHN HOLLANDER. Mr. Hollander's first volume of poetry, *A Crackling of Thorns,* won the Yale Series of Younger Poets Awards for 1958. He was a recipient of a National Institute of Arts and Letters grant (1963) and has been a member of the Wesleyan University Press Poetry Board and the Bollingen Poetry Translation Prize Board. Mr. Hollander is Professor of English at Hunter College.

THE SELECTED POETRY AND PROSE OF SIR PHILIP SIDNEY is edited by David Kalstone. Dr. Kalstone received his Ph.D. from Harvard in 1961. He has taught at Harvard and is currently an Associate Professor of English at Rutgers University. He has been a Fulbright Fellow and has authored a critical work on Sir Philip Sidney, as well as co-edited the text *Beginning with Poems.*

Sir Philip Sidney

SELECTED POETRY
AND
PROSE

Edited by David Kalstone

The Signet Classic Poetry Series
GENERAL EDITOR: JOHN HOLLANDER

A SIGNET MODERN CLASSIC from
NEW AMERICAN LIBRARY
TIMES MIRROR
New York and Toronto
The New English Library Limited, London

SIGNET TRADEMARK REG. U.S. PAT. OFF. AND FOREIGN COUNTRIES
REGISTERED TRADEMARK—MARCA REGISTRADA
HECHO EN CHICAGO, U.S.A.

SIGNET, SIGNET CLASSICS, MENTOR AND PLUME BOOKS
are published *in the United States* by The New American Library,
Inc., 1301 Avenue of the Americas, New York, New York 10019,
in Canada by The New American Library of Canada Limited,
295 King Street East, Toronto 2, Ontario,
in the United Kingdom by The New English Library Limited,
Barnard's Inn, Holborn, London, E.C. 1, England

First Printing, June, 1970

PRINTED IN THE UNITED STATES OF AMERICA

Contents

Introduction   *vii*

A General Note on the Text   *xxxi*

A Note on This Edition   *xxxiii*

Chronology   *xxxv*

Selected Bibliography   *xxxvii*

The Lady of May   39

From *The Countess of Pembroke's Arcadia*   53

From *Certain Sonnets*   105

Astrophel and Stella   121

From *The Psalms of David*   197

Other Poems   205

An Apology for Poetry   213

Introduction

In your letters I fancy I see a picture of the age in which we live: an age that resembles a bow too long bent, it must be unstrung or it will break. (Sidney to Hubert Languet)

For, both the mind itself must (like other things) sometimes be unbent, or else it will be either weakened or broken. . . . (Pyrocles to Musidorus, from *The Countess of Pembroke's Arcadia*)

Whether in the letters of others or in the speeches of his own created characters, Sidney's instinct is for the stresses of experience, all the adventurous possibilities and tense dangers represented by the tightly strung bow. But what is especially characteristic is his understanding a sense of danger not for opponents, but for those who wield the bow. His poems, whether spoken by the sonneteer Astrophel or by the heroic figures of the *Arcadia,* are marked by a rich sense of possibility, "great expectation," and by an equally sharp grasp of our resources for self-bafflement. The image, preserved in schoolboys' legends, of the noble courtier-poet, the hero of Zutphen, is not canceled but enriched by his acute sense of the mind's essential discords. The more one reads his work, particularly the love sonnets of *Astrophel and Stella*, the more one notices poems pointed toward the *discovery* of conflict—not, in other words, exercising the wise introspection of many of Shakespeare's sonnets ("When I consider everything that grows . . ."; "When I have seen by Time's fell hand defaced . . ."), but the pained acknowledgment of desire and will ("But ah, Desire still cries, give me some food").

It is useful to remind ourselves that such excitements are in store in sampling Sidney's work. For he did not so radically challenge poetic traditions as Donne did. He re-

vived and extended the accepted repertoire of lyric forms—
deserving to be called the "English Petrarke," though at
the same time he was calling Petrarchan energies into question. He wrote, in full accord with Renaissance theory, a
prose epic, though its principal action is a dangerous withdrawal from action. In other words, his success in renewing
Renaissance genres—heroic romance and pastoral lyric in
the *Arcadia*, the love sonnet in *Astrophel and Stella*—rests
on a lively awareness of the interplay between poetry's
visionary powers and the complicated impulses of a fallen
world. Himself a critic, Sidney provided in the *Apology
for Poetry* our definitive statement of the claims of poetry
to moral supremacy: the poet brings forth a "golden
world"; he is superior even to the philosopher who "replenisheth the memory with many infallible grounds of
wisdom: which notwithstanding, lie dark before the imaginative and judging power, if they be not illuminated or
figured forth by the speaking picture of poesy." It takes
some acquaintance with Sidney's own poetic practice to
understand how richly he interprets that role. He resists,
for example, any narrow definitions of the scope of the
heroic poem. Its moral intentions are, for him, still pri-
mary: "For as the image of each action stirreth and in-
structeth the mind, so the lofty image of such worthies,
most inflameth the mind with desire to be worthy." Heroic
literature (Sidney includes both poetry and prose) "maketh
magnanimity and justice shine, throughout all misty fearfulness and foggy desires." But he is alive to alternative
energies and particularly to the claims of love. To the
enemies of poetry who protest the demoralizing influence
of love in literature ("the lyric is larded with passionate
sonnets . . . even to the heroical, Cupid hath ambitiously
climbed"), to these objections Sidney can reply:

> Alas Love, I would, thou couldest as well defend thy-
> self, as thou canst offend others. I would those, on
> whom thou dost attend, could either put thee away, or
> yield good reason, why they keep thee. But grant love
> of beauty, to be a beastly fault, (although it be very hard,
> sith only man, and no beast, hath that gift, to discern
> beauty). Grant, that lovely name of Love, to deserve all

hateful reproaches: (although even some of my masters the philosophers, spent a good deal of their lamp-oil, in setting forth the excellency of it.) Grant, I say, whatsoever they will have granted; that not only love, but lust, but vanity, but (if they list) scurrility, possesseth many leaves of the poets' books: yet think I, when this is granted, they will find, their sentence may with good manners, put the last words foremost: and not say, that poetry abuseth man's wit, but that, man's wit abuseth poetry.

The animation and play of wit is characteristically Sidneyan. A definition of love emerges slyly through the play of parentheses, and the value of love as subject in Renaissance epic is triumphantly affirmed, while he gives a guarded account of its pitfalls. Looking with a fresh eye at the implications of the traditional genres—heroic and amatory—he discovers his own poetic subject in the competing energies of love and heroic obligation and in the lively interplay of the poetic forms that express them. Whether in love sonnets, pastoral poetry, or prose romance, such choices of life are proposed, sometimes self-consciously in debates, sometimes acted out in moments of difficulty and decision by characters caught in the toils of desire.

There is very little mistaking Sidney for his greater or lesser contemporaries. In an anthology of English pastoral poems, one would always recognize as his

> Come shepherd's weeds, become your master's mind:
> Yield outward show, what inward change he tries:
> Nor be abasht, since such a guest you find,
> Whose strongest hope in your weak comfort lies.
>
> Come shepherd's weeds, attend my woeful cries:
> Disuse yourselves from sweet Menalcas' voice:
> For other be those tunes which sorrow ties,
> From those clear notes which freely may rejoice.
>   Then pour out plaint, and in one word say this:
>   Helpless his plaint, who spoils himself of bliss.

The poem, from Book I of the *Arcadia,* marks the moment when one of the heroes, Musidorus, takes on a shepherd's

disguise in order to penetrate the forest retreat of King
Basilius and woo his daughter Pamela. Musidorus' song is
a grave version of pastoral lyric; it does not relax to possible pleasures as does a poem like Marlowe's "Come live
with me, and be my love." Musidorus reluctantly enters the
pastoral world, "spoils himself of bliss." Nor is the difference between Sidney's poem and Marlowe's simply the
difference between a pastoral lament and an invitation to
pastoral leisure; it has to do, as well, with the manner in
which each adopts a pastoral fiction. The speaker of "Come
live with me" is every bit as aware of his courtly identity
as Musidorus is:

> And I will make thee beds of roses,
> And a thousand fragrant po(e)sies,
> A cap of flowers, and a kirtle,
> Embroidered all with leaves of myrtle.
>
> A gown made of the finest wool,
> Which from our pretty lambs we pull,
> Fair linèd slippers for the cold:
> With buckles of the purest gold.

For all his retreat Marlowe's shepherd still offers the sophisticated pleasures of court: "Fair linèd slippers . . .
buckles of the purest gold . . . coral clasps and amber
studs." He includes gestures which would be, in the perfumed chambers of London, either trite (everyone has
golden buckles there) or decadent (beds of roses). He
freshens those gestures by placing them side by side with
reminders of the first innocence of love and of the freedom and playfulness which should accompany it. For a
moment in Marlowe's poem, we are invited to richness
worthy of court, but by the speaker's puns ("beds of
roses,/And a thousand fragrant poesies") and by his
charming awkwardness, purged of all jaded associations.
We are far from the heavily scented opulence of Cleopatra's
paradise, where souls "do couch on flowers."

Sidney's sober invocations alert us immediately to pastoral which is, for responsible heroes, almost entirely a
landscape of the mind. They do not enjoy the elegant
freshness of Marlowe's shepherd but, rather, welcome

pleasures that must be judiciously weighed against civilized
obligations. Shepherd's garb must, ambiguously, "become"
(complement? symbolize?) the speaker's mind; "outward
show" must express "inward change." Musidorus is, above
all, "master," self-conscious about his powers and aware
that he is only adopting a shepherd's role as fictive clothing. Through his stage directions ("Come shepherd's
weeds") he makes explicit what is implicit in most pastoral
love poetry: that pastoral deals in a sophisticated way with
problems which concern civilized people; that whatever
courtly or urban cares they cast aside, they still have their
own treacherous hearts to deal with. The confused feelings
of lovers in later plays like *As You Like It* and *Midsum-
mer Night's Dream* were to be dramatized and clarified by
means of their pastoral stays. What sets Sidney's Arcadian
heroes apart is their self-conscious adoption of such roles
(Musidorus carefully distinguishes his poem from that of
"sweet Menalcas"). They are not subject to embodiments
of willful love in the way that Shakespeare's young Athenian lovers are victims of the whims of Titania, Oberon,
and their servant Puck. Whatever wild confusions of identity occur are *willed* by the heroic lovers themselves. They
give themselves over to love, while judiciously marking its
stages and reminding us that pastoral poems are instruments of meditation, a way of describing and, to an extent,
controlling their feelings. Hence the hypnotic explicitness
of a lament Musidorus sings to the princess Pamela, "to
show what kind of shepherd I was":

> My sheep are thoughts, which I both guide and serve:
> Their pasture is fair hills of fruitless love:
> On barren sweets they feed, and feeding sterve:
> I wail their lot, but will not other prove.
> My sheephook is wan hope, which all upholds:
> My weeds, desire, cut out in endless folds.
> > What wool my sheep shall bear, while thus they live,
> > In you it is, you must the judgement give.
> > > > (*Arcadia*, Book II)

Sidney's pastoral lyrics are valuable to his heroes as part
of the education of their feelings. Nor can the reader of

the *Arcadia* mistake the clarity with which these early lyrics are written so as to guide us, always explicit about how we must read and interpret the pastoral experience. Sidney's acuteness as a literary critic is never far from the surface of his verse.

In retrospect it looks as if the first audience Sidney sought to instruct included the Queen herself. The pastoral entertainment which came to be known in the eighteenth century as *The Lady of May* was written—probably in 1578—for one of Elizabeth I's visits to Wanstead, an estate of the Earl of Leicester. "Here, as everywhere in his writings, Sidney is above all a critic, and so we find this masque returning constantly to questions of its own form."[1] So special was Sidney's point of view, so playful was he in using pastoral conventions, that much of his critical originality seems to have been lost on the occasion. At the conclusion, when the Queen is asked to choose between rival suitors for the hand of the young shepherdess, the May Lady, "it pleased her Majesty" to reward the shepherd Espilus rather than his rival, the forester Therion. The report of the masque gives us no explanations: "What words, what reasons she used for it, this paper, which carrieth so base names, is not worthy to contain." Yet her choice may well have come as a disappointment to the author, who had composed for the conclusion a song consoling the shepherd's god, Pan, for his defeat at the hands of the forest god Silvanus: "Poor Pan (he said) although thou beaten be,/It is no shame, since Hercules was he."

The triumph of Hercules, archetypal man of action, in a pastoral masque suggests the unexpected drifts and eddies of *The Lady of May*. Espilus (the Greek derivation appears to be "felt-presser") does much that he should do. The May Lady describes him "sitting under some sweet bush, sometimes they say he records my name in doleful verses." But like his comic ancestors, the bumptious Polyphemus of Theocritus and Corydon in Virgil's second eclogue, he

[1] Stephen Orgel, *The Jonsonian Masque* (Cambridge, 1965), p. 46.

assumes that his weight in wool will recommend him: "Two thousand sheep I have as white as milk/. . . All this I give, let me possess thy grace." In their singing contest Therion, the forester (his name means "wild beast") chooses to undercut the shepherd's conventional rhetoric ("shallow brooks do yield the greatest sound") and offer an alternative view of wealth and personality:

> Two thousand deer in wildest woods I have,
> Them can I take, but you I cannot hold:
> He is not poor who can his freedom save,
> Bound but to you, no wealth but you I would.

The lady is faced with a rather modern choice: "Whether the many deserts and many faults of Therion, or the very small deserts and no faults of Espilus be to be preferred." From the debate that follows it is clear that Sidney is asking the observer to judge freshly the "sad shepherd" of Renaissance complaints. The contest passes into a general argument between Rixus, a young forester, and Dorcas, an old shepherd, over the merits of their respective ways of life. When the May Lady tenders the decision to the Queen, she stresses "that in judging me, you judge more than me in it." Though the shepherds' claim to traditional contemplative joys is strong, a more inclusive alternative is offered by the young woodsman, Rixus:

> I was saying the shepherd's life had some goodness in it, because it borrowed of the country quietness something like ours, but that is not all, for ours besides that quiet part, doth both strengthen the body, and raise up the mind with this gallant sort of activity. O sweet contentation to see the long life of the hurtless trees, to see how in straight growing up, though never so high, they hinder not their fellows, they only enviously trouble, which are crookedly bent. What life is to be compared to ours where the very growing things are ensamples of goodness?

Offering a richer metaphor, Rixus envisions a life that has both "country quietness" and "gallant activity" which "doth both strengthen the body, and raise up the mind." Sidney's incorporation of both action and contemplation into the forester's life may have been a stroke lost on his noble audience. Perhaps the shepherd Espilus triggered precisely the familiar response that Sidney challenged and redefined. Perhaps the audience was prone to judge from spectacle and not pay elaborate attention to the poet's words, as Jonson so often complained in his efforts "to make the spectators understanders." Or, as Robert Kimbrough suggests,[2] the immediate political point of *The Lady of May* might have been an appeal for the more vigorous Protestant policies of Leicester—an appeal which displeased the Queen and dictated her choice of the safer shepherd. All we have to guide us is a report of her decision and Sidney's lively little text, which, from the moment it introduces the false rhetorician, the pedantic Rombus, sharpens our suspicion of the stock response, puts us off balance, widens the eyes a bit, like Yeats's dancer, who, as she is urged to new understandings, remembers that "they say such different things at school."

The Lady of May, with its refusal to separate the active and contemplative lives, proved to be a trial run for Sidney's major essay in pastoral, *The Countess of Pembroke's Arcadia.* The adventures of its text are in themselves illuminating. We now possess two versions: the original or *Old Arcadia,* which Sidney probably composed during visits to his sister, the Countess of Pembroke, from 1577 to 1580, and the *New Arcadia,* an incomplete recasting undertaken perhaps in 1584. The *Old Arcadia* was unknown until this century; the version rooted in English literary history—the one Charles I chose to take to the scaffold and Milton found "vain" and "amatorious"—proves to be a hybrid. Editions of 1593 and the canonical folio of 1598 —probably overseen by Sidney's sister—print the two and a half books Sidney had already revised and fill out the volume, slightly bowdlerized, with the final books of the old, unrevised *Arcadia.*

[2] Robert Kimbrough and Philip Murphy, "The Helmingham Hall ms. of Sidney's *The Lady of May,*" *Renaissance Drama: New Series I: Essays Principally on Masques and Entertainments* (Evanston, 1968).

In his revisions Sidney added heroic material and made alterations which help us understand the strange pressured nature of his Arcadian poems. The *New Arcadia* opens with the entrance of the heroes Pyrocles and Musidorus into that pastoral world where they are to test and be tested by love. The details of their heroic education and adventures (considerably expanded from the *Old Arcadia*) are told by the heroes themselves as part of their wooing. While it is true that they want the princesses Pamela and Philoclea to love them for the dangers they have passed, their courting narratives must overcome an even simpler obstacle. King Basilius has superstitiously withdrawn himself and his family into a forest retreat, given his kingdom to regents, and cloistered his daughters from the attentions of suitors. To reach the princesses, the two heroes must cast off their heroic attire and assume disguises, Pyrocles as the Amazon Zelmane, Musidorus as the shepherd Dorus. Their task in recounting the heroic tales of Pyrocles and Musidorus is, in part, to give away their secret, to allow their heroic identities to shine through their disguises. But their mosaic of tales, much of it added to the *New Arcadia,* serves a more interesting purpose: it allows the adventures to be told retrospectively, not struck out of the chaos of battle, but shaped, assimilated, understood, the princes' heroic image kept always before them.

Any reader of the *Apology for Poetry* will recognize the stress on memory and mastery that Pyrocles and Musidorus display in the telling of their tales. During their youthful training, they received "conceits not unworthy of the best speakers . . . images . . . then delivered to their memory, which after, their stronger judgements might dispense. . . ." What happens to them is what happens to the reader of literature as Sidney describes it in the *Apology:* "This purifying of wit, this enriching of memory, enabling of judgement, and enlarging of conceit, which commonly we call learning." Sidney's emphasis is never on simple participation in the stream of events, or even on simple delight and fear of the images before one, but rather on control and mastery. His heroes are not breathless storytellers; they become *readers* of their experience. Telling their adventures retrospectively allows the hidden connections of political disorder and sexual treachery to emerge for them. Spenser's knights, the heroic Britomart and Redcrosse, do not interpret themselves aloud for us; much more is discovered to the reader through their participation in the welter of events. What surprises us in the *Arcadia* is the degree to which Pyrocles and Musidorus are both participants in and interpreters of their experience.

Only against this background can one fully respond to the strange-sounding eclogues of the *Arcadia*. Their peculiarity has almost nothing to do with literary notions of an idealized pastoral world; Sidney's garden has real toads in it. The songs (excluding the eclogues written for the real shepherds of Arcadia) are designed for speakers whose entanglements in love are to be measured against the heroic careers which they recount with the measured assurance of the prepared mind. The poems have a choric function, the pursuits of love for a moment stilled in verse that bears the pressure of judgement. Obviously the fullest response to these poems comes when they are read within their prose frame. (I have tried in notes to give at least some indication of their dramatic context. To relish fully Pyrocles' song (p. 55) we need to realize that this is the first glimpse both Musidorus and the reader have of that hero rigged out as the Amazon Zelmane. Musidorus, who conceives a healthy lust for the attractive figure in the woods, stops short, realizing it is the disguised Pyrocles, and turns to give his companion a stern lecture about the dangers of desire. This is the song that warns him who the Amazon really is:

> Transformed in show, but more transformed in mind,
> I cease to strive, with double conquest foiled:
> For (woe is me) my powers all I find
> With outward force and inward treason spoiled.
>
> For from without came to mine eyes the blow,
> Whereto mine inward thoughts did faintly yield:
> Both these conspired poor Reason's overthrow;
> False in myself, thus have I lost the field.

Thus are my eyes still captive to one sight,
Thus all my thoughts are slaves to one thought still:
Thus Reason to his servants yields his right,
Thus is my power transformèd to your will:
  What marvel then I take a woman's hue,
  Since what I see, think, know is all but you?

Pyrocles' sonnet serves both as self-appraisal and as the appeal of a lamenting lover. Twice over, he surveys his "inward treason" and the orderly crumbling of command: eyes subdue thoughts, and the two conquer Reason. It is through elegant patterning that Pyrocles interprets his disguise and most precisely leads us into a landscape of the mind. The octave measures thoughts in two-line units, within lines or pairs of lines setting out clear oppositions: "transformed in show . . . transformed in mind"; "strive . . . double conquest"; "from without . . . inward thoughts." But this judiciousness is eased by a more delicate movement. Even before the sestet, he begins emphatic concessions in more rapid one-line units: "thus have I lost . . . thus are my eyes . . . thus all my thoughts . . . thus Reason . . . thus is my power." We soon forget that "thus" has a logical function and hear it not as part of a controlled deduction, but as an insistent repetition, tolling the spoils yielded finally at "your will." (This is a swelling of movement which Sidney made more intense by revising the version in the *Old Arcadia*, where the pattern was weakened in lines 9 and 10: "And thus mine eyes are placed still in one sight/And thus my thoughts can think but one thing still.") From rueful self-appraisal the sonnet finally moves toward more intimate direct address; the whole process becomes a tribute to his mistress. His disguise, first reflecting his fall from heroic control, is at the close slyly offered as a sign that he thinks only of his lady and so adopts, as compliment, "a woman's hue." As so many of the princes' poems do, this sonnet starts by finding in details of their pastoral retreat, emblems of their inner state. ("Come shepherd's weeds, become your master's mind"; "My sheep are thoughts, which I both guide and serve.") But Pyrocles' sonnet *becomes* a love poem before our eyes; it finally turns to compliment, though, as is so often true in the *Arcadia,* lyrical elements are strongly subordinated to sober evaluations of love.

Such poems are, as Neil Rudenstine has pointed out,[8] "essentially toneless." Their patterns suggest an unbreakable circle of desire.[4] Though not totally absent, the accents of individual speech and quickened feeling enter in quietly perceptible ways: in such effects as the measured acceleration of the sestet in "Transformed in show . . ."; or a momentary twist away from the dominant iambics ("This is thy work thou god for ever blind/Though thousands old, a boy entitled still"). The emphatic rhythm at the outset of this latter example prepares for an equally emphatic metaphor: "Thus children do the silly birds they find,/ With stroking hurt and too much cramming kill" (see p. 68). Yet this sonnet, like most of the Arcadian poems, deliberately limits variations of feeling, allows only a flash of indignation. It begins and ends by stressing the almost diagrammatic nature of love, in helplessly balanced paradox: "Lovèd I am, and yet complain of Love"; "Let me be lov'd, or else not lovèd be." For these heroes and heroines, love is a condition in which they are caught; they reflect upon and assimilate it by repeated celebrations of its pattern. This is the sense in which Sidney's rhetorical arrangements perform a choric function. The props of pastoral are for the royal figures only ways of performing these ceremonials, enacting the extremity of one of the *Certain Sonnets* (p. 114): "Infected minds infect each thing they see."

Sidney insistently marks the heroes off from the Arcadian shepherds and from the relief of a pastoral invitation like that of Thyrsis' promise to Kala (First Eclogues, p. 61):

> I will you music yield
> In flow'ry field, and as the day begins
> With twenty gins we will the small birds take,
> And pastimes make, as Nature things hath made.

[8] Neil Rudenstine, *Sidney's Poetic Development,* pp. 75-90.   [4] David Kalstone, *Sidney's Poetry* (Cambridge, 1965), pp. 85–88.

But when in shade we meet of myrtle boughs,
Then love allows our pleasures to enrich,
The thought of which doth pass all worldly pelf.

In the singing contest of which this is part, such pastoral pleasures are available to the princely shepherd Dorus— the disguised Musidorus—only as an inventory of his state, a litany of his troubles:

my tunes waymenting yield:
Despair my field; the flowers spirit's wars:
My day new cares; my gins my daily sight,
In which do light small birds of thoughts o'erthrown:

Here, as in "My sheep are thoughts" or "Over these brooks" (p. 68), Sidney's noble speakers are flailing for emblems and finding in their activity no relief. The effort demands an essentially static poetry, multiplying the effects of single-line units rather than drawing out the sense from line to line. The technique can generate great force, as in the most powerful of the *Arcadia*'s poems, the double sestina "Ye goatherd gods" (p. 71), where the ceaseless return to six key words prepares a crescendo of unbearable desire: "Meseems I hear, when I do hear sweet music,/ The dreadful cries of murd'red men in forests"; "Shamèd I hate myself in sight of mountains,/And stop mine ears, lest I grow mad with music."

Sidney has been praised, justly, for his experiments in domesticating European verse forms and meters. But it should be clear that such echoing forms as the double sestina served him in special ways, allowing him to convey the vivid sense of imprisonment which the Arcadian lovers feel. Sidney's interest in Italian prosody[5] (the *sdrucciola,* with its accent falling on the antepenultimate syllable of the line; the *femina,* or feminine rhyme) is a way of drawing out for himself certain potentialities of English rhythms, as he does in the dying fall of each of the six rhyme words in the double sestina: *mountains, valleys, forests, music, morning, evening;* or in the *sdrucciola* of one of the singing contests: "Shallow brooks murmur most, deep silent slide

[5] See *Apology,* p. 269.

away,/Nor true-love loves, his loves with other mingled be."

It would be hard to distinguish these effects from his experiments in applying classical prosody to English verse, had not several surviving manuscripts marked the quantities for us. In the *Apology* Sidney notes the value of accentual verse, "more fit lively to express divers passions, by the low or lofty sound of the well-weighed syllable." These asclepiadics ("O sweet woods the delight of solitariness"), anacreontics ("My muse what ails this ardor"), sapphics ("If mine eyes can speak to do hearty errand") prove a perfect medium for the effect of repeated gravity Sidney wants to obtain. The principal rule followed is that of vowels "long by position," that is, considered long because they precede two consonants, even if the sound in English would not be considered long, or the syllable itself not receive a stress. This guarantees a recurring pattern of thinning and thickening consonants and hence a weighty control of English lines.

So, for example, Pyrocles-Zelmane's eclogue, "If mine eyes can speak to do hearty errand" (p. 62). Hoping that Philoclea will penetrate his disguise, the warrior "as if . . . long restrained conceits had new burst out of prison . . . laying fast hold on her face with [his] eyes, . . . sang these sapphics." For all the passionate intensity of the stage directions, the song is partly a grave argument exploring, with its "if's" and "yet's" and "thus," and with its posing of alternatives from one stanza to another, the possibility that Philoclea will not recognize him, will not understand the feelings expressed directly to her. Even if she does not reward him, sober "soul" and "mind" ("Fleshly vail consumes; but a soul hath his life") will preserve her praise in a measured rhapsody:

> If the senseless spheres do yet hold a music,
> If the swan's sweet voice be not heard, but at death,
> If the mute timber when it hath the life lost,
>   Yieldeth a lute's tune:

We move to the measured sly relief of the last stanza, virtually a repeat of the first, a gasp of hope that the message will not go unheeded. The poem accommodates both lyric wooing and some impassioned theorizing about the way love poetry can matter more than the lover. But the argumentation and conceptual vocabulary are entirely controlled and given their lyric value by somber rhythms, by the thickening of the quantitative verse, by the dying fall of the feminine endings, and by the short line closing each sapphic stanza, a device that has the effect of a plangent English refrain. Sidney's Latin metrics, in other words, complement devices we have observed before: expression in single-line units; recurring patterns striking the combination of song and speculative gravity which is the poetry of his Arcadian aristocrats.

Knowing this, a reader will be less troubled by the sonnets of the *Arcadia,* free as they are of the panache and ease of *Astrophel and Stella.* In at least the first two books of the *Arcadia,* Sidney appears to have felt no need to explore the dramatic possibilities of sonnet form. He deliberately mutes the difference between sonnets and the gravely repeating lyrics already discussed. Sonnets too are planned out like songs, each of three quatrains as a stanza set to the same music. While they move forward, they seem to cover the same ground; they do not take the opportunities for surprise that shifts in the sestet might offer. Much depends upon rhythmic patterns and on declarative order—the suggestions of incantations—rather than on the compressed or jagged syntax Sidney exhibits in *Astrophel and Stella.* Yet, in the *Arcadia,* one can almost catch Sidney in the act of animating his sonnets and setting dramatic character free. Particularly in Book III, he comes to think of the complete sonnet as a unit of thought. Instead of quatrains tolling repeated patterns (rhymed *abab cdcd efef gg*), he returns to the Italian form with only two rhymes in the octave. More important, he puts the tighter, more unified form at the service of dramatic meditation, as in Philoclea's impatient "O stealing time the subject of delay" (p. 89). From simple irritation in that opening line, her sonnet moves to puzzle out words that stall the mind: "delay,/Delay, the rack of unrefrain'd desire"; "my hopes . . ./My hopes which do but to mine own aspire/Mine own? O word on whose sweet sound doth prey/My greedy soul. . . ." Philoclea's thoughts are clarified; she specifies her claims, launching the sonnet into the joyful anticipation of the sestet: "O time, become the chariot of my joys." It is the kind of language we shall hear from Juliet.

But the norm for the *Arcadia* is the lyric put at the service of lovers who are always aware of the possibilities of mastery and will, self-conscious about their devotions:

> O heaven and earth (said Musidorus) to what a pass are our minds brought, that from the right line of virtue, are wryed to these crooked shifts? But O love, it is thou that doost it: thou changest name upon name; thou disguisest our bodies, and disfigurest our minds. But indeed thou hast reason, for though the ways be foul, the journey's end is most fair and honorable.

The degree to which these assumptions prevail is clear when we look at the eclogues, those poems presented as royal entertainments between books of the *Arcadia,* poems that set the princes against shepherds who have a more relaxed view of love—some happy (like Thyrsis in the singing contest of the First Eclogues, the same shepherd whose wedding is celebrated in the epithalamium which sets the tone of the Third Eclogues), some with a wise view of cuckoldry (like Nico, who, with a "merry marriage look" recites the fabliau which follows and counters the marriage song, p. 94). These are windows into other worlds, into an earthier and happier pastoral than any available to the responsible heroes of the romance.

In the *Arcadia* Sidney paid his strictest tribute to the heroic ideal and to the *Apology*'s epic vision of literature. At the same time he was testing delightful alternatives. In the *Certain Sonnets,* written during the years 1577–1581, he offers love poems freer in courtly utterance than would have been proper to the dedicated princes of *Arcadia.* Neil Rudenstine[6] has made a good case for seeing many of these poems as closer to the conversational style of *Astrophel*

---

[6] Rudenstine, pp. 114–130.

and Stella and for viewing the whole set of thirty-two poems as occasional pieces collected over the years, then arranged to suggest the curve of a courtly love tale. Whether or not as a group they give a foretaste of *Astrophel and Stella,* certainly a lover with Astrophel's suspicion of mere literary loving makes his bow:

> Are poets then the only lovers true?
> Whose hearts are set on measuring a verse:
> Who think themselves well blest, if they renew
> Some good old dump, that Chaucer's mistress knew
> (p. 113)

We hear as well the witty lover who stays close to glittering danger—in a poem which takes as much pleasure in running lively counter to a fable of Sidney's friend Edward Dyer as it does in its sly flirtations with desire ("Better like I thy satyr dearest Dyer,/Who burnt his lips to kiss fair shining fire"). *Certain Sonnets* is very much Sidney in mid-passage. Side by side we find two songs to the same tune (pp. 107–108) but clearly not from the same world. An Italian lyric, now lost, provides the frame for both of these laments for unrequited love. One ("The fire to see my wrongs for anger burneth") uses the formulaic line of the Arcadian poems—the lyric, in fact, turns up in the *New Arcadia.* Fire, earth, air, and water: each element is called up in turn, part of a ritual invocation to cure the speaker's sufferings in love. To the very same music, Sidney produces quite a different, and better, poem. "The Nightingale" depends upon the same dying fall of feminine endings as its sister poem does, but a richer syntax keeps us from lingering over rhyme words:

> The nightingale as soon as April bringeth
> Unto her rested sense a perfect waking,
> While late bare earth, proud of new clothing springeth,
> Sings out her woes, a thorn her song-book making:

To have suspended the main verb so artfully was to keep the woes suspended as well. We are allowed a more delicate complication of feeling about the bird's song, intertwining it with "rested sense," "perfect waking," and the

proud rite of spring, an effect lost if the clauses are differently arranged. Though full weight is given the nightingale's
sadness, the speaker asserts his own. For him it is natural
that both the nightingale's sorrow and the spring with
which it in effect merges should seem distant enviable
states:

> But I who daily craving,
> Cannot have to content me,
> Have more cause to lament me,
> Since wanting is more woe than too much having.

In a poem that so subtly adjusts the reader's feelings and
sympathies and one that resists literary notions (Philomela)
that absorb or falsify desire, the muse of *Astrophel and
Stella* is clearly present.

We are told that Chaucer's *Troilus and Criseyde* was
one of "Astrophel's cordials." Chaucer's affectionate way
of both undercutting and animating courtly conventions
was not lost on Sidney; and the Elizabethan's sonnet sequence, though not at all a narrative, functions as a series
of recitatives and reflective arias which follow a dramatic
curve. "The tragicomedy of love . . . the argument cruel
chastity, the prologue hope, the epilogue despair" was
Nashe's way of describing it in a racy preface to one of
the first editions (1591). Not for Astrophel the rewards
of the *Arcadia,* whose heroes will, after all, return with
their princesses to a heroic life, their mastery having been
exercised through memory and the choric distancing of
almost every moment of their experience. They are able
to see that "though the ways be foul, the journey's end is
most fair and honorable." For Astrophel the pressures of
heroic experience and education operate differently; they
prepare him less successfully for life. Astrophel, by contrast
with the Arcadians, is a puzzled participant in his love for
Stella. The poetic mode of *Astrophel and Stella* allows for
an incomplete and developing experience. Astrophel is
engaged in discovery, testing the formulas with which
others characterize love and defining himself against them.

Many of his sorties are encounters with books: poets' phrases that do not seem adequate to the true voice of feeling (sonnets 1, 3, 6, 15, 74); the lessons of Reason, Virtue, and "great expectation" (4, 10, 21), which trouble his growing allegiance to Stella and the world of love; and finally Stella herself, "fairest book of Nature" (71), whose lessons are confusing and do not accommodate his strong desires. The sequence is filled with personifications from a textbook for lovers, figures whose importance Astrophel is always challenging: Hope (67); Patience (56); "traitor Absence" (88); Doctor Cupid (61). His chafings and probings create the pattern of *Astrophel and Stella;* Astrophel is continually defining and declaring his feelings against adversaries—one set no sooner defeated, others appear.

The opening brace of twenty-one sonnets offers a series of harried—sometimes guilty and rueful, sometimes jaunty and triumphant—defenses against Reason and Virtue. Astrophel's delightful posing and his witty assertions of love carry him beyond these opponents. Once committed to love, he alternately invokes the Petrarchan contraries ("Where Love is chasteness, Pain doth learn delight") and bristles at the artificialities of courtship ("Alas, if Fancy drawn by imag'd things,/Though false, yet with free scope more grace doth breed/Than servant's wrack . . ."). The pressures of desire challenge easy literary definitions of love: Stella imposes "a love not blind," one anchored "fast . . . on Virtue's shore," so leading Astrophel to new discriminations:

> Alas, if this the only metal be
> Of love, new-coin'd to help my beggary,
> Dear, love me not, that you may love me more.
>
> (p. 154)

The sequence follows Astrophel from one crossroad to another, each of his bright distinctions proving not to be the final one he had hoped it would be. New paths branch off constantly; new frustrations are discovered in his love until wearily he acknowledges the irreducible element of desire, by sonnet 72 his "old companion": "But thou

Desire, because thou wouldst have all,/Now banisht art,
but yet alas how shall?" Late in the series, sonnets give
way to lyric confrontation in eleven songs, both characters
now directly on stage, the impossibility of their love crystal-
lized as Stella, regretfully, banishes him in honor's name.
Astrophel and Stella ends with what amounts to a cere-
mony of grief; the last sonnets, more like songs than any
others in the series, invoke personifications of Woe, Sighs,
Thought, and Grief. After this clarification of feeling, the
sequence can do nothing but end on a note of exhaustion.
(The last two of the *Certain Sonnets* ["Thou blind man's
mark" and "Leave me O love, which reachest but to dust"],
as poems of renunciation, were often printed at the end of
the series, a fulfillment of nineteenth-century taste which
has no justification in sixteenth-century texts.)

The plot of *Astrophel and Stella* allows, then, an investi-
gation of feeling; Astrophel's probing and puzzlement
demand techniques which make these sonnets far different
from the Arcadian poems. Many of them are pitched toward an unexpected conclusion, the sonnet form filled out
as if, while Astrophel speaks, his counter feelings are
gathering, to burst out in the final lines. Majestic praise
of Stella as the "fairest book of Nature," drawing him
forcibly to Virtue (71), is suddenly challenged:

> So while thy beauty draws the heart to love,
> As fast thy Virtue bends that love to good:
> But ah, Desire still cries, give me some food.

Or the eloquent claims of the "inward light" (5)—"True,
that on earth we are but pilgrims made,/And should in
soul up to our country move"—crystallize a quiet counter-
ing resolve: "True, and yet true that I must Stella love."

But the true departure of *Astrophel and Stella*—what
points ahead to Shakespeare and to Donne—is its more
intense verbal activity: a liberation of sound, rhythm, and
syntax which vividly transmits the sense of Astrophel as
participant in, rather than heroic master of, his experience.
One can pose, for example, Pyrocles' judicious lament,
"Transformed in show, but more transformed in mind,"

against Astrophel's urgent discovery of what it is like to fall in love: "Fly, fly, my friends, I have my death wound; fly,/See there that boy, that murth'ring boy I say" (20). Familiar as the scene of Cupid's ambush may be in Renaissance poetry, Astrophel's sonnet still manages to sound <u>urgent and irritated</u>. He is <u>experiencing, in the present tense</u>, what Pyrocles has already weighed and assimilated before he begins his poem. A familiar conceit is animated by the rhythms of surprise, above all by the penetrating sounds ("Fly, fly . . . I . . . fly,/See . . . say")—the long "e's" and "i's" and "a's"—that keep those opening cries echoing through the poem (in all the rhyme words of the octave, for example), until the urgency is slowly damped down by the closed rhymes of the last lines.

<u>Syntax, too, follows the hesitations and urgencies of feeling</u> rather than marking and controlling emotions as the Arcadian sonnets do.

> Woe, having made with many fights his own
> Each sense of mine, each gift, each power of mind,
> Grown now his slaves, he forc'd them out to find
> The thorowest words, fit for woe's self to groan,
> Hoping that when they might find Stella alone. . . .
> (sonnet 57)

These lines have the <u>quality of breathy yet considered speech</u>. It is possible to read the phrases of line 2 as intensified objects of "made . . . his own"; or, spilling over into the following line, any or all of them as the subject of "grown now his slaves." Such deliberate fluidity makes it seem as if the battles and slavery to Woe are now, wearily and firmly, a part of life, telescoped quickly behind the redundant "he" as if to put these experiences in place. The rapid movement calls us back to the present, to a new frustration: as Stella receives his "plaints," she sings his poem and so removes the sting of its strong feeling. We must be alive to these syntactical pleasures which, slowing and quickening the flow of the poems, give privileged renditions of particular moments of feeling. Here is the octave of a more familiar sonnet:

> With how sad steps, O moon, thou climb'st the skies,
>   How silently, and with how wan a face,
>   What may it be, that even in heav'nly place
> That busy archer his sharp arrows tries?
> Sure if that long with love acquainted eyes
>   Can judge of love, thou feel'st a lover's case;
>   I read it in thy looks, thy languisht grace
> To me that feel the like, thy state descries.

One with the remarkable slow movement of the piece and the measured monosyllables is a quiet blurring of syntax. "Languisht grace" may serve as both object of "read" and subject of "descries," making the line of which it is part almost a floating syntactical unit and wafting Astrophel from what he observes to what he insists is its meaning. From speculation ("What may it be . . ./Sure if that long with love acquainted eyes/Can judge . . .") he moves to the hoped-for identification of feelings ("Then ev'n of fellowship, O moon, tell me . . .").

Astrophel and Stella often invites attention to such details; its resources, its more intense verbal activity, allow a psychological subtlety which would have been inappropriate to the willed evaluations of the *Arcadia*. The movement of mind, so often praised in Donne, is already present in many of the sonnets of Sidney's sequence, though perhaps without so intricate a representation of the snares of thought. Sidney, who helped domesticate the Petrarchan mode in England, also carried its habitual introspection to an extreme which helped undermine the tradition. The immediacy with which he follows the lover's turns of mind —from line to line or from sonnet to sonnet—draws us away from visions of the ideal mistress, the Lauras and Stellas, to the individualizing energy impatient with the worshipful stance the lover finds himself assuming. Where Petrarch's lover, imagining his mistress, is drawn by the brilliance of her image, his particular turbulence balanced and transformed by intense lyric presentations of Laura, Astrophel can only fitfully, without strain, transport himself into these moods.[7] By the end of the sequence—unlike

[7] See Kalstone, *Sidney's Poetry*, pp. 105–132.

Petrarch, and unlike the idealized heroes at the close of the *Arcadia*—he is irrevocably, even joyfully committed to the confusions of the fallen world. His understanding of love is not the purifying, gradual refinement of Petrarch's *Rime,* but rather an emerging definition of and commitment to his own fallen nature as an earthly lover. A sonnet like *Astrophel and Stella,* 38, makes this clear:

> This night while sleep begins with heavy wings
> To hatch mine eyes, and that unbitted thought
> Doth fall to stray, and my chief powers are brought
> To leave the scepter of all subject things,
> The first that straight my fancy's error brings
> Unto my mind, is Stella's image, wrought
> By Love's own self, but with so curious draught,
> That she, methinks, not only shines but sings.
> I start, look, hark, but what in clos'd up sense
> Was held, in open'd sense it flies away,
> Leaving me nought but wailing eloquence:
> I seeing better sights in sight's decay,
> Call'd it anew, and wooèd sleep again:
> But him her host that unkind guest had slain.

An orthodox Petrarchan might well have closed with the striking vision which "not only shines but sings." Shakespeare, by no means an orthodox Petrarchan, has his sonneteer sustain such a lover's vision to the very end of the poem and stresses its transforming power:

> Save that my soul's imaginary sight
> Presents thy shadow to my sightless view,
> Which like a jewel hung in ghastly night
> Makes black night beauteous, and her old face new.
> (Sonnets, 27)

But Sidney's dream is a stranger mixture of pressure and pleasure. It is first of all touched by that heroic gravity which Astrophel knew before his full involvement with Stella. The opening of Sidney's sonnet is much less straightforward than Shakespeare's "Weary with toil, I haste me to my bed." With its auxiliary constructions and passive verbs ("begins to hatch"; "doth fall to stray"; "are brought to leave") Sidney's poem enacts the silent process which is

an abdication of reason's powers as well as a privileged
vision of Stella. "Fancy's error" brings the relief of wandering, but hints glancingly at the possible dangers of love.
And the speaker's very intensity, climaxing at "Stella's
image, wrought/By Love's own self . . . not only shines but
sings," invites the immediate abrupt wakening of the sestet:
"I start, look, hark. . . ." He is left with "open'd sense,"
the waking awareness that his brilliant vision cannot be
maintained, that it troubles him to "wailing eloquence."
The pattern here is, in small, the pattern of *Astrophel and
Stella*: exploring possibilities of sustained praise and lyric
vision leads to a shattered recall to the desiring, unsatisfied
self.

Auden has called Sidney a poet's poet. Ambiguous
praise, it highlights an important truth—that Sidney's range
is not great, and that many of his self-conscious efforts at
formal effects are of interest only to those, like poets,
whose interests are highly technical. It was Auden and
Empson who called attention to the wonderful double
sestina "Ye goatherd gods," reprinting it for an audience
which might never have looked for it among the self-ab-
sorbed, sometimes drab lyrics of the *Arcadia*. Surely it
suggests one example of the heightened effects of form,
divorced from the individualized, errant, probing voices of
modern poetry. Yet Sidney himself was moving away from
his patterned performances. In *Astrophel and Stella* he
brought back into English poetry that very different kind of
voice which was to be heard in the spacious achievement
of the Elizabethan stage: dramatic speech, capable of leaps
from lyricism to the colloquial in a line's space, and committed to the wandering voices of the fallen world. Astrophel might easily have made his way into *Love's Labor's
Lost* and from there into *As You Like It* or *Much Ado
about Nothing*. Sidney had, triumphantly, discovered new
powers.

The sonnet form breeds its own antithesis

A General Note on the Text

The overall textual policy for the Signet Classic Poetry series attempts to strike a balance between the convenience and dependability of total modernization, on the one hand, and the authenticity of an established text on the other. Starting with the Restoration and Augustan poets, the General Editor has set up the following guidelines for the individual editors:

Modern American spelling will be used, although punctuation may be adjusted by the editor of each volume when he finds it advisable. In any case, syllabic final "ed" will be rendered with grave accent to distinguish it from the silent one, which is written out without apostrophe (e.g., "to gild refinèd gold," but "asked" rather than "ask'd"). Archaic words and forms are to be kept, naturally, whenever the meter or the sense may require it.

In the case of poets from earlier periods, the text is more clearly a matter of the individual editor's choice, and the type and degree of modernization has been left to his decision. But in any event, archaic typographical conventions ("i," "j," "u," "v," etc.) have all been normalized in the modern way.

JOHN HOLLANDER

A Note on This Edition

I have based my text of the poems and *The Lady of May* on the first collected edition of Sidney's writings, the folio of 1598, *The Countess of Pembroke's Arcadia*. The authoritative scholarly text is *The Poems of Sir Philip Sidney,* ed. W. A. Ringler, Jr. (Oxford, 1962), with full apparatus. To it all students of Sidney are deeply indebted; I have drawn upon it for many readings, textual references, and notes. (In this edition, the Oxford volume is designated as Ringler; the 1598 folio as 1598; Thomas Newman's two unauthorized editions of *Astrophel and Stella* in 1591 as Q1, Q2, or, in cases where they agree, as 1591; and the two earlier editions of the *Arcadia* as 1590 and 1593, respectively.) For Sidney's critical treatise, I have chosen the text published by Henry Olney in 1595 as *An Apology for Poetry,* but I have also consulted Ponsonby's alternate edition of the same year, published as *The Defense of Poesy.* The best modern edition, to whose extensive notes I am indebted, is that of Geoffrey Shepherd (London, 1965). For *The Psalms of David,* I have consulted the Bodleian MS. Rawlinson poet. 25 (designated by Ringler as B), as well as the readings of Ringler and of J. C. Rathmell, *The Psalms of Sir Philip Sidney and the Countess of Pembroke* (New York, 1963).

The texts are modernized, though I have kept features of the early editions which may help with the sound of the poems: contractions, some final "t's," and unusual spellings necessary for rhyming. Except in cases where it might create great confusion I have retained the punctuation of 1598 or of the quartos. Though we have no firm evidence for Sidney's own punctuation of the texts, early editions allow a flexibility destroyed in many overpunctuated modern reprints. Though we do not know enough about sixteenth-century punctuation, it will be seen that the pointing of Olney's text of the *Apology* has less concern for syntactical clarity and more for rhetorical pauses, perhaps with oral presentation in mind.

I give textual variants in cases where they are particularly interesting or may affect interpretation. The order of works is roughly chronological, except for the *Apology,* which is at the close of the volume; some critics have suggested that the *Psalms* were composed earlier, but I have adopted Ringler's placement. Numbering of the *Certain Sonnets* and *Astrophel and Stella* accords with Ringler's edition, as do the patterns of indentation of the sonnets. The poems from the *Arcadia* are arranged in the order in which they appear in the folio of 1598. Annotations are primarily glosses of unfamiliar words, particularly those not to be found in standard modern dictionaries.

Chronology

1554   30 November. Sidney born at Penshurst, Kent. Eldest son of Sir Henry Sidney and Lady Mary Sidney (sister of the Earl of Leicester).

1559   Sidney's father Lord President of the Marches of Wales; lives at Ludlow Castle.

1564   Sidney enters Shrewsbury School, where Greville is also enrolled.

1565   Sidney's father Lord Deputy of Ireland.

1568   Sidney enters Christ Church, Oxford.

1571   Leaves Oxford, without taking a degree.

1572   With the Queen's permission, goes abroad to learn languages. Spends three months in Paris, where he witnesses the St. Bartholomew's Day massacre.

1573   In Frankfurt, Heidelberg, Vienna (from which he visits Hungary). Meets Hubert Languet, an elderly Burgundian serving the Elector of Saxony. Languet, an ardent Protestant, becomes Sidney's Continental mentor. From November, Sidney in Italy, principally at Venice and Padua.

1574   Italy, Vienna, Poland.

1575   Prague, Dresden, Heidelberg. Returns to England.

1576   In Ireland with his father and at court.

1577   Serves as ambassador to the new Elector Palatine and new Emperor of Germany. Visits William of Orange. Explores possibilities for a league of Protestant princes. Back in England, probably begins writing *Arcadia* while visiting his sister Mary, the Countess of Pembroke, at Wilton.

1578   *The Lady of May* performed before Queen Elizabeth on a visit to the Earl of Leicester at Wanstead.

1579   Spenser's *Shepherds' Calendar* dedicated to Sidney.

1580   Sidney leaves court and stays at Wilton (March–August). Probably completes *Arcadia* and most of *Certain Sonnets*. *Apology for Poetry?*

1581   Becomes member of Parliament.

1582   Probable date of *Astrophel and Stella*.

1583   Knighted. Marries Frances Walsingham (age 15).

1584   Probably begins revision of *Arcadia*. Also begins translation of DuPlessis Mornay's *La Vérité de la Religion Chrestienne* (completed by Golding and published in 1587).

1585   Begins translations of the Psalms of David. (Another possible date: 1580.) Becomes governor of Flushing and leaves for the Netherlands.

1586   Dies of a wound at battle of Zutphen.

1587   Buried February 16 at public funeral in St. Paul's.

1590   Books I–III of the revised *Arcadia* published.

1591   *Astrophel and Stella* published. Three unauthorized editions.

1593   Revised *Arcadia* published, the last two and one-half books drawn from the *Old Arcadia*.

1595   Two editions, one entitled *An Apology for Poetry*, the other *The Defense of Poesy*.

1598   Folio edition, probably supervised by the Countess of Pembroke: includes *Arcadia, Defense of Poesy, Certain Sonnets, Astrophel and Stella, The Lady of May*.

Selected Bibliography

Editions:

The Complete Works of Sir Philip Sidney. Albert Feuillerat
(ed.). 4 volumes. Cambridge, Eng., 1912–26.
The Poems of Sir Philip Sidney. W. A. Ringler, Jr. (ed.).
Oxford, 1962.
An Apology for Poetry. Geoffrey Shepherd (ed.). London,
1965.

Life and Literary Career:

Buxton, John. *Sir Philip Sidney and the English Renais-
sance*. London, 1954.
Greville, Fulke. *Life of Sir Philip Sidney*, ed. Nowell Smith.
Oxford, 1907.
Myrick, Kenneth O. *Sir Philip Sidney as a Literary Crafts-
man*. Cambridge, Mass., 1935.
Stillinger, Jack. "The Biographical Problem of *Astrophel
and Stella*," *Journal of English and Germanic Philology*,
LIX (1960).
Van Dorsten, J. A. *Poets, Patrons, and Professors: Sir
Philip Sidney, Daniel Rogers, and the Leiden Humanists*.
Publications of the Sir Thomas Browne Institute, II.
Leiden, 1962.
Wallace, M. W. *The Life of Sir Philip Sidney*. London,
1915.

Criticism:

Davis, Walter, and Lanham, Richard A. *Sidney's Arcadia*.
New Haven, 1965.

Empson, William. *Seven Types of Ambiguity* (pp. 45–50). New York, 1931.

Hathaway, Baxter. *The Age of Criticism: The Late Renaissance in Italy*. New York, 1962.

Kalstone, David. *Sidney's Poetry*. Cambridge, Mass., 1965.

Lever, J. W. *The Elizabethan Love Sonnet*. London, 1956.

Montgomery, Robert L. *Symmetry and Sense*. Austin, 1961.

Orgel, Stephen. *The Jonsonian Masque* (pp. 44–57). Cambridge, Mass., 1965.

Rudenstine, Neil. *Sidney's Poetic Development*. Cambridge, Mass., 1967.

Smith, Hallett. *Elizabethan Poetry*. Cambridge, Mass., 1952.

Spencer, Theodore. "The Poetry of Sir Philip Sidney," *Journal of English Literary History*, XII (1945).

Thompson, John. *The Founding of English Metre*. New York, 1961.

Thorne, J. P. "A Ramistical Commentary on Sidney's *Apologie for Poetrie*," *Modern Philology*, LIV (1956).

Tuve, Rosemond. *Elizabethan and Metaphysical Imagery*. Chicago, 1947.

Young, Richard B. "English Petrarke: A Study of Sidney's *Astrophel and Stella*," in *Three Studies in the Renaissance: Sidney, Jonson, Milton*. New Haven, 1958.

THE LADY OF MAY

The Lady of May

grove, there came suddenly among the train, one apparelled like an honest man's wife of the country, where crying out for justice, and desiring all the lords and gentlemen to speak a good word for her, she was brought to the presence of her Majesty, to whom upon her knees she offered a supplication, and used this speech.

The Suitor.

Most fair lady, for as for other your titles of state statelier persons shall give you, and thus much mine own eyes are witnesses of, take here the complaint of my poor wretch, as deeply plunged in misery, as I wish to you the highest point of happiness.

One only daughter I have, in whom I had placed all the hopes of my good hap, so well had she with her good parts recompensed my pain of bearing of her, and care of bringing her up: but now alas that she is come to the time I should reap my full comfort of her, so is she troubled with that notable matter, which we in country call matrimony, as I cannot choose but fear the loss of her wits, at least of her honesty. Other women think they may be unhappily cumbered with one master husband, my poor daughter is oppressed with two, both loving her, both equally liked of her, both striving to deserve her. But now lastly (as this jealousy for sooth is a vile matter) each have brought their partakers with them, and are at this present, without your presence redress it, in some bloody controversy; now sweet lady help, your own way guides you to the place where they encumber her: I dare stay here no longer, for our men say in the country, the sight of you is infectious.

And with that she went away a good pace, leaving the supplication with her Majesty, which very formally contained this.

SUPPLICATION.

Most gracious Sovereign,

To one whose state is raisèd over all,
Whose face doth oft the bravest sort enchant,
Whose mind is such, as wisest minds appall,
Who in one self these diverse gifts can plant;
　　How dare I wretch seek there my woes to rest,
　　Where ears be burnt, eyes dazzled, hearts opprest?

Your state is great, your greatness is our shield,
Your face hurts oft, but still it doth delight,
Your mind is wise, your wisdom makes you mild,
Such planted gifts enrich even beggars' sight:
　　So dare I wretch, my bashful fear subdue,
　　And feed mine ears, mine eyes, my heart in you.

Herewith the woman-suitor being gone, there was heard in the woods a confused noise, and forthwith there came out six shepherds with as many fosters haling[1] and pulling, to whether side they should draw the Lady of May, who seemed to incline neither to the one nor other side. Among them was Master Rombus a schoolmaster of a village thereby, who being fully persuaded of his own learned wisdom, came thither, with his authority to part their fray; where for answer he received many unlearned blows. But the Queen coming to the place where she was seen of them, though they knew not her estate, yet something there was which made them startle aside and gaze upon her: till old father Lalus stepped forth (one of the substantialest shepherds) and making a leg or two, said these few words.

---

[1] haling dragging.

Lalus the old shepherd.

May it please your benignity to give a little superfluous intelligence to that, which with the opening of my mouth, my tongue and teeth shall deliver unto you. So it is right worshipful audience, that a certain she creature, which we shepherds call a woman, of a minsical[2] countenance, but by my white lamb not three quarters so beauteous as yourself, hath disannulled the brain pan of two of our featioust young men. And will you wo´ how? by my mother Kit's soul, with a certain fransical[3] malady they call Love, when I was a young man they called it flat folly. But here is a substantial schoolmaster can better disnounce the whole foundation of the matter, although in sooth for all his loquence our young men were nothing duteous to his clerkship; Come on, come on master schoolmaster, be not so bashless, we say, that the fairest are ever the gentlest: tell the whole case, for you can much better vent[4] the points of it than I.

Then came forward Master Rombus, and with many special graces made this learned oration.

Now the thunderthumping Jove transfund his dotes[5] into your excellent formosity,[6] which have with your resplendent beams thus segregated the emnity of these rural animals: I am *potentissima domina*,[7] a schoolmaster, that is to say, a pedagogue, one not a little versed in the disciplinating of the juvental fry, wherein (to my laud I say it) I use such geometrical proportion, as neither wanted mansuetude[8] nor correction, for so it is described.

parcare subjectos & debellire superbos.[9]

Yet hath not the pulchritude of my virtues protected me from the contaminating hands of these plebeians; for com-

---

[2] **minsical** dainty. [3] **fransical** frenzied. [4] **vent** give out. [5] **transfund . . . dotes** pour . . . gifts (Rombus' speeches are peppered with these comic and dubious Latinisms). [6] **formosity** beauty. [7] **potentissima domina** most powerful lady. [8] **mansuetude** clemency. [9] **parcare . . . superbos** one of Rombus' typically dubious quotations from the classics. Here he misquotes Virgil (*Aeneid*, VI, 853): "to spare the humble and conquer the proud."

ing, *solummodo*[10] to have parted their sanguinolent fray,
they yielded me no more reverence, than if I had been
some *pecorius asinus*. I, even I, that am, who am I? *Dixi
verbus sapiento satum est.*[11] But what said that Trojan
Aeneas, when he sojourned in the surging sulks of the
sandiferous seas, *Haec olim memonasse juvebit.*[12] Well well,
ad propositos revertebo,[13] the purity of the verity is, that a
certain *pulchra puella profecto*[14] elected and constituted by
the integrated determination of all this topographical
region, as the sovereign Lady of this Dame Maia's month,
hath been *quodammodo*[15] hunted, as you would say, pursued by two, a brace, a couple, a cast of young men, to
whom the crafty coward Cupid had *inquam*[16] delivered his
dire-dolorous dart.

*But here the May Lady interrupted his speech, saying to
him:*

Away away you tedious fool, your eyes are not worthy
to look to yonder princely sight, much less your foolish
tongue to trouble her wise ears.

At which Master Rombus in a great chafe cried out:

O tempori, ô moribus[17] in profession a child, in dignity
a woman, in years a lady, *in caeteris*[18] a maid, should thus
turpify[19] the reputation of my doctrine, with the superscrip-
tion of a fool, *ô tempori, ô moribus*!

But here again the May Lady saying to him,

Leave off good Latin fool, and let me satisfy the long

---

[10] **solummodo** for the sole reason.   [11] **Dixi . . . est** I have said, a word
to the wise is sufficient (like all Rombus' Latin, incorrectly put).
[12] **Haec . . . juvebit** "these things, some day, it will be a joy to recall"
(incorrectly quoted from *Aeneid*, I, 203).   [13] **ad . . . revertebo** to come
back to the main point.   [14] **pulchra . . . profecto** beautiful girl indeed.
[15] **quodammodo** in a certain measure.   [16] **inquam** I say.   [17] **O . . .
moribus** refers incorrectly to Cicero's *"O tempora! O mores."*   [18] **in
caeteris** in other things.   [19] **turpify** befoul.

desire I have had to feed mine eyes with the only sight this
age hath granted to the world.

*The poor schoolmaster went his way back, and the Lady
kneeling down said in this manner:*

Do not think (sweet and gallant lady) that I do abase
my self thus much unto you because of your gay apparel,
for what is so brave as the natural beauty of the flowers,
nor because a certain gentleman hereby seeks to do you all
the honor he can in his house; that is not the matter, he is
but our neighbor, and these be our own groves, nor yet
because of your great estate, since no estate can be compared to be the Lady of the whole month of May as I am.
So that since both this place and this time are my servants,
you may be sure I would look for reverence at your hands
if I did not see something in your face which makes me
yield to you; the troth is, you excel me in that wherein I
desire most to excel, and that makes me give this homage
unto you, as to the beautifulest lady these woods have ever
received. But now as old father Lalus directed me, I will
tell you my fortune, that you may be judge of my mishaps
and others worthiness. Indeed so it is, that I am a fair
wench or else I am deceived, and therefore by the consent
of all our neighbors have been chosen for the absolute
Lady of this merry month, with me have been (alas I am
ashamed to tell it) two young men, the one a forester
named Therion,[20] the other Espilus a shepherd very long
even in love forsooth, I like them both, and love neither,
Espilus is the richer, but Therion the livelier: Therion doth
me many pleasures, as stealing me venison out of these
forests, and many other such like pretty and prettier services, but withal he grows to such rages, that sometimes he
strikes me, sometimes he rails at me. This shepherd Espilus
of a mild disposition, as his fortune hath not been to do
me great service, so hath he never done me any wrong,
but feeding his sheep, sitting under some sweet bush, some-

[20] **Therion, Espilus** derivations from "wild beast" and "felt-presser,"
respectively.

times they say he records my name in doleful verses. Now the question I am to ask you fair lady, is, whether the many deserts and many faults of Therion, or the very small deserts and no faults of Espilus be to be preferred. But before you give your judgement (most excellent lady) you shall hear what each of them can say for themselves in their rural songs.

Thereupon Therion challenged Espilus to sing with him, speaking these six verses:

Therion.

Come Espilus, come now declare thy skill,
Show how thou canst deserve so brave desire,
Warm well thy wits, if thou wilt win her will,
For water cold did never promise fire:
    Great sure is she, on whom our hopes do live,
    Greater is she who must the judgement give.

But Espilus as if he had been inspired with the Muses, began forthwith to sing, whereto his fellow shepherds set in with their recorders, which they bare in their bags like pipes, and so of Therion's side did the foresters, with the cornets they wore about their necks like hunting horns in baudrics.[21]

Espilus.

Tune up my voice, a higher note I yield,
To high conceits the song must needs be high,
More high than stars, more firm than flinty field
Are all my thoughts, on which I live or die:
    Sweet soul, to whom I vowèd am a slave,
    Let not wild woods so great a treasure have.

Therion.

The highest note comes oft from basest mind,
As shallow brooks do yield the greatest sound,
Seek other thoughts thy life or death to find;

---

[21] **baudrics** belts slung from one shoulder across the breast and under the opposite arm.

Thy stars be fal'n, plowed is thy flinty ground:
    Sweet soul let not a wretch that serveth sheep,
    Among his flock so sweet a treasure keep.

Espilus.

Two thousand sheep I have as white as milk,
Though not so white as is thy lovely face,
The pasture rich, the wool as soft as silk,
All this I give, let me possess thy grace,
    But still take heed lest thou thyself submit
    To one that hath no wealth, and wants his wit.

Therion.

Two thousand deer in wildest woods I have,
Them can I take, but you I cannot hold:
He is not poor who can his freedom save,
Bound but to you, no wealth but you I would:
    But take this beast, if beasts you fear to miss,
    For of his beasts the greatest beast he is.

Espilus kneeling to the Queen.

Judge you to whom all beauty's force is lent.

Therion.

Judge you of love, to whom all love is bent.

But as they waited for the judgement her Majesty should give of their deserts, the shepherds and foresters grew to a great contention, whether of their fellows had sung better, and so whether the estate of shepherds or foresters were the more worshipful. The speakers were Dorcas an old shepherd, and Rixus a young foster, between whom the schoolmaster Rombus came in as moderator.

Dorcas the shepherd.

Now all the blessings of mine old grandam (silly Espilus) light upon thy shoulders for this honeycomb singing of thine; now of my honesty all the bells in the town could

not have sung better, if the proud heart of the harlotry lie
not down to thee now, the sheep's rot catch her, to teach
her that a fair woman hath not her fairness to let it grow
rustish.

Rixus the foster.

O Midas why art thou not alive now to lend thine ears
to this drivel, by the precious bones of a huntsman, he
knows not the bleaying of a calf from the song of a nightingale, but if yonder great gentlewoman be as wise as she is
fair, Therion thou shalt have the prize, and thou old Dorcas
with young master Espilus shall remain tame fools, as you
be.

Dorcas. And with cap and knee be it spoken, is it your
pleasure neighbor Rixus to be a wild fool?

Rixus. Rather than a sleepish dolt.

Dorcas. It is much refreshing to my bowels, you have
made your choice, for my share I will bestow your leavings
upon one of your fellows.

Rixus. And art not thou ashamed old fool, to liken
Espilus a shepherd to Therion of the noble vocation of
huntsmen, in the presence of such a one as even with her
eye only can give the cruel punishment?

Dorcas. Hold thy peace, I will neither meddle with her
nor her eyes, they sayn in our town they are dangerous both,
neither will I liken Therion to my boy Espilus, since one
is a thievish proller,[22] and the other is as quiet as a lamb
that new came from sucking.

Rombus the schoolmaster.

*Heu, Ehem, hei, Insipidum, Inscitium vulgorum & popu-
lorum.* Why you brute nebulons have you had my *corpusculum*[23] so long among you, and cannot yet tell how to edify
an argument? Attend and throw your ears to me, for I am
gravidated with child, till I have endoctrinated your plumbeous cerebrosities.[24] First you must divisionate your point,

---

[22] **proller** prowler. [23] **corpusculum** diminutive of *corpus,* body.
[24] **plumbeous cerebrosities** leaden arguments.

quasi[25] you should cut a cheese into two particles, for thus must I uniform my speech to your obtuse conceptions; for *Prius dividendum oratio antequam definiendum exemplum gratia,*[26] either Therion must conquer this Dame Maia's nymph, or Espilus must overthrow her, and that *secundum*[27] their dignity, which must also be subdivisionated into three equal species, either according to the penetrancy of their singing, or the meliority of their functions, or lastly the superancy of their merits *De* singing *satis. Nunc* are you to argumentate of the qualifying of their estate first, and then whether hath more infernally, I mean deeply deserved.

Dorcas. O poor Dorcas, poor Dorcas, that I was not set in my young days to school, that I might have purchased the understanding of master Rombus mysterious speeches. But yet thus much I concern of them, that I must even give up what my conscience doth find in the behalf of shepherds. O sweet honey milken lommes, and is there any so flinty a heart, that can find about him to speak against them, that have the charge of such good souls as you be, among whom there is no envy, and all obedience, where it is lawful for a man to be good if he list, and hath no outward cause to withdraw him from it, where the eye may be busied in considering the works of nature, and the heart quietly rejoiced in the honest using them. If templation as clerks say, be the most excellent, which is so fit a life for templers as this is, neither subject to violent oppression, nor servile flattery, how many courtiers think you I have heard under our field in bushes make their woeful complaints, some of the greatness of their mistress' estate, which dazzled their eyes and yet burned their hearts; some of the extremity of her beauty mixed with extreme cruelty, some of her too much wit, which made all their loving labors folly. O how often have I heard one name sound in many mouths, making our vales witnesses of their doleful agonies! So that with long lost labor finding their thoughts

bare no other wool but despair, of young courtiers they
grew old shepherds. Well sweet lambs I will end with you
as I began, he that can open his mouth against such innocent souls, let him be hated as much as a filthy fox, let
the taste of him be worse than musty cheese, the sound of
him more dreadful than the howling of a wolf, his sight
more odible[28] than a toad in one's porridge.

Rixus. Your life indeed hath some goodness.

Rombus the schoolmaster.

O *tace, tace,* or all the fat will be ignified, first let me
dilucidate the very intrinsical maribone[29] of the matter. He
doth use a certain rhetorical invasion into the point, as if
in deed he had conference with his lambs, but the troth is
he doth equitate you in the mean time master Rixus, for
thus he saith, that sheep are good, *ergo* the shepherd is
good, An *Enthimeme à loco contingentibus,*[30] as my finger
and my thumb are *Contingentes*: again he saith, who liveth
well is likewise good, but shepherds live well, *Ergo* they
are good; a Syllogism in Darius king of Persia a *Con-
jugatis;* as you would say, a man coupled to his wife, two
bodies but one soul: but do you but acquiescate to my
exhortation, and you shall extinguish him. Tell him his
major is a knave, his minor is a fool, and his conclusion
both, *Et ecce homo blancatus quasi liliu.*[31]

Rixus. I was saying the shepherd's life had some goodness in it, because it borrowed of the country quietness
something like ours, but that is not all, for ours besides that
quiet part, doth both strengthen the body, and raise up the
mind with this gallant sort of activity. O sweet contentation
to see the long life of the hurtless trees, to see how in
straight growing up, though never so high, they hinder not
their fellows, they only enviously trouble, which are
crookedly bent. What life is to be compared to ours where
the very growing things are ensamples of goodness? we
have no hopes, but we may quickly go about them, and

---

[28] **odible** hateful   [29] **maribone** marrowbone.   [30] **Enthimeme . . . contingentibus** a syllogism by juxtaposition.   [31] **Et . . . liliu** and behold a man
white as a lily.

going about them, we soon obtain them; not like those that have long followed one (in troth) most excellent chase, do now at length perceive she could never be taken: but that if she stayed at any time near the pursuers, it was never meant to tarry with them, but only to take breath to fly further from them. He therefore that doubts that our life doth not far excel all others, let him also doubt that the well deserving and painful Therion is not to be preferred before the idle Espilus, which is even as much to say, as that the roes are not swifter than sheep, nor the stags more goodly than goats.

Rombus. Bene bene, nunc de questione prepositus, that is as much to say, as well well, now of the proposed question, that was, whether the many great services and many great faults of Therion, or the few small services and no faults of Espilus, be to be preferred, incepted or accepted the former.

The May Lady.

No no, your ordinary trains shall not deal in that matter, I have already submitted it to one, whose sweet spirit hath passed through greater difficulties, neither will I that your blockheads lie in her way.

Therefore O lady worthy to see the accomplishment of your desires, since all your desires be most worthy of you, vouchsafe our ears such happiness, and me that particular favor, as that you will judge whether of these two be more worthy of me, or whether I be worthy of them: and this I will say, that in judging me, you judge more than me in it.

This being said, it pleased her Majesty to judge that Espilus did the better deserve her: but what words, what reasons she used for it, this paper, which carrieth so base names, is not worthy to contain. Sufficeth it, that upon the judgement given, the shepherds and foresters made a full consort of their cornets and recorders, and then did Espilus sing this song, tending to the greatness of his own joy, and yet to the comfort of the other side, since they were overthrown by a most worthy adversary. The song contained two short tales, and thus it was.

Silvanus long in love, and long in vain,
At length obtain'd the point of his desire,
When being askt, now that he did obtain
His wishèd weal, what more he could require:
    Nothing said he, for most I joy in this,
    That goddess mine, my blessèd being sees.

When wanton Pan deceiv'd with lion's skin,
Came to the bed, where wound for kiss he got,
To woe and shame the wretch did enter in,
Till this he took for comfort of his lot,
    Poor Pan (he said) although thou beaten be,
    It is no shame, since Hercules was he.

Thus joyfully in chosen tunes rejoice,
That such a one is witness of my heart,
Whose clearest eyes I bliss, and sweetest voice,
That see my good, and judgeth my desert:
    Thus woefully I in woe this salve do find,
    My foul mishap came yet from fairest mind.

The music fully ended, the May Lady took her leave in this sort.

Lady yourself, for other titles do rather diminish than add unto you. I and my little company must now leave you, I should do you wrong to beseech you to take our follies well, since your bounty is such, as to pardon greater faults. Therefore I will wish you good night, praying to God according to the title I possess, that as hitherto it hath excellently done, so hence forward the flourishing of May, may long remain in you and with you.

FINIS.

From

THE COUNTESS OF
PEMBROKE'S
ARCADIA

From Book I

*

Transformed° in show, but more transformed in mind,
I cease to strive, with double conquest foiled:
For (woe is me) my powers all I find
With outward force and inward treason spoiled.

For from without came to mine eyes the blow,   5
Whereto mine inward thoughts did faintly° yield:
Both these conspired poor Reason's overthrow;
False in myself, thus have I lost the field.

Thus are my eyes still captive to one sight,
Thus all my thoughts are slaves to one thought still: 10
Thus Reason to his servants yields his right,
Thus is my power transformèd to your will:
    What marvel then I take a woman's hue,
    Since what I see, think, know is all but you?

*

Come shepherd's° weeds, become° your master's mind:
Yield° outward show, what inward change he tries:°
Nor be abasht, since such a guest you find,
Whose strongest hope in your weak comfort lies.

5 Come shepherd's weeds, attend my woeful cries:
Disuse yourselves from sweet Menalcas'° voice:
For other be those tunes which sorrow ties,
From those clear notes which freely may rejoice.
    Then pour out plaint, and in one word say this:
10 Helpless his plaint, who spoils himself of bliss.

From the First Eclogues°

*

A) We love, and have our loves rewarded.

B) We love, and are no whit regarded.

A) We find most sweet affection's snare.

B) That sweet, but sour despairful care.

5 A) Who can despair, whom hope doth bear?°

B) And who can hope that feels despair?

A) As without breath no pipe doth move,

B) No music kindly° without love.

*

6 **Menalcas'** the shepherd with whom Musidorus changes clothes;
also, traditional Virgilian name, used here as contrast to suggest
that e prince is a different and special kind of shepherd (see Introduction, p. *xi*).
0 **First Eclogues** introduced by shepherds dancing and "singing some
short couplets, whereto the one half beginning, the other half answered." **5 bear** sustain. **8 kindly** natural.

Thyrsis.° Come Dorus, come, let songs thy sorrows
    signify,
And if for want of use thy mind ashamèd is,
That very shame with love's high title dignify.
    No style is held for base, where love well namèd is:
Each ear sucks up the words a true love scattereth,   5
And plain speech oft, than quaint phrase better
    framèd is.

Dorus. Nightingales seldom sing, the pie still chattereth,
    The wood cries most, before it throughly kindled be,
    Deadly wounds inward bleed, each slight sore
        mattereth.
    Hardly they herd, which by good hunters singled°   10
        be:
    Shallow brooks murmur most, deep silent slide away,
    Nor true-love loves, his loves with others mingled
        be.

Thyrsis. If thou wilt not be seen, thy face go hide away,
    Be none of us, or else maintain our fashion:
    Who frowns at others' feasts, doth better bide away.   15
        But if thou hast a love, in that love's passion,
    I challenge thee by show of her perfection,
    Which of us two deserveth most compassion.

Dorus. Thy challenge great, but greater my protection:
    Sing then, and see (for now thou hast inflamèd me)   20
    Thy health too mean a match for my infection.
        No, though the heav'ns for high attempts have
            blamèd me,
    Yet high is my attempt. O Muse historify
    Her° praise, whose praise to learn your skill hath
        framèd me.

---

1 **Thyrsis** One of the Arcadian shepherds challenges Dorus, the
prince disguised as a shepherd, to what becomes an elaborate singing
contest: first in *terza rima* with the *sdrucciola* or triple rhyme (see
Apology, p. 269); then, at line 71, feminine rhyme; and at line 98,
masculine rhyme. Lines 114–146 employ a complicated inner rhyme,
the Italian *frottola*.   10 **singled** in hunting, separated from the herd.
24 **Her** Pamela.

25 *Thyrsis.* Muse hold your peace: but thou my god Pan
         glorify
      My Kala's gifts: who with all good gifts fillèd is.
      Thy pipe, O Pan, shall help, though I sing sorrily.
         A heap of sweets she is, where nothing spilled is;
      Who though she be no bee, yet full of honey is:
30   A lily field, with plough of rose which tillèd is.
         Mild as a lamb, more dainty than a coney is:
      Her eyes my eyesight is, her conversation
      More glad to me, than to a miser money is.
         What coy account she makes of estimation?
35   How nice to touch? how all her speeches peizèd° be?
      A Nymph thus turn'd, but mended in translation.

Dorus. Such Kala is: but ah my fancies raisèd be
      In one, whose name to name were high presumption,
      Since virtues all, to make her title, pleasèd be.
40   O happy gods, which by inward assumption
      Enjoy her soul, in body's fair possession,
      And keep it join'd, fearing your seat's consumption.
         How oft with rain of tears skies make confession,
      Their dwellers rapt with sight of her perfection,
45   From heav'nly throne to her heav'n use digression?
         Of best things then what world can yield
            confection
      To liken her? Deck yours with your comparison:
      She is herself of best things the collection.

Thyrsis. How oft my doleful sire cried to me, tarry son
50   When first he spied my love? how oft he said to me,
      Thou art no soldier fit for Cupid's garrison.
         My son, keep this, that my long toil hath laid to
            me:
      Love well thine own: methinks wool's whiteness
            passeth all:
      I never found long love such wealth hath paid to me.
55   This wind he spent: but when my Kala glasseth
            all
      My sight in her fair limbs, I then assure myself.
      Not rotten sheep, but high crowns she surpasseth all.

35 **peizèd** weighed.

Can I be poor, that her gold hair procure myself?
Want I white wool, whose eyes her white skin
  garnishèd?
Till I get her, shall I to sheep inure myself?   60

Dorus. How oft, when Reason saw love of her
  harnishèd°
With armor of my heart, he cried, O vanity,
To set a pearl in steel so meanly varnishèd?
  Look to thyself, reach not beyond humanity.
Her mind, beams, state, far from thy weak wings   65
  banishèd:
And love, which lover hurts is unhumanity.
  Thus Reason said: but she came, Reason
  vanishèd;
Her eyes so mastering me, that such objection
Seem'd but to spoil the food of thoughts long
  famishèd.
  Her peerless height my mind to high erection   70
Draws up; and if hope failing end life's pleasure,
Of fairer death how can I make election?

Thyrsis. Once my well waiting eyes espied my treasure,
With sleeves turn'd up, loose hair, and breast
  enlargèd,°
Her father's corn (moving her fair limbs) measure.   75
  O, cried I, of so mean work be dischargèd:
Measure my case, how by thy beauty's filling
With seed of woes my heart brimful is chargèd.
  Thy father bids thee save, and chides for spilling.
Save then my soul, spill not my thoughts well   80
  heapèd,
No lovely praise was ever got by killing.
  These bold words she did hear, this fruit I reapèd,
That she whose look alone might make me blessèd,
Did smile on me, and then away she leapèd.

Dorus. Once, O sweet once, I saw with dread   85
  oppressèd
Her whom I dread: so that with prostrate lying

61 **harnishèd** armored.   74 **enlargèd** exposed, set free.

Her length the earth in Love's chief clothing dressèd.
   I saw that riches fall, and fell a crying;
Let not dead earth enjoy so dear a cover,
90 But deck therewith my soul for your sake dying:
   Lay all your fear upon your fearful lover:
Shine eyes on me that both our lives be guarded;
So I your sight, you shall yourselves recover.
   I cried, and was with open rays rewarded:
95 But straight they fled, summon'd by cruel honor,
Honor, the cause desert is not regarded.

Thyrsis. This maid, thus made for joys, O Pan bemoan
   her,
That without love she spends her years of love:
So fair a field would well become an owner.
100   And if enchantment can a hard heart move,
Teach me what circle may acquaint her sprite,
Affection's charms in my behalf to prove.
   The circle is my (round about her) sight,
The power I will invoke dwells in her eyes:
105 My charm should be she haunt me day and night.

Dorus. Far other case, O Muse, my sorrow tries,
Bent to such one in whom myself must say,
Nothing can mend one point that in her lies.
   What circle then in so rare force bears sway?
110 Whose sprite all sprites can spoil, raise, damn, or
   save:
No charm holds her, but well possess she may,
   Possess she doth, and makes my soul her slave,
My eyes the bands, my thoughts the fatal knot.
No thralls like them that inward bondage have.

115 *Thyrsis.* Kala at length conclude my ling'ring lot:
Disdain me not, although I be not fair.
Who is an heir of many hundred sheep
Doth beauties keep which never sun can burn,
Nor storms do turn: fairness serves oft to wealth.
120 Yet all my health I place in your good-will.
Which if you will (O do) bestow on me,
Such as you see, such still you shall me find,

Constant and kind, my sheep your food shall breed,
Their wool your weed, I will you music yield
In flow'ry field, and as the day begins   *125*
With twenty gins we will the small birds take,
And pastimes make, as Nature things hath made.
But when in shade we meet of myrtle boughs,
Then love allows our pleasures to enrich,
The thought of which doth pass all wordly pelf.   *130*

Dorus. Lady yourself whom neither name I dare,
And titles are but spots to such a worth,
Hear plaints come forth from dungeon of my mind.
The noblest kind rejects not others' woes.
I have no shows of wealth: my wealth is you,   *135*
My beauty's hue your beams, my health your deeds;
My mind for weeds your virtue's livery wears.
My food is tears, my tunes waymenting° yield:
Despair my field; the flowers spirit's wars:
My day new cares; my gins my daily sight,   *140*
In which do light small birds of thoughts o'erthrown:
My pastimes none: time passeth on my fall:
Nature made all, but me of dolors made:
I find no shade, but where my sun doth burn:
No place to turn; without, within it fries: *145*
Nor help by life or death who living dies.

Thyrsis. But if my Kala this my suit denies,
Which so much reason bears:
Let crows pick out mine eyes, which saw too much:
If still her mind be such,   *150*
My earthy mould doth melt in wat'ry tears.

Dorus. My earthy mould doth melt in wat'ry tears,
And they again resolve
To air of sighs, sighs to the heart's fire turn,
Which doth to ashes burn: *155*
So doth my life within itself dissolve.

Thyrsis. So doth my life within itself dissolve,
That I am like a flower
New pluckèd from the place where it did breed,

138 **waymenting** lamenting.

160   Life showing, dead indeed:
        Such force hath Love above poor Nature's power.

Dorus. Such force hath Love above poor Nature's
        power,
    That I grow like a shade,°
    Which being nought seems somewhat to the eyen,
165   While that one body° shine.
    Oh he is marr'd that is for others made.

Thyrsis. Oh he is marr'd that is for others made.
    Which thought doth mar my piping declaration,
    Thinking how it hath marr'd my shepherd's trade.
170   Now my hoarse voice doth fail this occupation,
    And others long to tell their loves' condition:
    Of singing take to thee the reputation.

Dorus. Of singing take to thee the reputation
    New friend of mine; I yield to thy hability:
175   My heart doth seek another estimation.
        But ah my Muse I would thou hadst facility,
    To work my goddess so by thy invention,
    On me to cast those eyes, where shine nobility.
        Seen, and unknown; heard but without attention.

*

If mine° eyes can speak to do hearty° errand,
Or mine eyes' language she do hap to judge of,
So that eyes' message be of her receivèd,
    Hope we do live yet.

5 But if eyes fail then, when I most do need them,
Or if eyes' language be not unto her known,
So that eyes' message do return rejected,
    Hope we do both die.

Yet dying, and dead, do we sing her honor;
10 So become our tombs monuments of her praise;

---

163 **shade** shadow.   165 **one body** the sun (Pamela).
1 **mine** Pyrocles, continuing in disguise as an Amazon, "sang these
sapphics, speaking as it were to her own hope."   1 **hearty** (1) cou-
rageous; (2) from the heart, heartfelt.

So becomes our loss the triumph of her gain;
    Hers be the glory.

If the senseless spheres do yet hold a music,
If the swan's sweet voice be not heard, but at death,
If the mute timber when it hath the life lost,   *15*
    Yieldeth a lute's tune:

Are then human minds privileg'd so meanly,
As that hateful death can abridge them of power
With the voice of truth to record to all worlds,
    That we be her spoils?   *20*

Thus not ending, ends the due praise of her praise;
Fleshly vail consumes;° but a soul hath his life,
Which is held in love, love it is, that hath join'd
    Life to this our soul.

But if eyes can speak to do hearty errand,   *25*
Or mine eyes' language she do hap to judge of,
So that eyes' message be of her receivèd,
    Hope we do live yet.

From Book II

*

In vain, mine eyes, you labor to amend
    With flowing tears your fault of hasty sight:
Since to my heart her° shape you so did send,
    That her I see, though you did lose your light.

In vain, my heart, now you with sight are burn'd,   *5*
    With sighs you seek to cool your hot desire:
Since sighs (into mine inward furnace turn'd)
    For bellows serve to kindle more the fire.

---

22 vail consumes (1) the veil of flesh decays; (2) fleshly worth (vail)
decays.
3 my . . . her Pyrocles singing of his love for Philoclea.

Reason, in vain (now you have lost my heart)
10   My head you seek, as to your strongest fort:
Since there mine eyes have played so false a part,
        That to your strength your foes have sure resort.
            Then since in vain I find were all my strife,
            To this strange death I vainly yield my life.

*

Let not old age° disgrace my high desire,
        O heavenly soul, in human shape contain'd:
Old wood inflam'd, doth yield the bravest fire,
        When younger doth in smoke his virtue° spend.

5   Ne let white hairs, which on my face do grow,
        Seem to your eyes of a disgraceful hue:
Since whiteness doth present the sweetest show,
        Which makes all eyes do honor unto you.

Old age is wise, and full of constant truth;
10   Old age well stayed, from ranging humor° lives:
Old age hath known what ever was in youth:
        Old age o'ercome, the greater honor gives.
            And to old age since you yourself aspire,
            Let not old age disgrace my high desire.

*

Since so mine eyes are subject to your sight,°
That in your sight they fixèd have my brain;
Since so my heart is fillèd with that light,
That only light° doth all my life maintain;

5   Since in sweet you all goods so richly reign,
That where you are no wishèd good can want;°
Since so your living image lives in me,
That in myself yourself true love doth plant;
        How can you him unworthy then decree,
10   In whose chief part your worths implanted be?

*

1 old age sung by the king, Basilius, who has fallen in love with the
Amazon, not realizing she is Pyrocles in disguise.   4 virtue also,
strength.   10 humor fancy.
1 your sight pretending to court Pamela's servant, Mopsa, Musidorus really directs this song to the princess.   4 only light light
alone.   6 want be lacking.

My sheep are thoughts, which I both guide and serve:°
Their pasture is fair hills of fruitless love:
On barren sweets they feed, and feeding sterve:°
I wail their lot, but will not other prove.°
My sheephook is wan hope,° which all upholds: 5
My weeds, desire, cut out in endless folds.
    What wool my sheep shall bear, while thus they live,
    In you it is, you must the judgement give.

*

Ye living powers enclosed in stately shrine°
Of growing trees; ye rural gods that wield
Your scepters here, if to your ears divine
A voice may come, which troubled soul doth yield:
    This vow receive, this vow O gods maintain;   5
    My virgin life no spotted thought shall stain.

Thou purest stone, whose pureness doth present°
My purest mind; whose temper hard doth show
My temp'red heart; by thee my promise sent
Unto my self let after-livers know.   10
    No fancy mine, nor others' wrong suspect°
    Make me, O virtuous shame, thy laws neglect.

O Chastity, the chief of heavenly lights,
Which makes us most immortal shape to wear,
Hold thou my heart, establish thou my sprights: 15
To only thee my constant course I bear.
    Till spotless soul unto thy bosom fly,
    Such life to lead, such death I vow to die.

*

1 **serve** Musidorus, in his shepherd's disguise, to Pamela: hoping to
"mollify . . . her silent imaginations . . . as is the nature of music
to do and withal, to show what kind of shepherd I was." 3 **sterve**
starve. 4 **prove** experience. 5 **wan hope** or, as one word, wanhope
(despair).

1 **shrine** words written by Philoclea—before the arrival of Pyrocles
—on a white marble stone "that should seem had been dedicated in
ancient time to the sylvan gods." 7 **present** i.e., represent. 11 **sus-
pect** suspicion.

My words,° in hope to blaze° my steadfast mind,
This marble chose, as of like temper known:
But lo, my words defac'd, my fancies blind,
Blots to the stone, shame to myself I find:
5   And witness am, how ill agree in one,
    A woman's hand with constant marble stone.

My words full weak, the marble full of might;
My words in store,° the marble all alone;
My words black ink, the marble kindly white;
10 My words unseen, the marble still in sight,
    May witness bear, how ill agree in one,
    A woman's hand, with constant marble stone.

*

Poor painters° oft with silly poets join,
To fill the world with strange but vain conceits:
One brings the stuff, the other stamps the coin,
Which breeds nought else but glozes of deceits.
5   Thus painters Cupid paint, thus poets do
    A naked god, young blind with arrows two.

Is he a god, that ever flies the light?
Or naked he, disguis'd in all untruth?
If he be blind, how hitteth he so right?
10 How is he young, that tam'd old Phoebus'° youth?
    But arrows two, and tipp'd with gold or lead?
    Some hurt accuse a third with horny head.°

No, nothing so; an old false knave he is,
By Argus° got on Io, then a cow:

1 **My words** The preceding poem, which Philoclea had written on
white marble. Revisiting the spot, "there came into her head certain
verses, which if she had had present commodity, she would have ad-
joined as a retraction to the other."   1 **blaze** emblazon.   8 **in store**
in abundance.
1 **Poor painters** Miso, wife of the clownish Dametas, shows the princesses her "prayer book" which closes with this satirical genealogy
of Love.   10 **Phoebus'** whom Cupid forced to fall in love with
Daphne.   12 **horny head** cuckoldry. Sidney's addition to the traditional gold arrow of love and lead arrow of disdain.   14 **Argus** the
hundred-eyed guardian of Io, who, after her visitation from Jove,
had been transformed into a cow.

What time for her Juno her Jove did miss,   15
And charge of her to Argus did allow.
   Mercury kill'd his false sire for this act,
   His dam a beast was pardon'd beastly fact.

With father's death, and mother's guilty shame,
With Jove's disdain at such a rival's seed: 20
The wretch compell'd a runnagate° became,
And learn'd what ill a miser state doth breed:
   To lie, feign, gloze, to steal, pry, and accuse,
   Naught in himself each other to abuse.

Yet bears he still his parents' stately gifts,   25
A horn'd head, cloven foot, and thousand eyes,
Some gazing still, some winking wily shifts,
With long large ears, where never rumor dies.
   His hornèd head doth seem the heaven to spite,
   His cloven foot doth never tread aright.   30

Thus half a man, with man he daily haunts,
Cloth'd in the shape which soonest may deceive:
Thus half a beast, each beastly vice he plants,
In those weak hearts that his advice receive.
   He prowls each place still in new colors deckt,   35
   Sucking one's ill, another to infect.

To narrow breasts he comes all wrapt in gain:
To swelling hearts he shines in honor's fire:
To open eyes all beauties he doth rain;
Creeping to each with flattering of desire,   40
   But for that Love's desire most rules the eyes,
   Therein his name, there his chief triumph lies.

Millions of years this old drivel Cupid lives;
While still more wretch, more wicked he doth prove:
Till now at length that Jove him office gives,   45
(At Juno's suit, who much did Argus love)
   In this our world a hang-man for to be,
   Of all those fools, that will have all they see.

*

21 **runnagate** vagabond.

Lovèd I am, and yet complain of Love:°
As loving not, accus'd,° in Love I die.
When pity most I crave, I cruel prove:
Still seeking Love, Love found as much I fly.
5   Burnt in myself, I muse at others' fire:
What I call wrong, I do the same, and more:
Barr'd of my will, I have beyond desire:
I wail for want, and yet am chokt with store.
    This is thy work, thou god for ever blind:
10 Though thousands old, a boy entitled still.
Thus children do the silly birds they find,
With stroking hurt, and too much cramming kill.
    Yet thus much Love, O Love, I crave of thee:
    Let me be lov'd, or else not lovèd be.

*

Over these brooks° trusting to ease mine eyes,
(Mine eyes even great in labor with their tears)
I laid my face; my face wherein there lies
Clusters of clouds, which no sun ever clears.
5   In wat'ry glass my wat'ry eyes I see:
    Sorrows ill eas'd, where sorrows painted be.

My thoughts imprison'd in my secret woes,
With flamy breath do issue oft in sound:
The sound to this strange air no sooner goes,
10 But that it doth with Echo's force rebound,
    And make me hear the plaints I would refrain:
    Thus outward helps my inward griefs maintain.

Now in this sand I would discharge my mind,
And cast from me part of my burd'nous cares:
15 But in the sand my tales° foretold I find,

---

1 **Lovèd . . . Love** Pyrocles, in love with Philoclea, is being wooed
by Basilius and by the queen Gynecia, who has penetrated his
Amazon disguise. 2 **accus'd** i.e., of not loving Gynecia and
Basilius.
1 **brooks** Pyrocles "took a willow stick and wrote in a sandy bank
these verses." 15 **tales** *Old Arcadia*—"pains."

And see therein how well the writer fares.
    Since stream, air, sand, mine eyes and ears conspire:
    What hope to quench, where each thing blows the
        fire?

*

With two strange fires of equal heat possest,°
The one of love, the other jealousy,
Both still do work, in neither find I rest:
For both, alas, their strengths together tie:
The one aloft doth hold° the other high.   5
    Love wakes the jealous eye lest thence it moves:
    The jealous eye, the more it looks, it loves.

These fires increase: in these I daily burn:
They feed on me, and with my wings do fly:
My lively° joys to doleful ashes turn: 10
Their flames mount up, my powers prostrate lie:
They live in force, I quite consumèd die.
    One wonder yet far passeth my conceit:
    The fuel small: how be the fires so great?

From the Second Eclogues

*

Reason.° Thou rebel vile, come, to thy master yield.
Passion. No, tyrant, no; mine, mine shall be the field.
R. Can Reason then a tyrant counted be?
P. If Reason will, that Passions be not free.

1 With . . . possest Gynecia, who loves Pyrocles, is jealous of her
daughter whom he pursues. 5 hold 1590 punctuation: "hold, the."
10 lively 1590, 1593: "lovely."

1 Reason The opening of the second set of eclogues, a skirmish between Reason and Passion, each side represented by seven shepherds "four of them making a square, and the other two going a
little wide of either side, like wings for the main battle; and the
seventh man foremost, like the forlorn hope to begin the skirmish."

5   *R.* But Reason will, that Reason govern most.
      P. And Passion will, that Passion rule the rost.
      R. Your will is will; but Reason reason is.
      P. Will hath his will, when Reason's will doth miss.
      R. Whom Passion leads unto his death is bent.
10   *P.* And let him die, so that he die content.
      R. By nature you to Reason faith have sworn.
      P. Not so, but fellowlike together born.
      R. Who Passion doth ensue, lives in annoy.
      P. Who Passion doth forsake, lives void of joy.
15   *R.* Passion is blind, and treads an unknown trace.
      P. Reason hath eyes to see his own ill case.
      R. Dare Passions then abide in Reason's light?
      P. And is not Reason dimm'd with Passion's might?
      R. O foolish thing, which glory doth destroy.
20   *P.* O glorious title of a foolish toy.
      R. Weakness you are, dare you with our strength fight?
      P. Because our weakness weakeneth all your might.
      R. O sacred Reason, help our virtuous toils.
      P. O Passion, pass on feeble Reason's spoils.
25   *R.* We with ourselves abide a daily strife.
      P. We gladly use the sweetness of our life.
      R. But yet our strife sure peace in end doth breed.
      P. We now have peace, your peace we do not need.
      R. We are too strong: but Reason seeks not blood.
30   *P.* Who be too weak, do feign they be too good.
      R. Though we cannot o'ercome, our cause is just.
      P. Let us o'ercome, and let us be unjust.
      R. Yet Passion, yield at length to Reason's stroke.
      P. What shall we win by taking Reason's yoke?
35   *R.* The joys you have shall be made permanent.
      P. But so we shall with grief learn to repent.
      R. Repent indeed, but that shall be your bliss.
      P. How know we that, since present joys we miss?
      R. You know it not: of Reason therefore know it.
40   *P.* No Reason yet had ever skill to show it.
      R. P. Then let us both to heavenly rules give place,
             Which Passions kill, and Reason do deface.

*

Strephon.° Ye goatherd gods, that love the grassy
          mountains,
     Ye Nymphs that haunt the springs in pleasant
          valleys,
     Ye Satyrs joy'd with free and quiet forests,
     Vouchsafe your silent ears to plaining music,
     Which to my woes gives still an early morning: 5
     And draws the dolor on till weary evening.

Klaius. O Mercury, foregoer to the evening,
     O heavenly huntress of the savage mountains,
     O lovely star, entitled of the morning,°
     While that my voice doth fill these woeful valleys,   10
     Vouchsafe your silent ears to plaining music,
     Which oft hath Echo tir'd in secret forests.

Strephon. I that was once free-burgess of the forests,
     Where shade from sun, and sport I sought in
          evening,
     I that was once esteem'd for pleasant music   15
     Am banisht now among the monstrous mountains
     Of huge despair, and foul affliction's valleys,
     Am grown a shrich-owl° to myself each morning.

Klaius. I that was once delighted every morning,
     Hunting the wild inhabiters of forests: 20
     I that was once the music of these valleys,
     So darkened am, that all my day is evening,
     Heart-broken so, that molehills seem high
          mountains,
     And fill the vales with cries in stead of music.

---

1 ff. **Strephon, Klaius** In the original version, two gentlemen who
become shepherds for the love of Urania, "thought a shepherd's
daughter, but indeed of far greater birth." The *New Arcadia*
opens with a prose lament commemorating her departure for
"Cithera," and thus more clearly establishing her as a figure of de-
parted, ideal love. The form, following Italian models, is the double
sestina. 7–9 **Mercury . . . morning** referring both to the gods and
to their astrological representatives: Mercury (evening star); Diana
(the moon); Venus (the morning star). 18 **shrich-owl** shriek-owl.

25 *Strephon.* Long since alas, my deadly swannish music°
    Hath made itself a crier of the morning,
    And hath with wailing strength climb'd highest
       mountains:
    Long since my thoughts more desert° be than forests:
    Long since I see my joys come to their evening,
30   And state thrown down to overtrodden valleys.

Klaius. Long since the happy dwellers of these valleys,
    Have pray'd me leave my strange exclaiming music,
    Which troubles their day's work, and joys of
       evening:
    Long since I hate the night, more hate the morning:
35   Long since my thoughts chase me like beasts in
       forests,
    And make me wish myself laid under mountains.

Strephon. Meseems I see the high and stately
       mountains,
    Transform themselves to low dejected° valleys:
    Meseems I hear in these ill-changèd forests,
40   The nightingales do learn of owls their music:
    Meseems I feel the comfort of the morning
    Turn'd to the mortal serene° of an evening.

Klaius. Meseems I see a filthy cloudy evening,
    As soon as sun begins to climb the mountains:
45   Meseems I feel a noisome scent, the morning
    When I do smell the flowers of these valleys:
    Meseems I hear, when I do hear sweet music,
    The dreadful cries of murd'red men in forests.

Strephon. I wish to fire the trees of all these forests,
50   I give the sun a last farewell each evening,
    I curse the fiddling finders out of music:
    With envy I do hate the lofty mountains;
    And with despite despise the humble valleys:
    I do detest night, evening, day, and morning.

---

25 deadly . . . music the swan was said to sing only at the moment
of death.   **28 desert** desolate.   **38 dejected** thrown down.   **42 mortal serene** noxious vapor that falls after sunset.

Klaius. Curse to myself my prayer is, the morning: 55
  My fire is more than can be made with forests;
  My state more base, than are the basest valleys:
  I wish no evenings more to see, each evening;
  Shamèd I hate° myself in sight of mountains,
  And stop mine ears, lest I grow mad with music.   60

Strephon. For she, whose parts maintain'd a perfect
      music,
  Whose beauty shin'd more than the blushing
      morning,
  Who much did pass in state the stately mountains,
  In straightness past the cedars of the forests,
  Hath cast me wretch into eternal evening,   65
  By taking her two suns from these dark valleys.

Klaius. For she, to whom compar'd, the Alps are
      valleys,
  She, whose least word brings from the spheres their
      music,
  At whose approach the sun rose in the evening,
  Who, where she went, bare in her forehead morning,   70
  Is gone, is gone from these our spoilèd forests,
  Turning to deserts our best pastur'd mountains.

Strephon. These mountains witness shall, so shall these
      valleys,
Klaius. These forests eke, made wretched by our
      music,
  Our morning hymn this is, and song at evening.   75

*

Strephon.° I joy in grief, and do detest all joys:
  Despise delight, am tir'd with thought of ease:
  I turn my mind to all forms of annoys,
  And with the change of them my fancy please.
  I study that which most may me displease,   5

---

59 hate 1590, 1593: "have."
1 **Strephon** another lament, this time a "dizaine" or "Crown," in
which the last line of a stanza becomes the first line of the next.

And in despite of that displeasure's might,
Embrace that most, that most my soul destroys.
Blinded with beams, fell darkness is my sight:
Dwell in my ruins, feed with sucking smart,
10   I think from me, not from my woes to part.

Klaius. I think from me, not from my woes to part,
And loathe this time, call'd life, nay think, that life
Nature to me for torment did impart;
Think, my hard haps have blunted death's sharp
    knife,
15 Not sparing me, in whom his works be rife:
And thinking this, think nature, life, and death
Place sorrow's triumph on my conquer'd heart:
Whereto I yield, and seek no other breath,
But from the scent of some infectious grave:
20 Nor of my fortune ought, but mischief crave.

Strephon. Nor of my fortune ought, but mischief crave,
And seek to nourish that, which now contains
All what I am: if I myself will save,
Then must I save, what in me chiefly reigns,
25 Which is the hateful web of sorrow's pains.
Sorrow then cherish me, for I am sorrow:
No being now, but sorrow I can have:
Then deck me as thine own; thy help I borrow,
Since thou my riches art, and that thou hast
30 Enough to make a fertile mind lie waste.

Klaius. Enough to make a fertile mind lie waste
Is that huge storm, which pours itself on me:
Hailstones of tears, of sighs a monstrous blast,
Thunders of cries; lightnings my wild looks be,
35 The darken'd heav'n my soul which nought can see;
The flying sprites which trees by roots up tear
Be those despairs, which have my hopes quite wast.°
The diff'rence is; all folks those storms forbear:
But I cannot; who then myself should fly,
40 So close unto myself my wracks do lie.

37 **wast** wasted.

Strephon. So close unto myself my wracks do lie;
   Both cause, effect, beginning, and the end
   Are all in me: what help then can I try?
   My ship, myself, whose course to love doth bend,
   Sore beaten doth her mast of Comfort spend: 45
   Her cable, Reason, breaks from anchor, Hope:
   Fancy, her tackling, torn away doth fly:
   Ruin, the wind, hath blown her from her scope:°
   Bruisèd with waves of Care, but broken is
   On rock, Despair, the burial of my bliss.   50

Klaius. On rock, Despair, the burial of my bliss
   I long do plow with plough of deep Desire:
   The seed Fast-meaning° is, no truth to miss:
   I harrow it with Thoughts, which all conspire
   Favor to make my chief and only hire.   55
   But, woe is me, the year is gone about,
   And now I fain would reap, I reap but this,
   Hate fully grown, Absence new sprongen out.
   So that I see, although my sight impair,
   Vain is their pain, who labor in Despair.   60

Strephon. Vain is their pain, who labor in Despair.
   For so did I, when with my angle, Will,
   I sought to catch the fish Torpedo° fair.
   Ev'n then Despair did Hope already kill:
   Yet Fancy would perforce employ his skill,   65
   And this hath got; the catcher now is caught,
   Lam'd with the angle, which itself° did bear,
   And unto death, quite drown'd in Dolors, brought
   To death, as then disguis'd in her fair face.
   Thus, thus alas, I had my loss in chase.°   70

Klaius. Thus, thus alas, I had my loss in chase,
   When first that crownèd basilisk° I knew,
   Whose footsteps I with kisses oft did trace,
   Till by such hap, as I must ever rue,

48 **scope** goal. 53 **Fast-meaning** firm or established meaning.
63 **Torpedo** the electric ray, a fish which paralyzes the angler as he
catches it. 67 **itself** the catcher himself. 70 **in chase** while chasing.
72 **basilisk** a fabulous reptile whose breath and look are fatal.

75   Mine eyes did light upon her shining hue,
   And hers on me, astonisht with that sight.
   Since then my heart did loose his wonted place,
   Infected so with her sweet poison's might,
   That, leaving me for dead, to her it went:
80   But ah her flight hath my dead reliques spent.

Strephon. But ah her flight hath my dead reliques
       spent,
   Her flight from me, from me, though dead to me,
   Yet living still in her, while her beams lent
   Such vital spark, that her mine eyes might see.
85   But now those living lights absented be,
   Full dead before, I now to dust should fall,
   But that eternal pains my soul have hent,°
   And keep it still within this body thrall:
   That thus I must, while in this death I dwell,
90   In earthly fetters feel a lasting hell.

Klaius. In earthly fetters feel a lasting hell
   Alas I do; from which to find release,
   I would the earth, I would the heavens sell.
   But vain it is to think these pains should cease,
95   Where life is death, and death cannot breed peace.
   O fair, O only fair, from thee, alas,
   These foul, most foul, disasters to me fell;
   Since thou from me (O me) O sun didst pass.
   Therefore esteeming all good blessings toys,
100 I joy in grief, and do detest all joys.

Strephon. I joy in grief, and do detest all joys.
   But now an end, (O Klaius) now an end:
   For even the herbs our hateful music 'stroys,
   And from our burning breath the trees do bend.

*

My muse what ails this ardor°
To blaze° my only secrets?
Alas it is no glory

1 My . . . ardor Zelmane (Pyrocles) "threw down the burden of her
mind in Anacreon's kind of verses." **2 blaze** emblazon.

To sing my own decay'd state.
Alas it is no comfort,   5
To speak without an answer.
Alas it is no wisdom
To show the wound without cure.

My muse what ails this ardor?
My eyes be dim, my limbs shake,   10
My voice is hoarse, my throat scorcht,
My tongue to this my roof cleaves,
My fancy amaz'd, my thoughts dull'd,
My heart doth ache, my life faints,
My soul begins to take leave.   15
So great a passion all feel,
To think a sore so deadly
I should so rashly rip up.

My muse what ails this ardor?
If that to sing thou art bent,   20
Go sing the fall of old Thebes,
The wars of ugly Centaurs,
The life, the death of Hector,
So may thy song be famous,
Or if to love thou art bent,   25
Recount the rape of Europe,
Adonis' end, Venus' net,
The sleepy kiss° the moon stale:
So may thy song be pleasant.

My muse what ails this ardor   30
To blaze my only secrets?
Wherein do only flourish
The sorry fruits of anguish.
The song thereof a last will,
The tunes be cries, the words plaints,   35
The singer is the song's theme,
Wherein no ear can have joy,
Nor eye receive due object
Ne pleasure here, ne fame get.

28 sleepy kiss the goddess of the moon kisses the shepherd boy
Endymion, while he is asleep.

40 My muse what ails this ardor?
    Alas, she° saith, I am thine,
    So are thy pains my pains too.
    Thy heated heart my seat is
    Wherein I burn, thy breath is
45 My voice, too hot to keep in,
    Besides lo here the author
    Of all thy harms: Lo here she,°
    That only can redress thee,
    Of her I will demand help.

50 My muse I yield, my muse sing,
    But all thy song herein knit,
    The life we lead is all love:
    The love we hold is all death,
    Nor ought I crave to feed life,
55 Nor ought I seek to shun death,
    But only that my goddess
    My life my death do count hers.

*

O sweet woods the delight of solitariness!°
O how much I do like your solitariness!
Where man's mind hath a freed consideration
Of goodness to receive lovely direction.
5 Where senses do behold th'order of heav'nly host,
   And wise thoughts do behold what the creator is:
   Contemplation here holdeth his only seat:
   Bounded with no limits, borne with a wing of hope
   Climbs even unto the stars, Nature is under it.
10 Nought disturbs thy quiet, all to thy service yield,
    Each sight draws on a thought, thought mother of
              science,
    Sweet birds kindly do grant harmony unto thee,
    Fair trees' shade is enough fortification,
    Nor danger to thyself if be not in thyself.

41 she his muse, whose speech ends at line 49.   47 she his mistress,
Philoclea.

1 O . . . solitariness Dorus, "singing these verses called Asclepiadics."

O sweet woods the delight of solitariness!   15
O how much I do like your solitariness!
Here no treason is hid, veilèd in innocence,
Nor envy's snaky eye, finds any harbor here,
Nor flatterers' venomous insinuations,
Nor conning humorists'° puddled opinions,   20
Nor courteous ruin of proffered usury,
Nor time prattled away, cradle of ignorance,
Nor causeless duty, nor comber of arrogance,
Nor trifling title of vanity dazzleth us,
Nor golden manacles, stand for a paradise,   25
Here wrong's name is unheard: slander a monster is.
Keep thy sprite from abuse, here no abuse doth haunt.
What man grafts in a tree dissimulation?

O sweet woods the delight of solitariness!
O how well I do like your solitariness!   30
Yet dear soil, if° a soul closed in a mansion°
As sweet as violets, fair as a lily is,
Straight as cedar, a voice stains the Canary birds,
Whose shade safety doth hold, danger avoideth her:
Such wisdom, that in her lives speculation: 35
Such goodness that in her simplicity triumphs:
Where envy's snaky eye, winketh or else dieth,
Slander wants a pretext, flattery gone beyond:
Oh! if such a one have bent to a lonely life
Her steps, glad we receive, glad we receive her eyes.   40
    And think not she doth hurt our solitariness,
    For such company decks such solitariness.

---

20 humorists' persons subject to humors or fancies; faddists.   **31 if**
. . . sentence completed at line 39.   **31 mansion** i.e., her body.

From Book III

*

Now was our heav'nly vault deprivèd of the light°
With sun's depart: and now the darkness of the night
Did light those beamy stars which greater light did
    dark:
Now each thing which enjoy'd that fiery quick'ning
    spark
5 (Which life is call'd) were mov'd their spirits to repose,
And wanting° use of eyes, their eyes began to close:
A silence sweet each where with one consent embrac'd
(A music sweet to one in careful musing plac'd)
And mother Earth, now clad in mourning weeds, did
    breathe
10 A dull desire to kiss the image of our death:
When I, disgracèd wretch, not wretched then, did give
My senses such release, as they which quiet live,
Whose brains boil not in woes, nor breasts with
    beatings ache,
With nature's praise are wont in safest home to take.
15 Far from my thoughts was ought, whereto their minds
    aspire,
Who under courtly pomps do hatch° a base desire.
Free all my powers were from those captiving snares,
Which heavn'ly purest gifts defile in muddy cares.
Ne could my soul itself accuse of such a fault,
20 As tender conscience might with furious pangs assault.

1 Originally given to Philisides, Sidney's thinly disguised *persona*
in the *Old Arcadia*, this dream vision was transferred in the *New
Arcadia* to the warrior Amphialus as a dream vision which he sees
the night before falling in love with the princess Philoclea.
6 wanting deprived of. 16 hatch also, close (see *Astrophel and
Stella*, 38).

But like the feeble flower (whose stalk cannot sustain
His weighty top) his top doth downward drooping lean:
Or as the silly bird in well acquainted nest
Doth hide his head with cares but only how to rest:
So I in simple course, and unentangled mind   25
Did suffer drowsy lids mine eyes then clear to blind;
And laying down my head, did nature's rule observe,
Which senses up doth shut the senses to preserve.
They first their use forgot, then fancies lost their force;
Till deadly sleep at length possest my living corse.°   30
A living corse I lay: but ah, my wakeful mind
(Which made of heav'nly stuff no mortal change doth
        bind)
Flew up with freer wings of fleshly bondage free;
And having plac'd my thoughts, my thoughts thus
        placèd me.
Methought, nay sure I was, I was in fairest wood   35
Of Samothea land; a land, which whilom stood
An honor to the world, while honor was their end,
And while their line of years they did in virtue spend.
But there I was, and there my calmy thoughts I fed
On nature's sweet repast, as healthful senses led.   40
Her gifts my study was, her beauties were my sport:
My work her works to know, her dwelling my resort.
Those lamps of heav'nly fire to fixèd motion bound,
The ever-turning spheres, the never-moving ground;
What essence dest'ny hath; if fortune be or no;   45
Whence our immortal souls to mortal earth do flow:
What life it is, and how that all these lives do gather,
With outward maker's force, or like an inward father.
Such thoughts, methought, I thought, and strain'd my
        single mind,
Then void of nearer cares, the depth of things to find;   50
When lo with hugest noise (such noise a tower makes
When it blown down with wind a fall of ruin takes)
(Or such a noise it was, as highest thunder send,
Or cannons thunderlike, all shot together, lend)
The moon asunder rent (O gods, O pardon me,   55

30 corse corpse.

That forced with grief reveals what grievèd eyes did
    see)
The moon asunder rent; whereat with sudden fall
(More swift than falcon's stoop to feeding falconer's
    call)
There came a chariot fair by doves and sparrows
    guided,
60 Whose stormlike course stay'd not till hard by me it
    bided.
I wretch astonisht was, and thought the deathful
    doom
Of heaven, of earth, of hell, of time and place was
    come.
But straight there issued forth two ladies (ladies sure
They seem'd to me) on whom did wait a virgin pure.
65 Strange were the ladies' weeds; yet more unfit than
    strange.
The first with cloth's tuckt up as nymphs in woods do
    range;
Tuckt up even with the knees, with bow and arrows
    prest:°
Her right arm naked was, discovered was her breast.
But heavy was her pace, and such a meagre cheer,°
70 As little hunting mind (God knows) did there appear.
The other had with art (more than our women know,
As stuff meant for the sale set out to glaring show)
A wanton woman's face, and with curl'd knots had
    twin'd
Her hair, which by the help of painter's cunning,
    shin'd.
75 When I such guests did see come out of such a house,
The mountains great with child I thought brought forth
    a mouse.
But walking forth, the first thus to the second said,
Venus come on: said she, Diane you are obey'd.
Those names abasht me much, when those great names
    I heard:

67 prest in readiness. **69 cheer** expression.

Although their fame (meseem'd) from truth had   80
    greatly jarr'd.
As I thus musing stood, Diana call'd to her
Her waiting nymph, a nymph that did excel as far
All things that erst I saw, as orient pearls exceed
That which their mother hight,° or else their silly seed.°
Indeed a perfect hue, indeed a sweet consent   85
Of all those Graces' gifts the heavens have ever lent.
And so she was attir'd, as one that did not prize
Too much her peerless parts, not yet could them
    despise.
But call'd, she came apace; a pace wherein did move
The band of beauties all, the little world of love.   90
And bending humbled eyes (O eyes the sun of sight)
She waited mistress' will: who thus disclos'd her sprite.
Sweet Mira mine (quoth she) the pleasure of my mind,
In whom of all my rules the perfect proof I find,
To only thee thou seest we grant this special grace   95
Us to attend, in this most private time and place.
Be silent therefore now, and so be silent still
Of what thou seest: close up in secret knot thy will.
She answer'd was with look, and well perform'd behest:
And Mira I admir'd: her shape sank in my breast.   100
But thus with ireful eyes, and face that shook with spite
Diana did begin. What mov'd me to invite
Your presence (sister dear) first to my moony sphere,
And hither now, vouchsafe to take with willing ear.
I know full well you know, what discord long hath   105
    reign'd
Betwixt us two; how much that discord foul hath
    stain'd
Both our estates, while each the other did deprave,°
Proof speaks too much to us that feeling trial have.
Our names are quite forgot, our temples are defac'd:

83–84 **orient . . . seed** distinguishing the lustrous pearl (usually
from the Indian Ocean) from mother-of-pearl (a pearl-like substance found in shells) and from tiny seed pearls.   84 **hight** named.
107 **deprave** slander.

110 Our off'rings spoil'd, our priests from priesthood are
         displac'd.
     Is this the fruit of strife? those thousand churches high,
     Those thousand altars fair now in the dust to lie?
     In mortal minds our minds but planets' names preserve:
     No knee once bowed, forsooth, for them they say we
         serve.
115 Are we their servants grown? no doubt a noble stay:°
     Celestial powers to worms, Jove's children serve to
         clay.
     But such they say we be: this praise our discord bred,
     While we for mutual spite a striving passion fed.
     But let us wiser be; and what foul discord brake,
120 So much more strong again let fastest concord make.
     Our years do it require: you see we both do feel
     The weak'ning work of Time's for ever-whirling wheel.
     Although we be divine, our grandsire Saturn is
     With age's force decay'd, yet once the heaven was his.
125 And now before we seek by wise Apollo's skill
     Our young years to renew (for so he saith he will)
     Let us a perfect peace betwixt us two resolve:
     Which lest the ruinous want of government dissolve;
     Let one the princess be, to her the other yield:
130 For vain equality is but contention's field.
     And let her have the gifts that should in both remain:
     In her let beauty both, and chasteness fully reign.
     So as if I prevail, you give your gifts to me:
     If you, on you I lay what in my office be.
135 Now resteth only this, which of us two is she,
     To whom precedence shall of both accorded be.
     For that (so that you like) hereby doth lie a youth
     (She beck'ned unto me) as yet of spotless truth,
     Who may this doubt discern: for better, wit, than lot
140 Becometh us: in us fortune determines not.°
     This crown of amber fair (an amber crown she held)
     To worthiest let him give, when both he hath beheld:
     And be it as he saith. Venus was glad to hear

115 **stay** condition.   140 **fortune . . . not** not left to mere fortune.

Such proffer made, which she well show'd with smiling
    cheer.
As though she were the same, as when by Paris' doom   *145*
She had chief goddesses in beauty overcome.
And smirkly thus gan say. I never sought debate
Diana dear; my mind to love and not to hate
Was ever apt: but you my pastimes did despise.
I never spited you, but thought you overwise.   *150*
Now kindness proff'red is, none kinder is than I:
And so most ready am this mean of peace to try.
And let him be our judge: the lad doth please me well.
Thus both did come to me, and both began to tell
(For both together spake, each loth to be behind)   *155*
That they by solemn oath their deities would bind
To stand unto my will: their will they made me know.
I that was first aghast, when first I saw their show,
Now bolder waxt, waxt proud, that I such sway might
    bear:
For near acquaintance doth diminish reverent fear.   *160*
And having bound them fast by Styx,° they should
    obey
To all what I decreed, did thus my verdict say.
How ill both you can rule, well hath your discord
    taught:
Ne yet for what I see, your beauties merit ought.
To yonder nymph therefore (to Mira I did point)   *165*
The crown above you both for ever I appoint.
I would have spoken out; but out they both did cry;
Fie, fie, what have we done? ungodly rebel fie.
But now we must needs yield, to what our oaths
    require.
Yet thou shalt not go free (quoth Venus) such a fire   *170*
Her beauty kindle shall within thy foolish mind,
That thou full oft shalt wish thy judging eyes were blind.
Nay then (Diana said) the chasteness I will give
In ashes of despair (though burnt) shall make thee live.
Nay thou (said both) shalt see such beams shine in her   *175*
    face

161 **Styx** by an oath invoking the river Styx.

That thou shalt never dare seek help of wretched case.
And with that cursèd curse away to heaven they fled,
First having all their gifts upon fair Mira spread.
The rest I cannot tell, for therewithal I wak'd
180 And found with deadly fear that all my sinews shak'd.
Was it a dream? O dream, how hast thou wrought in
        me,
That I things erst unseen should first in dreaming see?
And thou O traitor Sleep, made for to be our rest,
How hast thou fram'd the pain wherewith I am
        opprest?
185 O coward Cupid thus dost thou thy honor keep,
Unarm'd (alas) unwarn'd to take a man asleep?

*

Phoebus farewell,° a sweeter saint I serve,
The high conceits thy heav'nly wisdoms breed
My thoughts forget: my thoughts which never swerve
From her, in whom is sown their freedom's seed,
5 And in whose eyes my daily doom° I read.

Phoebus farewell, a sweeter saint I serve.
Thou art far off, thy kingdom is above:
She heav'n on earth with beauties doth preserve.
Thy beams I like, but her clear rays I love:
10 Thy force I fear, her force I still do prove.

Phoebus yield up thy title in my mind.
She doth possess, thy image is defac'd,
But if thy rage some brave revenge will find,
On her, who hath in me thy temple raste,°
15 Employ thy might, that she my fires may taste.
        And how much more her worth surmounteth thee,
        Make her as much more base by loving me.

*

Since that the stormy rage of passions dark
(Of passions dark, made dark by beauty's light)

1 **Phoebus farewell** Basilius, following a birthday prayer to Apollo,
turns again to wooing Pyrocles-Zelmane. 5 **doom** judgement. 14
raste razed.

With rebel force, hath clos'd in dungeon dark
My mind ere now led forth by reason's light:

Since all the things which give mine eyes their light   5
Do foster still the fruits of fancies dark:
So that the windows° of my inward light
Do serve, to make my inward powers dark:

Since, as I say, both mind and senses dark
Are hurt, not helpt, with piercing of the light: 10
While that the light may show the horrors dark
But cannot make resolvèd darkness light:
 I like this place,° where at the least the dark
 May keep my thoughts, from thought of wonted
   light.

*

Like those sick folks, in whom strange humors flow,°
Can taste no sweets, the sour only please:
So to my mind, while passions daily grow,
Whose fiery chains, upon his freedom seize,
 Joys strangers seem, I cannot bide their show,   5
 Nor brook ought else but well acquainted woe.
 Bitter grief tastes me best, pain is my ease,
 Sick to the death, still loving my disease.

*

My true love° hath my heart, and I have his,
By just exchange, one for the other giv'n.
I hold his dear, and mine he cannot miss:°
There never was a better bargain driv'n.

His heart in me, keeps me and him in one,   5
My heart in him, his thoughts and senses guides:
He loves my heart, for once it was his own:
I cherish his, because in me it bides.

7 **windows** the senses.   13 **this place** a cave near which Pyrocles is
singing this song.
1 **Like . . . flow** Gynecia, complaining of her love for Pyrocles.
1 **My true love . . .** The prose frame for the song is an ironic one:
Musidorus invents a pastoral scene in which the cloddish Dametas
is wooed by a shepherdess singing this song. His purpose is to divert
Dametas' wife while he courts Pamela.   3 **miss** lack.

His heart his wound receivèd from my sight:
10 My heart was wounded, with his wounded heart,
For as from me, on him his hurt did light,
So still methought in me his hurt did smart:
    Both equal hurt, in this change° sought our bliss:
    My true love hath my heart and I have his.

*

Do not disdain, O straight up-raisèd pine,°
That wounding thee, my thoughts in thee I grave:
Since that my thoughts, as straight as straightness thine
No smaller wound, alas! far deeper have.

5 Deeper engrav'd, which salve nor time can save,
Giv'n to my heart, by my fore° wounded eyne:°
Thus cruel to myself how canst thou crave
My inward hurt should spare thy outward rine?

Yet still fair tree, lift up thy stately line,°
10 Live long, and long witness my chosen smart,
Which barred desires, (barred by myself) impart.

And in this growing bark grow verses mine.
My heart my word, my word hath giv'n my heart.
The giver giv'n from gift shall never part.

*

Why dost thou haste away
O Titan fair the giver of the day?
Is it to carry news
To Western wights, what stars in East appear?
5 Or dost thou think that here
Is left a sun,° whose beams thy place may use?
Yet stay and well peruse,
What be her gifts, that make her equal thee,
Bend all thy light to see

---

13 change also, exchange.

1 pine Pamela, who has fled with Musidorus, engraves these verses
in the bark of a tree. 6 fore before. 6 eyne eyes. 9 line (1) its
height; (2) its descendants, its race.

6 sun Pyrocles-Zelmane, in whose praise Basilius sings this madrigal.

In earthly clothes enclosed a heavenly spark.   10
Thy running course cannot such beauties mark:
No, no, thy motions be
Hastened from us with bar of shadow dark,
Because that thou the author of our sight
Disdainst we see thee stain'd with other's light.   15

                                    *

O stealing time° the subject° of delay,
(Delay, the rack of unrefrain'd° desire)
What strange design hast thou my hopes to stay,
My hopes which do but to mine own aspire?

Mine own? O word on whose sweet sound doth prey   5
My greedy soul, with gripe° of inward fire:
Thy title great, I justly challenge may,
Since in such phrase his faith he did attire.

O time, become the chariot of my joys:
As thou drawest on, so let my bliss draw near.   10
Each moment lost, part of my hap destroys.

Thou art the father of occasion° dear:
Join with thy son, to ease my long annoys.
In speedy help, thank-worthy friends appear.

                                    *

My lute° within thyself thy tunes enclose,
Thy mistress' song is now a sorrow's cry,
Her hand benumb'd with fortune's daily blows,
Her mind amaz'd can neither's help apply.
Wear these my words as mourning weeds of woes,   5

---

1 0 . . . time Philoclea, urged by her father Basilius to "divert his
thoughts," sings a companion piece to his madrigal (see previous
poem), "not unwilling to disburden her secret passion." 1 the
subject ruled by. 2 unrefrain'd not abstained from. 6 gripe vulture. 12 occasion opportunity.

1 My lute Gynecia's song, engraved on her lute "under which veil
she . . . had made the lute a monument of her mind"; Philoclea, dis-
covering it, realizes her mother is a rival for the love of Pyrocles-
Zelmane.

Black ink becomes the state wherein I die.°
   And though my moans be not in music bound,
   Of written griefs, yet be the silent ground.°

The world doth yield such ill consorted° shows,
10 With circled course, which no wise stay can try,
That childish stuff which knows not friends from foes,
(Better despis'd) bewonder gazing eye.
Thus noble gold, down to the bottom goes,
When worthless cork, aloft doth floating lie.
15   Thus in thyself, least strings are loudest found,
   And lowest stops do yield the highest sound.

*

Get hence° foul Grief, the canker of the mind:
Farewell Complaint, the miser's only pleasure:
Away vain Cares, by which few men do find
   Their sought-for treasure.

5 Ye helpless Sighs, blow out your breath to nought,
Tears, drown yourselves, for woe (your cause) is
      wasted,
Thought, think to end, too long the fruit of thought
   My mind hath tasted.

But thou, sure Hope, tickle my leaping heart.
10 Comfort, step thou in place of wonted sadness.
Fore-felt Desire, begin to savor part
   Of coming gladness.

Let voice of Sighs into clear music run,
Eyes, let your Tears with gazing now be mended,
15 Instead of Thought, true pleasure be begun,
   And never ended.

---

6 **die** original spelling, "dye," preserves the pun. 8 **ground** (1) accompaniment, musical bass; (2) writing surface. 9 **consorted** harmonized.

1 **Get hence** Basilius, on the way to what he thinks will be a rendezvous with Pyrocles-Zelmane, deeming himself "in the chief tower of his desires."

From the Third Eclogues

*

Let mother earth now deck herself in flowers,°
To see her offspring seek a good increase,
Where justest love doth vanquish Cupid's powers
And war of thoughts is swallow'd up in peace
    Which never may decrease   5
    But like the turtles° fair
    Live one in two, a well united pair,
    Which that no chance may stain,
    O Hymen° long their coupled joys maintain.

O heav'n awake show forth thy stately face,   10
Let not these slumb'ring clouds thy beauties hide,
But with thy cheerful presence help to grace
The honest bridegroom, and the bashful bride,
    Whose loves may ever bide,
    Like to the elm and vine,   15
    With mutual embracements them to twine:
    In which delightful pain,
    O Hymen long their coupled joys maintain.

Ye Muses all which chaste affects° allow,
And have to Thyrsis show'd your secret skill,   20
To this chaste love your sacred favors bow,
And so to him and her your gifts distill,
    That they all vice may kill:
    And like to lilies pure
    May please all eyes, and spotless may endure.   25
    Where that all bliss may reign,
    O Hymen long their coupled joys maintain.

1 **Let . . . flowers** An epithalamium for the wedding of Thyrsis and
Kala, this opens the third set of eclogues. 6 **turtles** turtledoves,
traditionally representing forms of constancy. 9 **Hymen** god of
marriage. 19 **affects** affection.

Ye Nymphs which in the waters empire have,
Since Thyrsis' music oft doth yield you praise,
30 Grant to the thing which we for Thyrsis crave.
Let one time (but long first) close up their days,
    One grave their bodies seize:
    And like two rivers sweet,
    When they though divers do together meet:
35   One stream both streams contain,
    O Hymen long their coupled joys maintain.

Pan, father Pan, the god of silly sheep,
Whose care is cause that they in number grow,
Have much more care of them that them do keep,
40 Since from these good the others' good doth flow,
    And make their issue show
    In number like the herd
    Of younglings, which thyself with love hast rear'd,
    Or like the drops of rain.
45   O Hymen long their coupled joys maintain.

Virtue (if not a god) yet god's chief part,
Be thou the knot of this their open vow,
That still he be her head, she be his heart,
He lean to her, she unto him do bow:
50   Each other still allow:
    Like oak and mistletoe.
    Her strength from him, his praise from her do grow.
    In which most lovely train,
    O Hymen long their coupled joys maintain.

55 But thou foul Cupid, sire to lawless lust,
Be thou far hence with thy empoisn'd dart,
Which though of glitt'ring gold, shall here take rust
Where simple love, which chasteness doth impart,
    Avoids thy hurtful art,
60   Not needing charming skill,
    Such minds with sweet affections for to fill,
    Which being pure and plain,
    O Hymen long their coupled joys maintain.

All churlish words, shrewd answers, crabbèd looks,
All privateness, self-seeking, inward spite,   65
All waywardness, which nothing kindly brooks,
All strife for toys, and claiming master's right:
  Be hence aye put to flight,
  All stirring husband's hate
  Gainst neighbors good for womanish debate   70
  Be fled as things most vain,
  O Hymen long their coupled joys maintain.

All peacock pride, and fruits of peacock's pride,
Longing to be with loss of substance gay,
With recklessness what may thy house betide,   75
So that you may on higher slippers stay,
  For ever hence away:
  Yet let not sluttery,
  The sink of filth, be counted huswifery:
  But keeping wholesome mean,   80
  O Hymen long their coupled joys maintain.

But above all, away vile jealousy,
The evil of evils, just cause to be unjust,
(How can he love suspecting treachery?
How can she love where love cannot win trust?)   85
  Go snake hide thee in dust,
  Ne dare once show thy face,
  Where open hearts do hold so constant place,
  That they thy sting restrain,
  O Hymen long their coupled joys maintain.   90

The earth is deckt with flowers, the heav'ns display'd,
Muses grant gifts, Nymphs long and joinèd life,
Pan store of babes, virtue their thoughts well stay'd.
Cupid's lust gone, and gone is bitter strife,
  Happy man, happy wife.   95
  No pride shall them oppress,
  Nor yet shall yield to loathsome sluttishness,
  And jealousy is slain:
  For Hymen will their coupled joys maintain.

*

A neighbor mine not long ago there was,°
(But nameless he, for blameless he shall be)
That married had a trick° and bonny lass
As in a summer day a man might see:
5   But he himself a foul unhandsome groom,
       And far unfit to hold so good a room.

Now whether mov'd with self unworthiness,
Or with her beauty fit to make a prey,
Fell jealousy did so his brain oppress,
10   That if he absent were but half a day,
       He guessed the worst (you wot what is the worst)
       And in himself new doubting causes nurst.

While thus he fear'd the silly innocent,
Who yet was good, because she knew none ill,
15   Unto his house a jolly shepherd went,
To whom our prince did bear a great good will,
       Because in wrestling and in pastoral
       He far did pass the rest of shepherds all.

And therefore he a courtier was benamed,
20   And as a courtier was with cheer received,
(For they have tongues to make a poor man blamed,
If he to them his duty misconceived)
       And for this courtier should well like his table,
       The goodman bade his wife be serviceable.

25   And so she was, and all with good intent,
But few days past while she good manner us'd,
But that her husband thought her service bent
To such an end as he might be abus'd.
       Yet like a coward fearing stranger's pride,
30   He made the simple wench his wrath abide.

With chumpish° looks, hard words, and secret nips,
Grumbling at her when she his kindness sought,
Asking her how she tasted courtier's lips,

---

1 A neighbor . . . was Sung by Nico, one of the Arcadian shepherds, "with a merry marriage look"; following the epithalamium,
this fabliau is intended "to keep a husband from jealousy." 3
trick trim. 31 chumpish sullen.

He forc'd her think that which she never thought.
 In fine he made her guess, there was some sweet *35*
 In that which he so fear'd that she should meet.

When once this ent'red was, in woman's heart,
And that it had inflam'd a new desire,
There rested then, to play a woman's part,
Fuel to seek and not to quench the fire: *40*
 But (for his jealous eye she well did find)
 She studied cunning how the same to blind.

And thus she did. One day to him she came,
And (though against his will) on him she lean'd,
And out gan cry, ah well away for shame, *45*
If you help not our wedlock will be stain'd.
 The goodman starting, askt what did her move?
 She sigh'd and said, the bad guest sought her love.

He little looking that she should complain
Of that, whereto he fear'd she was inclin'd, *50*
Bussing her oft, and in his heart full fain,
He did demand what remedy to find;
 How they might get that guest, from them to wend,
 And yet the prince (that lov'd him) not offend.

Husband, quoth she, go to him by and by, *55*
And tell him that you find I do him love:
And therefore pray him that of courtesy
He will absent himself, lest he should move
 A young girl's heart, to that were shame for both,
 Whereto you know, his honest heart were loath. *60*

Thus shall you show that him you do not doubt,°
And as for me (sweet husband) I must bear.
Glad was the man when he had heard her out,
And did the same, although with mickle fear.
 For fear he did, lest he the young man might *65*
 In choler put, with whom he would not fight.

The courtly shepherd much aghast at this,
Not seeing erst such token in the wife,

61 **doubt** fear.

Though full of scorn, would not his duty miss,
70 Knowing that evil becomes a household strife,
Did go his way, but sojourn'd near thereby,
That yet the ground hereof he might espy.

The wife thus having settled husband's brain,
Who would have sworn his spouse Diana was,
75 Watchèd when she a further point might gain,
Which little time did fitly bring to pass.
For to the court her man was call'd by name,
Whither he needs must go for fear of blame.

Three days before that he must sure depart,
80 She written had (but in a hand disguis'd)
A letter such, which might from either part°
Seem to proceed, so well it was devis'd.
She seal'd it first, then she the sealing brake,
And to her jealous husband did it take.

85 With weeping eyes (her eyes she taught to weep)
She told him that the courtier had it sent:
Alas (quoth she) thus women's shame doth creep.
The goodman read on both sides the content,
It title had, *Unto my only love:*
90 Subscription was, *Yours most, if you will prove.*

The pistle self such kind of words it had,
My sweetest joy, the comfort of my sprite,
So may thy flock's increase thy dear heart glad,
So may each thing, even as thou wishest light,
95 As thou wilt deign to read, and gently read
This mourning ink, in which my heart doth bleed.

Long have I lov'd (alas thou worthy art)
Long have I lov'd (alas love craveth love)
Long have I lov'd thyself, alas my heart
100 Doth break, now tongue unto thy name doth move,
And think not that thy answer answer is,
But that it is my doom of bale or bliss.

81 **either part** herself or the courtier.

The jealous wretch must now to court be gone:
Ne can he fail, for prince hath for him sent:
Now is the time we may be here alone,   *105*
And give a long desire a sweet content.
    Thus shall you both reward a lover true,
    And eke revenge his wrong suspecting you.

And this was all, and this the husband read
With chafe enough, till she him pacified: *110*
Desiring, that no grief in him he bred
Now that he had her words so truly tried:
    But that he would, to him the letter show
    That with his fault he might her goodness know.

That straight was done with many a boist'rous threat,   *115*
That to the king he would his sin declare,
But now the courtier gan to smell the feat,
And with some words which showèd little care,
    He stay'd until the goodman was departed,
    Then gave he him the blow which never smarted.   *120*

Thus may you see, the jealous wretch was made
The Pandar of the thing he most did fear,
Take heed therefore, how you ensue that trade,
Least the same marks of jealousy you bear.
    For sure, no jealousy can that prevent,   *125*
    Whereto two parties once be full content.

*

As I° my little flock on Ister° bank
(A little flock; but well my pipe they couthe°)
Did piping lead, the sun already sank
Beyond our world, and ere I gatt° my booth°
Each thing with mantle black the night doth soothe;   *5*
    Saving the glow worm, which would courteous be
    Of that small light oft watching shepherds see.

1 As I Is sung by the courtier Philisides during the wedding eclogues; it appears to be a deliberate exercise in "pastoral style,"
using archaisms similar to those of *The Shepheardes Calendar*.
1 Ister the Danube. 2 couthe knew. 4 gatt arrived at. 4 booth
temporary dwelling covered with leaves, etc.

The welkin had full niggardly enclosed
In coffer of dim clouds his silver groats,°
10 Iclepèd° stars; each thing to rest disposed:
The caves were full, the mountains void of goats:
The birds' eyes clos'd, closèd their chirping notes.
    As for the nightingale woodmusic's king,
    It August was, he deign'd not then to sing.

15 Amid my sheep, though I saw nought to fear,
Yet (for I nothing saw) I fearèd sore;
Then found I which thing is a charge to bear
As for my sheep I dreaded mickle more
Than ever for myself since I was bore.
20   I sat me down: for see to go ne could,
    And sang unto my sheep lest stray they should.

The song I sang old Languet° had me taught,
Languet, the shepherd best swift Ister knew,
For clerkly rede,° and hating what is naught,
25 For faithful heart, clean hands, and mouth as true:
With his sweet skill my skilless youth he drew,
    To have a feeling taste of him that sits
    Beyond the heaven, far more beyond your wits.

He said, the music best thilke° powers pleas'd
30 Was jump° concord between our wit and will:
Where highest notes to godliness are rais'd,
And lowest sink not down to jot of ill:
With old true tales he wont mine ears to fill,
    How shepherds did of yore, how now they thrive,
35   Spoiling their flock, or while twixt them they strive.

He likèd me, but pitied lustful youth:
His good strong staff my slipp'ry years upbore:
He still hop'd well, because I lovèd truth;
Till forc'd to part, with heart and eyes even sore,
40 To worthy Coriden he gave me o'er,
    But thus in oak's true shade recounted he,
    Which now in night's deep shade sheep heard of me.

9 **groats** coins of small denomination.   10 **Iclepèd** called.   22 **Languet** Protestant statesman, Sidney's mentor during European travels,
and later his correspondent.   24 **clerkly rede** scholarly advice.   29
thilke these.   30 **jump** exact.

Such manner time there was (what time I n'ot°)
When all this earth, this dam or mould of ours
Was only won'd° with such as beasts begot: 45
Unknown as then were they that builden towers:
The cattle wild, or tame, in nature's bowers
    Might freely roam, or rest, as seemèd them:
    Man was not man their dwellings in to hem.

The beasts had sure some beastly policy:°   50
For nothing can endure where order n'is.
For once the lion by the lamb did lie.
The fearful hind the leopard did kiss.
Hurtless was tiger's paw and serpent's hiss.
    This think I well, the beasts with courage clad   55
    Like senators a harmless empire had.

At which whether the others did repine,
(For envy harb'reth most in feeblest hearts)
Or that they all to changing did incline,
(As even in beasts their dams leave changing parts)   60
The multitude to Jove a suit imparts,
    With neighing, blaying, braying, and barking,
    Roaring, and howling for to have a king.

A king, in language theirs they said they would:
(For then their language was a perfect speech)   65
The birds likewise with chirps, and pewing could
Cackling, and chatt'ring, that of Jove beseech.
Only the owl still warn'd them not to seech°
    So hastily that which they would repent:
    But saw they would, and he to deserts went.   70

Jove wisely said (for wisdom wisely says)
O beasts, take heed what you of me desire.
Rulers will think all things made them to please,
And soon forget the swink° due to their hire,
But since you will, part of my heav'nly fire   75
    I will you lend; the rest yourselves must give,
    That it both seen and felt may with you live.

43 **no't** know not. 45 **won'd** inhabited. 50 **policy** government.
68 **seech** seek. 74 **swink** toil.

Full glad they were and took the naked sprite,
Which straight the Earth yclothèd in his clay:
80 The lion, heart; the ounce° gave active might:
The horse, good shape; the sparrow, lust to play;
Nightingale, voice, enticing songs to say.
 Elephant gave a perfect memory:
 And parrot, ready tongue, that to apply.

85 The fox gave craft; the dog gave flattery;
Ass, patience; the mole, a working thought;
Eagle, high look; wolf secret cruelty;
Monkey, sweet breath; the cow, her fair eyes brought;
The ermion, whitest skin, spotted with nought;
90   The sheep, mild-seeming face; climbing, the bear;
 The stag did give the harm eschewing fear.

The hare, her sleights; the cat, his melancholy;
Ant, industrie; and coney, skill to build;
Cranes, order; storks, to be appearing holy;
95 Chameleon, ease to change; duck, ease to yield;
Crocodile, tears, which might be falsely spill'd;
 Ape great thing gave, though he did mowing° stand,
 The instrument of instruments, the hand.

Each other beast likewise his present brings:
100 And (but they drad° their prince they oft should want)
They all consented were to give him wings;
And aye more awe towards him for to plant,
To their own work this privilege they grant,
 That from thenceforth to all eternity,
105   No beast should freely speak, but only he.

Thus man was made; thus man their lord became:
Who at the first, wanting, or hiding pride,
He did to beasts' best use his cunning frame;
With water drink, herbs meat, and naked hide,
110 And fellow-like let his dominion slide;
 Not in his sayings saying I, but we:
 As if he meant his lordship common be.

---

80 ounce lynx. **97 mowing** grimacing. **100 drad** dreaded.

But when his seat so rooted he had found,
That they now skill'd not, how from him to wend;
Then gan in guiltless earth full many a wound,   115
Iron to seek, which gainst itself should bend,
To tear the bowels, that good corn should send.
    But yet the common dam none did bemoan;
    Because (thought hurt) they never heard her groan.

Then gan he factions in the beasts to breed;   120
Where helping weaker sort, the nobler beasts,
(As tigers, leopards, bears, and lions' seed)
Disdain'd with this, in deserts sought their rests;
Where famine ravine taught their hungry chests,   125
    That craftily he forc'd them to do ill,
    Which being done he afterwards would kill.

For murder done, which never erst was seen,
By those great beasts, as for the weaker's good,
He chose themselves his guarders for to been,
Gainst those of might, of whom in fear they stood,   130
As horse and dog, not great, but gentle blood:
    Blithe were the commons cattle of the field,
    Tho'° when they saw their foen of greatness° kill'd.

But they or spent, or made of slender might,
Then quickly did the meaner cattle find,   135
The great beams gone, the house on shoulders light:
For by and by the horse fair bits did bind:
The dog was in a collar taught his kind.
    As for the gentle birds like case might rue
    When falcon they, and goshawk saw in mew.   140

Worst fell to smallest birds, and meanest heard,
Who now his own, full like his own he used,
Yet first but wool, or feathers off he tear'd:
And when they were well us'd to be abused,
For hungry throat their flesh with teeth he bruised: 145
    At length for glutton taste he did them kill:
    At last for sport their silly lives did spill.

133 Tho' then.   133 foen of greatness foes, the great beasts.

But yet O man, rage not beyond thy need:
Deem it no gloire to swell in tyranny.
150 Thou art of blood; joy not to make things bleed:
Thou fearest death; think they are loath to die.
A plaint of guiltless hurt doth pierce the sky.
    And you poor beasts, in patience bide your hell,
    Or know your strengths, and then you shall do well.

155 Thus did I sing, and pipe eight sullen hours
To sheep, whom love, not knowledge, made to hear,
Now fancy's fits, now fortune's baleful stours.°
But then I homeward call'd my lambkins dear:
For to my dimmèd eyes began t'appear
160   The night grown old, her black head waxen gray,
    Sure shepherd's sign, that morn would soon fetch
        day.

From Book IV

*

O night,° the ease of care, the pledge of pleasure,
Desire's best mean, harvest° of hearts affected,
The seat of peace, the throne which is erected
Of human life to be the quiet measure,

5 Be victor still of Phoebus' golden treasure:
Who hath our sight with too much sight infected,
Whose light is cause we have our lives neglected,
Turning all nature's course of self displeasure.

---

157 **stours** uproars.

1 **nigh**: Basilius, who has slept with his wife, but assumes it was
Pyrocles-Zelmane. He sings in praise of night which allows him such
escapes.   2 **harvest** 1593: harnest (harnessed).

These stately stars in their now shining faces,
With sinless sleep, and silence wisdom's mother,   *10*
Witness his wrong which by thy help is easèd:

Thou art therefore of these our desert places
The sure refuge, by thee and by no other
My soul is blist, sense joy'd, and fortune raisèd.

From Book V

*

Since nature's works be good, and death doth serve°
As nature's work: why should we fear to die?
Since fear is vain, but when it may preserve,
Why should we fear that which we cannot fly?

Fear is more pain, than is the pain it fears,   *5*
Disarming human minds of native might:
While each conceit an ugly figure bears,
Which were not evil, well view'd in reason's light.

Our owly eyes, which dimm'd with passions be,
And scarce discern the dawn of coming day,   *10*
Let them be clear'd, and now begin to see,
Our life is but a step in dusty way.
    Then let us hold the bliss of peaceful mind,
    Since this we feel, great loss we cannot find.

1 **Since . . . serve** sung by Musidorus to Pyrocles, as the two wait,
in prison, to be sentenced to death for their approaches to an ab-
duction of the princesses.

From

CERTAIN
SONNETS

1

Since shunning pain, I ease can never find:
Since bashful dread seeks where he knows me harmed:
Since will is won, and stoppèd ears are charmed:
Since force doth faint, and sight doth make me blind:

Since loosing long, the faster still I bind: 5
Since naked sense can conquer reason armed:
Since heart in chilling fear with ice is warmed:
In fine, since strife of thought but mars the mind,

I yield, O Love, unto thy loathèd yoke,
Yet craving law of arms, whose rule doth teach,   10
That hardly us'd,° who ever prison broke,
In justice quit, of honor made no breach:
    Whereas if I a grateful° guardian have,
    Thou art my lord, and I thy vowèd slave.

3

To the tune of *Non credo gia che piu infelice amante*°

The fire° to see my wrongs for anger burneth:
The air in rain for my affliction weepeth:
The sea to ebb for grief his flowing turneth:
The earth with pity dull the center° keepeth:
    Fame is with wonder blazèd:°   5
    Time runs away for sorrow:
    Place standeth still amazèd
    To see my night of evils, which hath no morrow.
        Alas, all only she no pity taketh,
        To know my miseries, but chaste and cruel: 10
        My fall her glory maketh,
        Yet still her eyes give to my flames their fuel.

Fire burn me quite, till sense of burning leave me:
Air let me draw no more thy breath in anguish:

11 **hardly us'd** cruelly treated.   13 **grateful** pleasing.
0 **To the . . . amante** See Introduction, p. *xxiii*.   1–4 **fire . . . earth**
See *Arcadia*, p. 68.   4 **center** of the universe.   5 **blazèd** See *Astrophel and Stella*, 13, line 13.

15 Sea drown'd in thee, of tedious life bereave me:
  Earth take this earth, wherein my spirits languish.
      Fame say I was not born:
      Time haste my dying hour:
      Place see my grave uptorn:
20   Fire, air, sea, earth, fame, time, place, show your
          power.
        Alas, from all their helps I am exilèd,
        For hers am I, and death fears her displeasure.
        Fie death, thou are beguilèd,
        Though I be hers, she makes of me no treasure.

4

To the same tune°

The nightingale as soon as April bringeth
Unto her rested sense a perfect waking,
While late bare earth, proud of new clothing springeth,
Sings out her woes,° a thorn° her song-book making:
5   And mournfully bewailing,
    Her throat in tunes expresseth
    What grief her breast oppresseth,
    For Tereus' force on her chaste will prevailing.
      O Philomela fair, O take some gladness,
10   That here is juster cause of plaintful sadness:
      Thine earth now springs, mine fadeth,
      Thy thorn without, my thorn my heart invadeth.

Alas she hath no other cause of anguish
But Tereus' love, on her by strong hand wroken,°
15 Wherein she suff'ring all her spirits' languish,

0 **To the same tune** See Introduction, p. *xxiii*. 4 **woes** Philomela,
ravished by Tereus, husband of her sister Procne, had her tongue
cut out in order to prevent her revealing the tale; she wove the
story into a tapestry and escaped Tereus' wrath, when she was transformed into a nightingale. 4 **thorn** perhaps relating to prick-song,
pricked-out or written music as opposed to that held in memory
(hence, *thorn* as "pricker" of the songbook). Prick-song is also an
ornamented descant as opposed to simple melody. 14 **wroken** in-
flicted.

Full womanlike complains her will was broken.
   But I who daily craving,
   Cannot have to content me,
   Have more cause to lament me,
   Since wanting is more woe than too much having.   20
     O Philomela fair, O take some gladness,
     That here is juster cause of plaintful sadness:
     Thine earth now springs, mine fadeth:
     Thy thorn without, my thorn my heart invadeth.

6

To the tune of *Basciami vita mia*

Sleep baby mine, Desire, nurse Beauty singeth:
Thy cries, O baby set mine head on aching:
The babe cries way,° thy love doth keep me waking.

Lully, lully, my babe, hope cradle bringeth
Unto my children alway good rest taking: 5
The babe cries way, thy love doth keep me waking.

Since baby mine, from me thy watching springeth,
Sleep then a little, pap° content is making:
The babe cries nay, for that abide I waking.

12

Translated out of Horace, which begins *Rectiùs vives*°

You better sure shall live, not evermore
   Trying high seas, nor while sea rage you flee,
   Pressing too much upon ill harbor'd shore.

The golden mean who° loves, lives safely free
   From filth of forworn° house, and quiet lives,   5
   Released from court, where envy needs must be.

---

3 **way** away. 8 **pap** (¹) the breast; (2) soft or semi-liquid food for
infants.

---

0 **Translated . . . vives** from *Odes*, II, x. 4 **who** i.e., the man who
(subject of verbs in lines 4 and 5). 5 **forworn** exhausted, decayed.

The wind most oft the hugest pine-tree grieves:
    The stately towers come down with greater fall:
    The highest hills the bolt of thunder cleaves:

10 Evil haps do fill with hope, good haps appall
        With fear of change, the courage° well prepar'd;
        Foul winters as they come, away they shall.

Though present times and past with evils be snar'd,
    They shall not last: with cithern° silent muse
15 Apollo wakes, and bow° hath sometime spar'd.

In hard estate with stout show valor use,
    The same man still in whom wisdom prevails,
    In too full wind draw in thy swelling sails.

15

Upon the device° of a seeled° dove, with this word of
Petrarch: *Non mi vuol e non mi trahe d'impaccio*

Like as the dove which seelèd up doth fly,
    Is neither freed, nor yet to service bound,
But hopes to gain some help by mounting high,
    Till want of force do force her fall to ground.

5 Right so my mind caught by his guiding eye,
        And thence cast off, where his sweet hurt he found,
    Hath neither leave to live, nor doom to die,
        Nor held in evil, nor suffered to be sound,

But with his wings of fancies up he goes,
10   To high conceits whose fruits are oft but small,
    Till wounded, blind, and wearied spirits, lose

11 **courage** heart or spirit (object of "fill" and "appall"). 14
cithern ancient instrument resembling guitar. 15 **bow** i.e., Apollo
sometimes spares the bow.
0 **device** emblem, illustrating the motto from Petrarch: "He (love)
does not want me and does not release me from my trouble."
0 **seeled** its eyes closed by stitching the lids, the thread held behind
its head (part of the training process in falconry, the bird flying
higher and higher while blinded).

Both force to fly and knowledge where to fall.
O happy dove if she no bondage tried:
More happy I, might I in bondage bide.

16a

Edward Dyer°

Prometheus when first from heaven high,
He brought down fire, ere then on earth not seen,
Fond of delight, a satyr standing by,
Gave it a kiss, as it like sweet had been.

Feeling forthwith the other burning power,   5
Wood° with the smart, with shouts and shrieking
shrill,
He sought his ease in river, field, and bower,
But for the time his grief went with him still.

So silly I, with that unwonted sight
In human shape, an angel from above,   10
Feeding mine eyes, the impression there did light,°
That since I run and rest as pleaseth love,
The difference is, the satyr's lips, my heart,
He for a while, I evermore have smart.

16

A satyr once did run away for dread,
With sound of horn, which he himself did blow,
Fearing and fear'd thus from himself he fled,
Deeming strange evil in that he did not know.

Such causeless fears when coward minds do take,   5
It makes them fly that which they fain would have:
As this poor beast who did his rest forsake,
Thinking not why, but how himself to save.

0 **Dyer** courtier and friend of Sidney, author of this first sonnet,
to which Sidney's, the second, is a reply. 6 **Wood** mad. 11 **light**
(1) set fire to; (2) alight.

Even thus might I, for doubts which I conceive
10   Of mine own words, my own good hap betray,
And thus might I for fear of may be, leave
    The sweet pursuit of my desirèd prey.
        Better like I thy satyr dearest Dyer,
        Who burnt his lips to kiss fair shining fire.

17

My mistress lours and saith I do not love:
    I do protest and seek with service due,
    In humble mind a constant faith to prove,
    But for all this I can not her remove
5   From deep vain thought that I may not be true.

If oaths might serve, even by the Stygian lake,
    Which poets say, the gods themselves do fear,
    I never did my vowèd word forsake:
    For why should I, whom free choice slave doth
        make,
10   Else what° in face, than in my fancy bear?

My Muse therefore for only thou canst tell,
    Tell me the cause of this my causeless woe,
    Tell how ill thought disgrac'd my doing well:
    Tell how my joys and hopes thus foully fell
15   To so low ebb that wonted were to flow.

O this it is, the knotted straw° is found
    In tender hearts, small things engender hate:
    A horse's worth laid waste the Troyan ground:
    A three foot stool° in Greece, made trumpets sound,
20   An ass's shade° ere now hath bred debate.

---

10 **Else what** anything else (object of "bear"). 16 **knotted straw**
"to seek the knot in a bulrush"; proverbial, for inventing petty difficulties. 19 **stool** the tripod at Delphi, from which sacred oracles
were given before involvements in war. 20 **shade** referring to
Plutarch's fable of the man who was not permitted to rest in the
shadow of an ass he had hired for a journey, on grounds that he
had hired the beast but not its shadow.

If Greeks themselves were mov'd with so small cause,
   To twist those broils, which hardly would untwine:
   Should ladies fair be tied to such hard laws,
   As in their moods to take a ling'ring pause?
   I would it not, their metal is too fine.   25

My hand doth not bear witnesse with my heart,
   She saith, because I make no woeful lays,
   To paint my living death, and endless smart:
   And so for one that felt god Cupid's dart
   She thinks I lead and live too merry days.   30

Are poets then the only lovers true?
   Whose hearts are set on measuring a verse:
   Who think themselves well blest, if they renew
   Some good old dump,° that Chaucer's mistress
      knew,
   And use but you for matters to rehearse.   35

Then good Apollo do away thy bow:
   Take harp and sing in this our versing time:
   And in my brain some sacred humor flow:
   That all the earth my woes, sighs, tears may know,
   And see you not that I fall now to rhyme?   40

As for my mirth, how could I but be glad,
   Whilst that methought I justly made my boast
   That only I the only mistress had:
   But now, if ere my face with joy be clad:
   Think Hannibal did laugh when Carthage lost.   45

Sweet lady, as for those whose sullen cheer,
   Compar'd to me, made me in lightness found:
   Who Stoic-like in cloudy hue appear:
   Who silence force to make their words more dear:
   Whose eyes seem chaste, because they look on   50
      ground:
   Believe them not for physic true doth find,
   Choler adust° is joyed in woman-kind.

---

34 **dump** plantive song.   52 **Choler adust** a form of melancholy.

18

In wonted walks, since wonted fancies change,
    Some cause there is, which of strange cause doth rise:
For in each thing whereto mine eye doth range,
    Part of my pain meseems engravèd lies.

5   The rocks which were of constant mind the mark
       In climbing steep, now hard refusal show:
The shading woods seem now my sun to dark,
    And stately hills disdain to look so low.

The restful caves now restless visions give,
10   In dales I see each way a hard ascent:°
Like late mown meads, late cut from joy I live.
    Alas sweet brooks do in my tears augment:
       Rocks, woods, hills, caves, dales, meads, brooks,
          answer me,
       Infected minds infect each thing they see.

19

If I could think how these my thoughts to leave,
    Or thinking still my thoughts might have good end:
    If rebel sense would reason's law receive;
    Or reason foil'd would not in vain contend:
5   Then might I think what thoughts were best to
          think:
       Then might I wisely swim or gladly sink.

If either you would change your cruel heart,
    Or cruel (still) time did your beauty stain:
    If from my soul this love would once depart,
10   Or for my love some love I might obtain,
       Then might I hope a change or ease of mind,
       By your good help, or in myself to find.

But since my thoughts in thinking still are spent,
    With reason's strife, by senses overthrown,
15   You fairer still, and still more cruel bent,

10 **ascent** original spelling "assent," allowing possible pun.

I loving still a love that loveth none,
 I yield and strive, I kiss and curse the pain:
 Thought, reason, sense, time, you, and I, maintain.

20

A Farewell

Oft have I mus'd, but now at length I find,
 Why those that die, men say they do depart:
Depart, a word so gentle to my mind,
 Weakly did seem to paint death's ugly dart.

But now the stars with their strange course do bind   5
 Me one to leave, with whom I leave my heart.
I hear a cry of spirits faint and blind,
 That parting thus my chiefest part I part.

Part of my life, the loathèd part to me,
 Lives to impart my weary clay some breath.   10
But that good part, wherein all comforts be,
 Now dead, doth show departure is a death,
  Yea worse than death, death parts both woe and
   joy,
  From joy I part still living in annoy.

24

To the tune of *The Smokes of Melancholy*

Who hath ever felt the change of love,
And known those pangs that the losers prove,
 May paint my face without seeing me,
 And write the state how my fancies be,
 The loathsome buds grown on sorrow's tree.   5
But who by hearsay speaks, and hath not fully felt
What kind of fires they be in which those spirits melt,
 Shall guess, and fail, what doth displease,
 Feeling my pulse, miss my disease.

10   O no, O no, trial only shows
      The bitter juice of forsaken woes,
          Where former bliss present evils do stain,
          Nay former bliss adds to present pain,
          While remembrance doth both states contain.
15   Come learners then to me, the model of mishap,
      Engulfèd in despair, slid down from fortune's lap:
          And as you like my double lot,
          Tread in my steps, or follow not.

      For me alas I am full resolv'd,
20   Those bands alas shall not be dissolv'd,
          Nor break my word though reward come late,
          Nor fail my faith in my failing fate,
          Nor change in change, though change change my
              state.
      But always one myself with eagle-eyed truth to fly,
25   Up to the sun, although the sun my wings do fry:
          For if those flames burn my desire,
          Yet shall I die in Phoenix fire.

                        29

The same Sireno in Montemaior° holding his mistress'
            glass before her,
looking upon her while she viewed her self, thus sang:

Of this high grace with bliss conjoin'd
    No further debt on me is laid,
Since that in self same metal coin'd,
    Sweet lady you remain well paid.
5   For if my place give me great pleasure,
             Having before me Nature's treasure,
             In face and eyes unmatchèd being,
             You have the same in my hands, seeing
             What in your face mine eyes do measure.

0 **Montemaior** author of the Spanish romance *Diana*, from which
this song is translated. Sireno is a shepherd, another of whose lyrics
Sidney translated as number 28 of this collection.

Nor think the match unev'nly made,   10
  That of those beams in you do tarry:
The glass to you but gives a shade,
  To me mine eyes the true shape carry.
    For such a thought most highly prizèd,
    Which ever hath Love's yoke despisèd: 15
    Better then one captiv'd perceiveth,
    Though he the lively form receiveth:
    The other sees it but disguisèd.

30

Ring out your bells, let mourning shows be spread,
  For Love is dead:
    All Love is dead, infected
    With plague of deep disdain:
    Worth as nought worth rejected,   5
    And faith fair scorn doth gain.
      From so ungrateful fancy,
      From such a female franzy,
      From them that use men thus,
      Good Lord deliver us.   10

Weep neighbors, weep, do you not hear it said,
  That Love is dead:
    His death-bed peacock's folly,
    His winding sheet is shame,
    His will false-seeming holy,   15
    His sole exec'tor blame.
      From so ungrateful fancy,
      From such a female franzy,
      From them that use men thus,
      Good Lord deliver us.   20

Let dirge be sung, and trentals° rightly read,
  For Love is dead:
    Sir wrong his tomb ordaineth,
    My mistress' marble heart,

21 **trentals** a set of thirty requiem masses.

25   Which epitaph containeth,
     Her eyes were once his dart.
       From so ungrateful fancy,
       From such a female franzy,
       From them that use men thus,
30   Good Lord deliver us.

   Alas, I lie: rage hath this error bred,
     Love is not dead.
     Love is not dead, but sleepeth
     In her unmatchèd mind:
35   Where she his counsel keepeth,
       Till due desert she find.
       Therefore from so vile fancy,
       To call such wit a franzy,
       Who love can temper thus,
40   Good Lord deliver us.

31

Thou blind man's mark,° thou fool's self chosen snare,
Fond fancy's scum, and dregs of scatt'red thought,
Band° of all evils, cradle of causeless care,
Thou web of will, whose end is never wrought.

5   Desire, desire I have too dearly bought,
With price of mangled mind thy worthless ware,
Too long, too long asleep thou hast me brought,
Who should my mind to higher things prepare.

But yet in vain thou hast my ruin sought,
10   In vain thou madest me to vain things aspire,
In vain thou kindlest all thy smoky fire.

For virtue hath this better lesson taught,
Within myself to seek my only hire:
Desiring nought but how to kill desire.

1 **mark** target.　3 **Band** for swaddling.

32

Leave me O Love, which reachest but to dust,
And thou my mind aspire to higher things:
Grow rich in that which never taketh rust:
What ever fades, but fading pleasure brings.

Draw in thy beams, and humble all thy might,   5
To that sweet yoke, where lasting freedoms be:
Which breaks the clouds and opens forth the light,
That doth both shine and give us sight to see.

O take fast hold, let that light be thy guide,
In this small course which birth draws out to death,   10
And think how evil becometh him to slide,
Who seeketh heav'n, and comes of heav'nly breath.
     Then farewell world, thy uttermost I see,
     Eternal Love maintain thy life in me.

Splendidis longum valedico nugis.°

15 **Splendidis . . . nugis.** I bid goodbye forever to brilliant trifles.

ASTROPHEL AND STELLA

1

Loving in truth, and fain in verse my love to show,
That the dear she° might take some pleasure of my
      pain:
Pleasure might cause her read, reading might make her
      know,
Knowledge might pity win, and pity grace obtain,
  I sought fit words to paint the blackest face of woe,   *5*
Studying inventions fine, her wits to entertain:
Oft turning others' leaves, to see if thence would flow
Some fresh and fruitful showers upon my sun-burn'd°
      brain.
    But words came halting forth, wanting Invention's
      stay,
Invention Nature's child, fled step-dame Study's blows,   *10*
And others' feet° still° seem'd but strangers in my way.
Thus great with child to speak, and helpless in my
      throes,
    Biting my truand°pen, beating myself for spite,
    Fool, said my Muse to me, look in thy heart° and
      write.

2

Not at first sight, nor with a dribbèd° shot
    Love gave the wound, which while I breathe will
      bleed:
    But known worth did in mine° of time proceed,
Till by degrees it had full conquest got.
I saw and liked, I liked but lovèd not,   *5*
    I loved, but straight did not what Love decreed:
    At length to Love's decrees, I forc'd, agreed,

2 **the dear she** 1598: "she (dear she)"—a reading more in accord
with the pattern of alliteration and rhetorical repetitions (*gradatio*).
8 **sun-burn'd** (1) "sun" of Stella's beauty; (2) "sun" of the ancients; others' writings. 11 **feet** also, poetic feet or measure. 11
still always. 13 **truand** truant, idle. 14 **heart** source of Stella's
image (see sonnet 32).
1 **dribbèd** random. 3 **mine** tunneling operation under besieged
walls.

Yet with repining at so partial° lot.
 Now even that footstep of lost liberty
10 Is gone, and now like slave-born Muscovite,
 I call it praise to suffer tyranny;
 And now employ the remnant of my wit,
  To make myself believe, that all is well,
  While with a feeling skill I paint my hell.

3

Let dainty wits cry on the Sisters nine,°
 That bravely maskt,° their fancies° may be told:
 Or Pindar's apes,° flaunt they in phrases fine,
 Enam'ling with pied flowers their thoughts of gold:
5 Or else let them in statelier glory shine,
 Ennobling new found tropes° with problems° old:
 Or with strange similes enrich each line,
 Of herbs or beasts,° which Ind or Afric hold.
  For me in sooth, no Muse but one I know:
10 Phrases and problems from my reach do grow,
 And strange things cost too dear for my poor sprites.
  How then? even thus: in Stella's face I read,
  What love and beauty be, then all my deed
 But copying is, what in her Nature writes.

4

Virtue alas, now let me take some rest,
 Thou setst a bate° between my will and wit,
 If vain love have my simple soul opprest:
 Leave what thou likest not, deal not thou with it.
5 Thy scepter use in some old Cato's° breast;
 Churches or schools are for thy seat more fit:
 I do confess, pardon a fault confest:

8 **partial** (1) excluding other activities; (2) unrequited by the lady.
1 **Sisters nine** the Muses. 2 **bravely maskt** splendidly (1) decked out; (2) hidden. 2 **fancies** loves. 3 **Pindar's apes** imitators of Pindar's grand style. 6 **tropes** rhetorical figures. 6 **problems** questions for disputation. 8 **herbs or beasts** as in Lyly's *Euphues*.
2 **bate** discord. 5 **old Cato** "a bitter punisher of faults" (see *Apology*, p. 253).

My mouth too tender is for thy hard bit.
  But if that needs thou wilt usurping be,
  The little reason that is left in me,   *10*
And still th'effect of thy persuasions prove:°
  I swear, my heart such one shall show to thee,
  That shrines in flesh so true a deity,
That Virtue, thou thyself shalt be in love.

5

It is most true, that eyes are form'd to serve
The inward light:° and that the heavenly part
Ought to be king, from whose rules who do swerve,
Rebels to Nature strive for their own smart.
  It is most true, what we call Cupid's dart,   *5*
An image is, which for ourselves we carve;
And, fools, adore in temple of our heart,
Till that good god make church and churchman starve.
  True, that true Beauty Virtue is indeed,
Whereof this beauty can be but a shade,°   *10*
Which elements with mortal mixture breed:
True, that on earth we are but pilgrims made,
  And should in soul up to our country move:
  True, and yet true that I must Stella love.

6

Some lovers speak when they their Muses entertain,
Of hopes begot by fear, of wot not what desires:
Of force of heav'nly beams, infusing hellish pain:
Of living deaths, dear wounds, fair storms and freezing
    fires:°
  Some one his song in Jove, and Jove's strange tales   *5*
    attires,
Bordered° with bulls and swans, powdered with golden
    rain:°

11 **prove** try.

2 **inward light** reason (see sonnet 71). 10 **shade** shadow.

2–4 **hopes . . . fires** oxymorons of Petrarchan love poetry. 5–6 **Jove . . . rain** material of Ovidian or mythological poetry. Jove came to Europa as a bull; to Leda as a swan; to Danae as a golden shower. 6 **Bordered** Ringler emends to "brodered" (embroidered).

Another humbler wit to shepherd's pipe retires,
Yet hiding royal blood full oft in rural vein.°
    To some a sweetest plaint, a sweetest style affords,
10   While tears pour out his ink, and signs breathe out his
        words:
His paper pale despair, and pain his pen doth move.
    I can speak what I feel, and feel as much as they,
    But think that all the map of my state I display,
When trembling voice brings forth that I do Stella love.

7

When Nature made her chief work, Stella's eyes,
In color black, why wrapt she beams so bright?
Would she in beamy° black, like painter wise,
Frame daintiest lustre, mixt of shades and light?
5   Or did she else that sober hue devise,
In object° best to knit and strength our sight,
Lest if no veil these brave gleams did disguise,
They sun-like should more dazzle than delight?
    Or would she her miraculous power show,
10 That whereas black seems Beauty's contrary,
She even in black doth make all beauties flow?
Both so and thus, she minding Love should be
    Placed ever there, gave him his mourning weed,
    To honor all their deaths, who for her bleed.

8

Love born in Greece, of late fled from his native
    place,°
    Forc'd by a tedious proof, that Turkish hardened
    heart,
    Is no fit mark to pierce with his fine pointed dart:
And pleased with our soft peace, stayed here his
    flying race.

7–8 shepherd's . . . vein pastoral love poetry.
3 beamy radiant. 6 In object with purpose.
1 native place Cyprus, one of the traditional homes of his mother
Venus, had been captured by the Turks in 1573.

But finding these North climes do coldly him embrace,   5
  Nor used to frozen clips,° he strave to find some
      part,
  Where with most ease and warmth he might employ
     his art:
At length he perch'd himself in Stella's joyful face,
  Whose fair skin, beamy eyes like morning sun on
     snow,
Deceiv'd the quaking boy, who thought from so pure   10
     light,
Effects of lively heat, must needs in nature grow.
But she most fair, most cold, made him thence take
     his flight
  To my close° heart, where while some firebrands
     he did lay,
  He burnt unwares his wings, and cannot fly away.

9

Queen Virtue's court, which some call Stella's face,
  Prepar'd by Nature's chiefest° furniture,°
  Hath his front° built of alablaster pure;
Gold is the covering of that stately place.
The door by which sometimes comes forth her grace,   5
  Red porphyr is, which lock of pearl makes sure:
  Whose porches rich (which name of cheeks endure)
Marble mixt red and white do enterlace.
  The windows now through which this heav'nly
     guest
Looks over the world, and can find nothing such,   10
Which dare claim from those lights the name of best.
Of touch° they are that without touch doth touch,
  Which Cupid's self from Beauty's mine did draw:
  Of touch they are, and poor I am their straw.

6 **clips** embraces. 13 **close** (1) nearby; (2) confined or secret.
2 **chiefest** 1598: "choicest." 2 **furniture** furnishing. 3 **front** also,
face or forehead. 12–14 **touch** the touchstone: (1) a fine-grained
black quartz used to test ("touch") the quality of gold and silver
alloy, and (2) associated with the jet, which when rubbed attracts
light materials, like straw.

10

Reason, in faith thou art well serv'd, that still
Wouldst brabbling° be with sense and love in me:
I rather wisht thee climb the Muses' hill,
Or reach the fruit of Nature's choicest tree,
5   Or seek heav'n's course, or heav'n's inside to see:
Why shouldst thou toil our thorny soil to till?
Leave sense, and those which sense's objects be:
Deal thou with powers of thoughts, leave love to will.
    But thou wouldst needs fight both with love and
       sense,
10 With sword of wit, giving wounds of dispraise,
Till down-right blows did foil thy cunning fence:°
For soon as they strake thee with Stella's rays,
    Reason thou kneel'dst, and offeredst straight to
      prove
    By reason good, good reason her to love.

11

In truth, O Love, with what a boyish kind
    Thou doest proceed in thy most serious ways:
    That when the heav'n to thee his best displays,
Yet of that best thou leav'st the best behind.
5 For like a child that some fair book doth find,
    With gilded leaves or color'd vellum plays,
    Or at the most on some fine picture stays,
But never heeds the fruit of writer's mind:
    So when thou saw'st in Nature's cabinet
10 Stella, thou straight lookst babies° in her eyes,
In her cheek's pit thou didst thy pitfold° set:
And in her breast bopeep° or couching lies,
    Playing and shining in each outward part:
    But, fool, seekst not to get into her heart.

---

2 **brabbling** quarreling.   11 **fence** swordmanship.
10 **babies** (1) small image of oneself seen in the pupil of another's
eye; (2) pictures in books, perhaps so named from ornamental
borders with Cupids.   11 **pitfold** snare for animals.   12 **bopeep**
from the nursery game.

12

Cupid, because thou shin'st in Stella's eyes,
   That from her locks, thy day-nets,° none scapes free,
   That those lips swell, so full of thee they be,
That her sweet breath makes oft thy flames to rise,
That in her breast thy pap well sugared lies,   5
   That her grace gracious makes thy wrongs, that she
   What words soe'er she speak persuades for thee,
That her clear voice lifts thy fame to the skies.
   Thou countest Stella thine, like those whose powers
Having got up a breach by fighting well,   10
Cry, Victory, this fair day all is ours.
O no, her heart is such a citadel,
   So fortified with wit, stor'd with disdain,
   That to win it, is all the skill and pain.

13

Phoebus was judge between Jove, Mars, and Love,
   Of those three gods, whose arms the fairest were:
   Jove's golden shield did eagle sables° bear,
Whose talents° held young Ganymede above:
But in vert field Mars bare a golden spear,   5
   Which through a bleeding heart his point did shove:
   Each had his crest, Mars carried Venus' glove,
Jove on his helm the thunderbolt did rear.
Cupid then smiles, for on his crest there lies
   Stella's fair hair, her face he makes his shield,   10
   Where roses gules are borne in silver field.
Phoebus drew wide the curtains of the skies
   To blaze° these last, and sware devoutly then,
   The first, thus matcht, were scarcely gentlemen.

2 **day-nets** a way of capturing larks, by attracting them to nets with
bright pieces of mirror.
3 ff. **sables . . . vert . . . gules** in heraldry, black, green, and red,
respectively. 4 **talents** (eagle's talons) alluding to the infatuated
Jove's disguise as an eagle in carrying off Ganymede to be cupbearer of the gods. 13 **blaze** (1) technically, the proper display of
heraldic devices to which gentlemen are entitled; (2) to publish or
proclaim.

14

Alas have I not pain enough my friend,
    Upon whose breast a fiercer gripe° doth tire,°
    Than did on him who first stale down the fire,°
While Love on me doth all his quiver spend,
5   But with your rhubarb° words you must contend,
    To grieve me worse, in saying that desire
    Doth plunge my well-form'd soul even in the mire
Of sinful thoughts, which do in ruin end?
    If that be sin which doth the manners frame,
10 Well stay'd with truth in word and faith of deed,
Ready of wit and fearing nought but shame:
If that be sin which in fix⁺ hearts doth breed
    A loathing of all loose unchastity,
    Then love is sin, and let me sinful be.

15

You that do search for every purling spring,
    Which from the ribs of old Parnassus° flows,
    And every flower° not sweet perhaps, which grows
Near thereabouts, into your poesy° wring.°
5   You that do dictionary's method° bring
    Into your rhymes, running in rattling rows:
    You that poor Petrarch's long deceasèd woes,
With new-born sighs and denizen'd° wit do sing.
    You take wrong ways, those far-fet helps be such,
10 As do bewray a want of inward touch:
And sure at length stol'n goods do come to light.
    But if (both for your love and skill) your name
    You seek to nurse at fullest breasts of Fame,
Stella behold, and then begin to indite.°

---

2 **gripe** vulture. 2 **tire** tear with the beak. 3 **him . . . fire** Prometheus, punished by Jove. 5 **rhubarb** bitter, also purgative.
2 **Parnassus** home of the Muses. 3 **flower** also, rhetorical figure ("flowers of rhetoric"). 4 **poesy** also, a nosegay or bunch of flowers (posy). 4 **wring** wreathe, insinuate. 5 **dictionary's method** esp. alliteration (line 6). 8 **denizen'd** domesticated. 14 **indite** compose.

16

In nature apt to like when I did see
   Beauties, which were of many carats fine,
   My boiling sprites° did thither soon incline,
And, Love, I thought that I was full of thee:
But finding not those restless flames in me,   *5*
   Which others said did make their souls to pine:
   I thought those babes of some pin's hurt did whine,
By my love judging what Love's pain might be.
   But while I thus with this young lion played,
Mine eyes (shall I say curst or blest) beheld   *10*
Stella; now she is named, need more be said?
In her sight I a lesson new have spell'd,
   I now have learn'd love right, and learn'd even so,
   As who by being poison'd doth poison know.

17

His mother dear Cupid offended late,
   Because that Mars grown slacker in her love,
   With pricking shot he did not throughly move,
To keep the pace of their first loving state.
The boy refused for fear of Mars's hate,   *5*
   Who threaten'd stripes, if he his wrath did prove:°
   But she in chafe him from her lap did shove,
Brake bow, brake shafts, while Cupid weeping sat:
   Till that his grandame Nature pitying it,
Of Stella's brows made him two better bows,   *10*
And in her eyes of arrows infinite.
O how for joy he leaps, O how he crows,
   And straight therewith like wags new got to play,
   Falls to shrewd° turns, and I was in his way.

3 **sprites** spirits.
6 **prove** try.   14 **shrewd** naughty.

18

With what sharp checks I in myself am shent,°
   When into Reason's audit I do go:
   And by just counts myself a bankrout know
Of all those goods, which heav'n to me hath° lent:
5 Unable quite to pay even Nature's rent,
   Which unto it by birthright I do owe:
   And which is worse, no good excuse can show,
But that my wealth I have most idly spent.
    My youth doth waste, my knowledge brings forth
      toys,
10 My wit doth strive those passions to defend,
Which for reward spoil it with vain annoys.
I see my course to lose myself doth bend:
   I see and yet no greater sorrow take,
   Than that I lose no more for Stella's sake.

19

On Cupid's bow how are my heart-strings bent,
   That see my wrack, and yet embrace the same?
   When most I glory, then I feel most shame:
I willing run, yet while I run, repent.
5 My best wits still their own disgrace invent:
   My very ink turns straight to Stella's name;
   And yet my words, as them my pen doth frame,
Avise themselves that they are vainly spent.
    For though she pass° all things, yet what is all
10 That unto me, who fare like him° that both
Looks to the skies, and in a ditch doth fall?
O let me prop my mind yet in his growth,
   And not in nature, for best fruits unfit:
   Scholar, saith Love, bend hitherward your wit.

1 **shent** shamed. 4 **hath** 1598: "have" (allowing "goods" to be subject).
9 **pass** surpass. 10 **him** the philosopher Thales who, according to Plato, fell into a well while looking at the stars.

20

Fly, fly, my friends, I have my death wound; fly,
See there that boy, that murth'ring boy I say,
Who like a thief, hid in dark bush doth lie,
Till bloody bullet get him wrongful prey.
    So tyran he no fitter place could spy,   *5*
Nor so fair level° in so secret stay,°
As that sweet black which veils the heav'nly eye:
There himself with his shot he close doth lay.
    Poor passenger,° pass now thereby I did,
And stayed pleas'd with the prospect of the place,   *10*
While that black hue from me the bad guest hid:
But straight I saw motions of lightning grace,
    And then descried the glist'ring of his dart:
    But ere I could fly thence, it pierced my heart.

21

Your words my friend (right healthful caustics) blame
    My young mind marr'd, whom Love doth windlass°
        so,
    That mine own writings like bad servants show
My wits, quick in vain thoughts, in virtue lame:
That Plato I read for nought, but if he tame   *5*
    Such coltish gyres,° that to my birth I owe
    Nobler desires, least else that friendly foe,
Great expectation, wear a train of shame.
    For since mad March great promise made of me,
If now the May of my years much decline,   *10*
What can be hoped my harvest time will be?
Sure you say well, your wisdom's golden mine
    Dig deep with learning's spade, now tell me this,
    Hath this world ought so fair as Stella is?

---

6 **level** line of fire. 6 **stay** stopping place. 9 **passenger** passer-by.
2 **windlass** snare (in hunting, a circuit made to intercept game).
6 **gyres** rapid turnings (1598: "years").

22

In highest way° of heav'n the sun did ride,
  Progressing° then from fair twins' gold'n place:
  Having no scarf° of clouds before his face,
But shining forth of heat in his chief pride;
5 When some fair ladies by hard promise tied,
  On horseback met him in his furious race,
  Yet each prepar'd with fan's well-shading grace,
From that foe's wounds their tender skins to hide.
Stella alone with face unarmèd marcht,
10 Either to do like him which open shone,
  Or careless of the wealth because her own:
Yet were the hid and meaner beauties parcht,
  Her daintiest bare went free; the cause was this,
  The sun which others burn'd, did her but kiss.

23

The curious wits seeing dull pensiveness
  Bewray itself in my long settled eyes,
  Whence those same fumes of melancholy rise,
With idle pains, and missing aim, do guess.
5 Some that know how my spring I did address,
  Deem that my Muse some fruit of knowledge plies:°
  Others, because the Prince my service tries,
Think that I think state errors to redress.
  But harder judges judge ambition's rage,
10 Scourge of itself, still climbing slipp'ry place,
Holds my young brain captiv'd in golden cage.
  O fools, or over-wise, alas the race
  Of all my thoughts hath neithe. stop nor start,
  But only Stella's eyes and Stella's heart.

---

1 **highest way** its position under sign of Gemini (the "fair twins"
of line 2); in June.   2 **Progressing** with overtones of a royal expe-
dition or progress.   3 **scarf** Quartos: "mask."
6 **plies** works busily at.

24

Rich° fools there be, whose base and filthy heart
Lies hatching still the goods wherein they flow:
And damning their own selves to Tantal's° smart,
Wealth breeding want, more blist, more wretched grow.
　　Yet to those fools heav'n such wit doth impart,　　　5
As what their hands do hold, their heads do know,
And knowing love, and loving lay apart,
As sacred things, far from all danger's show.
　　But that rich fool who by blind Fortune's lot,
The richest gem of love and life enjoys,　　　　　　　10
And can with foul abuse such beauties blot;
Let him deprived of sweet but unfelt joys,
　　(Exil'd for aye from those high treasures, which
　　He knows not) grow in only folly rich.

25

The wisest scholar of the wight most wise,
By Phoebus' doom,° with sug'red sentence° says,
That Virtue if it once met with our eyes,
Strange flames of Love it in our souls would raise.
　　But for that° man with pain this truth descries,　　5
Whiles he each thing in sense's balance weighs,
And so nor will, nor can behold those skies,
Which inward sun° to heroic mind displays,
　　Virtue of late with virtuous care to stir
Love of herself, takes Stella's shape, that she　　　　10
To mortal eyes might sweetly shine in her.
It is most true, for since I her did see,
　　Virtue's great beauty in that face I prove,°
　　And find th'effect, for I do burn in love.

1 **Rich** probably a reference to Lord Rich, who became the husband
of Penelope Devereux (thought to be the original of Stella).
3 **Tantal's** Tantalus, punished by starving with plentiful food and
drink just beyond his reach.

1-2 **wisest . . . doom** Plato ("wisest scholar"); Socrates ("wight most
wise"—so judged by Apollo's oracle at Delphi). 2 **sug'red sentence**
in *Phaedrus* (see Sidney's *Apology*, p. 256). 5 **for that** because.
8 **inward sun** See sonnet 71. 13 **prove** (1) in logical sense; (2)
experience.

26

Though dusty° wits dare scorn astrology,
And fools can think those lamps of purest light,
Whose numbers, ways, greatness, eternity,
Promising wonders, wonder do invite,
5   To have for no cause birthright in the sky,
But for to spangle the black weeds of night:
Or for some brawl,° which in that chamber high,
They should still dance to please a gazer's sight.
    For me, I do Nature unidle know,
10 And know great causes, great effects procure:
And know those bodies high reign on the low.
And if these rules did fail, proof makes me sure,
    Who oft fore-judge my after-following race,
    By only those two stars in Stella's face.

27

Because I oft in dark abstracted guise,
    Seem most alone in greatest company:
With dearth of words, or answers quite awry,
To them that would make speech of speech arise,
5   They deem, and of their doom the rumor flies,
    That poison foul of bubbling pride doth lie
    So in my swelling breast that only I°
Fawn on myself, and others do despise:
    Yet pride I think doth not my soul possess,
10 Which looks too oft in his unflatt'ring glass:
But one worse fault ambition I confess,
That makes me oft my best friends overpass,
    Unseen, unheard, while thought to highest place
    Bends all his powers, even unto Stella's grace.

1 **dusty** earthbound.   **7 brawl** French dance form, involving circular movement.
7 only I I do nothing but.

28

You that with allegory's curious° frame,°
   Of others' children changelings use to make,
   With me those pains for God's sake do not take:
I list not dig so deep for brazen fame.
When I say, Stella, I do mean the same   5
   Princess of beauty, for whose only sake
   The reins of Love I love, though never slack,
And joy therein, though nations count it shame.
   I beg no subject to use eloquence,°
Nor in hid ways to guide philosophy: 10
Look at my hands for no such quintessence;°
But know that I in pure simplicity,
   Breathe out the flames which burn within my heart,
   Love only reading unto me this art.

big theme of sonnets (see Louis Martz)

29

Like some weak lords, neighbor'd by mighty kings,
   To keep themselves and their chief cities free,
   Do eas'ly yield, that all their° coasts may be
Ready to store their° camps of needful things:
So Stella's heart finding what power Love brings,   5
   To keep itself in life and liberty,
   Doth willing grant, that in the frontiers he
Use all to help his other conquerings:
And thus her heart escapes, but thus her eyes
   Serve him with shot, her lips his heralds are: 10
   Her breasts his tents, legs his triumphal car:
Her flesh his food, her skin his armor brave,
And I, but for because my prospect° lies
Upon that coast, am giv'n up for a slave.

---

1 **curious** (1) studious, inquisitive; (2) intricate. 1 **frame** (1) formula of words, syllogism; (2) contrivance. 9 **subject . . . eloquence** topic needed to inspire to eloquence. 11 **quintessence** the fifth element, basic to all matter, and of which the heavenly bodies were said to be made. Alchemists labored to extract it.

3 **their** "weak lords." 4 **their** "mighty kings." 13 **prospect** gaze.

30

Whether the Turkish new-moon° minded be
  To fill his horns this year on Christian coast:
  How Poles' right king° means without leave of host,
To warm with ill-made fire cold Moscovy.
5 If French can yet three parts° in one agree,
  What now the Dutch in their full diets boast,
  How Holland hearts, now so good towns be lost,
Trust in the shade of pleasing Orange tree.°
  How Ulster likes of that same golden bit,°
10 Wherewith my father once made it half tame,
If in the Scottish court be welt'ring yet.
  These questions busy wits to me do frame;
  I cumb'red with good manners, answer do,
  But know not how, for still I think of you.

31

With how sad steps, O moon, thou climb'st the skies,
  How silently, and with how wan a face,
  What may it be, that even in heav'nly place
That busy archer his sharp arrows tries?
5 Sure if that long with love acquainted eyes
  Can judge of love, thou feel'st a lover's case;
  I read it in thy looks, thy languisht grace
To me that feel the like, thy state descries.
  Then ev'n of fellowship, O moon, tell me
10 Is constant love deem'd there but want of wit?
Are beauties there as proud as here they be?
Do they above love to be lov'd, and yet
  Those lovers scorn whom that love doth possess?
  Do they call Virtue there ungratefulness?°

1 **new-moon** referring to the Turkish flag and a feared attack on
Spain. 3 **Poles' . . . king** Maximilian II claimed the Polish throne
and had invaded Muscovy. 5 **three parts** factions of Catholics,
Huguenots, and *politiques.* 8 **Orange tree** William of Orange had
been ruler of Holland from 1576. In 1581–82 several towns had been
lost to the Spanish armies. 9 **golden bit** Sir Henry Sidney as Lord
Deputy had succeeded in imposing a levy on Irish landowners.
14 **ungratefulness** (1) do they, above, call ungratefulness (the
lady's) a virtue? (2) "ungrateful" means unpleasing or distasteful:
is Virtue (the lover's) considered unpleasing there?

32

Morpheus° the lively son of deadly sleep,
   Witness of life to them that living die:
   A prophet oft, and oft an history,
A poet eke, as humours fly or creep,
Since thou in me so sure a power doest keep,   *5*
   That never I with clos'd-up sense do lie,
   But by thy work my Stella I descry,
Teaching blind eyes both how to smile and weep,
   Vouchsafe of all acquaintance this to tell;
Whence hast thou ivory, rubies, pearl and gold,   *10*
To show her skin, lips, teeth and head so well?
Fool, answers he, no Inds such treasures hold,
    But from thy heart, while my sire charmeth thee,
    Sweet Stella's image I do steal to me.

33

I might, unhappy word, O me, I might,
And then would not, or could not see my bliss:
Till now wrapt in a most infernal night,
I find how heav'nly day wretch I did miss.
   Heart rent thyself, thou doest thyself but right,   *5*
No lovely Paris made thy Helen his:
No force, no fraud, robb'd thee of thy delight,
Nor Fortune of thy fortune author is:
   But to myself myself did give the blow,
While too much wit (forsooth) so troubled me,   *10*
That I respects° for both our sakes must show:
And yet could not by rising morn foresee
    How fair a day was near, O punisht eyes,
    That I had been more foolish or more wise.

---

1 **Morpheus** son of Somnus (sleep), responsible for appearance of
humans in dreams (hence "lively").
11 **respects** prudential considerations, caution.

34

Come let me write, and to what end? To ease
    A burth'ned heart, how can words ease, which are
    The glasses° of thy daily vexing care?°
Oft cruel fights well pictured forth do please.
5 Art not ashamed to publish thy disease?
    Nay, that may breed my fame, it is so rare:
    But will not wise men think thy words fond° ware?
Then be they° close,° and so none shall displease.
    What idler thing, than speak and not be hard?°
10 What harder thing than smart, and not to speak?
Peace foolish wit, with wit my wit is marred.
Thus write I while I doubt° to write, and wreak
    My harms on ink's poor loss, perhaps some find
    Stella's great pow'rs, that so confuse my mind.

35

What may words say, or what may words not say,
Where truth itself must speak like flattery?
Within what bounds can one his liking stay,
Where Nature doth with infinite agree?
5 What Nestor's° counsel can my flames allay,
Since Reason's self doth blow the coal in me?
And ah what hope, that hope should once see day,
Where Cupid is sworn page to Chastity?
Honor is honor'd, that thou doest possess
10 Him as thy slave, and now long needy Fame
    Doth even grow rich, naming my Stella's name.°
Wit learns in thee perfection to express,
    Not thou by praise, but praise in thee is rais'd:
    It is a praise to praise, when thou art prais'd.

1–3 **Come . . . care** usually read as series of staccato declarations
and questions ("and . . . end? . . . how . . . care?"), but the Folio
punctuation allows other possibilities. 3 **glasses** mirrors. 7 **fond**
foolish. 8 **they** i.e., words. 8 **close** secret. 9 **hard** heard. 12
doubt hesitate.

---

5 **Nestor's** the Greeks' wise counselor. 11 **rich . . . name** See
sonnet 24.

36

Stella, whence doth this new assault arise,
A conquer'd, yelden,° ransackt heart to win?
Whereto long since through my long batt'red eyes,
Whole armies of thy beauties ent'red in.
    And there long since, Love thy lieutenant lies,   *5*
My forces razed,° thy banners rais'd within:
Of conquest, do not these effects suffice,
But wilt new war upon thine own begin?
    With so sweet voice, and by sweet nature so
In sweetest strength, so sweetly skill'd withal,   *10*
In all sweet stratagems, sweet art can show,
That not my soul,° which at thy foot did fall,
    Long since forc'd by thy beams, but stone nor tree
    By sense's privilege,° can scape from thee.

37°

My mouth doth water, and my breast doth swell,
    My tongue doth itch, my thoughts in labor be:
    Listen then lordings with good ear to me,
For of my life I must a riddle tell.
Toward Aurora's court° a nymph doth dwell,   *5*
    Rich in all beauties which man's eye can see:
    Beauties so far from reach of words, that we
Abase her praise, saying she doth excel:
    Rich in the treasure of deserv'd renown,
Rich in the riches of a royal heart,   *10*
Rich in those gifts which give th'eternal crown;
Who though most rich in these and every part,
    Which make the patents° of true worldly bliss,
    Hath no misfortune, but that Rich she is.

2 **yelden** (archaic past participle): (1) yielded; (2) wearied.
6 **razed** completely destroyed. 12 **not . . . soul** not only my soul.
14 **By . . . privilege** (1) usually unaffected, being free of senses;
(2) given sense's privilege (parallel construction to "by thy beams").

0 **Sonnet 37** omitted in Thomas Newman's Quarto printing, 1591,
perhaps because of its reference to Penelope Rich. 5 **Aurora's
court** in the east (the seat of Lord Rich was in Essex). 13 **patents**
titles to possession.

38

This night while sleep begins with heavy wings
　　To hatch° mine eyes, and that unbitted° thought
　　Doth fall to stray, and my chief powers are brought
To leave° the scepter of all subject things,
5　　The first that straight my fancy's error° brings
　　Unto my mind, is Stella's image, wrought
　　By Love's own self, but with so curious draught,°
That she, methinks, not only shines but sings.
　　I start, look, hark, but what in clos'd up sense
10　Was held, in open'd sense it flies away,
Leaving me nought but wailing eloquence:
　　I seeing better sights in sight's decay,
　　　Call'd it anew, and wooèd sleep again:
　　　But him her host that unkind guest had slain.

39

Come sleep, O sleep, the certain knot of peace,
The baiting place° of wit, the balm of woe,
The poor man's wealth, the prisoner's release,
Th' indifferent judge between the high and low;
5　　With shield of proof° shield me from out the prease°
Of those fierce darts, despair at me doth throw:
O make in me those civil wars to cease;
I will good tribute pay if thou do so.
　　Take thou of me smooth pillows, sweetest bed,
10　A chamber deaf to noise, and blind to light:
A rosy garland,° and a weary head:
And if these things, as being thine by right,
　　　Move not thy heavy grace, thou shalt in me
　　　Livelier than elsewhere Stella's image see.

---

2 **hatch** close. 2 **unbitted** unbridled. 4 **leave** relinquish. 5 **error** wandering. 7 **draught** drawing.
2 **baiting place** wayside resting place. 5 **of proof** of tested strength (used of armor). 5 **prease** throng. 11 **rosy garland** rose as emblem of silence (*sub rosa*), having been dedicated by Cupid to Harpocrates, god of silence, who helped in the intrigues of Venus.

40

As good to write as for to lie and groan,
   O Stella dear, how much thy power hath wrought,
   That hast my mind, none of the basest, brought
My still kept course, while others sleep to moan.°
Alas, if from the height of Virtue's throne,   5
   Thou canst vouchsafe the influence of a thought
   Upon a wretch, that long thy grace hath sought;
Weigh then how I by thee am overthrown:
   And then, think thus, although thy beauty be
   Made manifest by such a victory,   1°
Yet noblest conquerors do wrecks avoid.
   Since then thou hast so far subduèd me,
   That in my heart I offer still° to thee,
O do not let thy temple be destroy'd.

41

Having this day my horse, my hand, my lance
   Guided so well, that I obtain'd the prize,
   Both by the judgement of the English eyes,
And of some sent from that sweet enemy France,
Horsemen my skill in horsemanship advance,°   5
   Town-folks my strength: a daintier° judge applies
   His praise to sleight,° which from good use° doth
      rise:
Some lucky wits impute it but to chance:
   Others, because of both sides° I do take
My blood from them, who did excel in this,   10
Think nature me a man of arms did make.
How far they shoot awry; the true cause is,
   Stella lookt on, and from her heavenly face
   Sent forth the beams, which made so fair my race.°

3–4 **That ... moan** syntax: brought my mind to moan my still kept
course (love for Stella).   13 **still** always.

---
5 **advance** praise.   6 **daintier** more demanding.   7 **sleight** dexterity.
7 **good use** practice.   9 **both sides** i.e., of family.   14 **race** course in
a tournament.

42

O eyes, which do the spheres of beauty move,
Whose beams be joys, whose joys all virtues be,
Who while they make Love conquer, conquer Love,
The schools where Venus hath learn'd chastity.
5   O eyes, where humble looks most glorious prove,
Only lov'd tyrants, just in cruelty,
Do not, O do not from poor me remove,
Keep still my zenith, ever shine on me.
    For though I never see them, but straightways
10 My life forgets to nourish languisht sprites;
Yet still on me, O eyes, dart down your rays:
And if from majesty of sacred lights,
    Oppressing mortal sense, my death proceed,
    Wracks triumphs be, which Love (high set) doth
      breed.

43

Fair eyes, sweet lips, dear heart, that foolish I
Could hope by Cupid's help on you to prey;
Since to himself he doth your gifts apply,
As his main force, choice sport, and easeful stay.
5   For when he will see who dare him gainsay,
Then with those eyes he looks, lo by and by°
Each soul doth at Love's feet his weapons lay,
Glad if for her he give them leave to die.
    When he will play, then in her lips he is,
10 Where blushing red, that Love's self them doth love,
With either lip he doth the other kiss:
But when he will for quiet's sake remove
    From all the world, her heart is then his rome,°
    Where well he knows, no man to him can come.

6 **by and by** at once. 13 **rome** obsolete spelling of both "room" and "roam."

44

My words I know do well set forth my mind,
　My mind bemoans his sense of inward smart;
　Such smart may pity claim of any heart,
Her heart, sweet heart, is of no tiger's kind:
And yet she hears, yet I no pity find;　　　　　　　5
　But more I cry, less grace she doth impart,
　Alas, what cause is there so overthwart,°
That nobleness° itself makes thus unkind?°
　I much do guess, yet find no truth save this,
That when the breath of my complaints doth touch　10
Those dainty doors unto the court of bliss,
The heav'nly nature of that place is such,
　That once come there, the sobs of mine annoys
　Are metamorphos'd straight to tunes of joys.

45

Stella oft sees the very face of woe
　Painted in my beclouded stormy face:
　But cannot skill° to pity my disgrace,
Not though thereof the cause herself she know:
Yet hearing late a fable, which did show　　　　　5
　Of lovers never known, a grievous case,
　Pity thereof gat in her breast such place,
That from that sea deriv'd tears' spring did flow.°
　Alas, if Fancy drawn by imag'd things,
Though false, yet with free scope more grace doth breed　10
Than servant's wrack, where new doubts honor brings;°
Then think my dear, that you in me do read
　Of lover's ruin some sad tragedy:
　I am not I, pity the tale of me.

---

7 **overthwart** in opposition. 8 **nobleness** may be taken as subject
of "makes," or as object with "cause" as subject. 8 **unkind** also,
unnatural.

3 **cannot skill** does not know how (or, perhaps, volitional: "will
not bother to"). 8 **That . . . flow** 1591 Quartos read: "As from
her eyes, a spring of tears did flow." 11 **new . . . brings** his honorable behavior (resulting in "servant's wrack") only creates in her
new doubts or fears.

46

I curst thee oft, I pity now thy case,
   Blind-hitting boy, since she that thee and me
   Rules with a beck, so tyrannizeth thee,
That thou must want or food, or dwelling place.
5 For she protests to banish thee her face,
   Her face? O Love, a rogue° thou then shouldst be!
   If Love learn not alone° to love and see,
Without desire to feed of further grace.
   Alas poor wag, that now a scholar art
10 To such a school-mistress, whose lessons new
Thou needs must miss,° and so thou needs must smart.
   Yet dear, let me his pardon get of you,
   So long° (though he from book myche° to desire)
Till without fuel you can make hot fire.

[handwritten left margin: This is a classical-rhetorical argument with the SELF. He "loses" the argument to a larger rhetorical aim — i.e. persuasion, of Stella's charms + power of love]

47

[handwritten right margin: These questions are quaesitio (a battery of opening questions)]

What, have I thus betrayed my liberty?
   Can those black beams° such burning marks° engrave
In my free side? or am I born a slave,
Whose neck becomes° such yoke of tyranny?
5 Or want I sense to feel my misery?
   Or sprite, disdain of such disdain to have?
   Who for long faith, tho' daily help I crave,
May get no alms but scorn of° beggary.

[handwritten: verbs ascend in strength]

   Virtue awake, Beauty but beauty is,
10 I may, I must, I can, I will, I do
Leave following that, which it is gain to miss.

[handwritten: anaphora (2's) + parison]

   Let her go: soft, but here she comes, go to,
   Unkind, I love you not: O me, that eye
Doth make my heart give to my tongue the lie. *

[handwritten: l.10 is exaggerated + shows us his heart isn't in it]

6 **rogue** legally, a vagrant (without dwelling place). 7 **If ... alone**
unless Love learn only to love and see. 11 **needs ... miss** (1) neg-
lect; (2) fail to apprehend. 13 **So long** until ... (a reminder that
Stella herself is fuel of Cupid's fire). 13 **myche** play truant.

2 **black beams** Stella's glance. 2 **burning marks** brands of slavery.
4 **becomes** suits. 8 **scorn** of scorn for.

*[handwritten bottom: * cp. HAMLET, III. ii, ll. 88-153]*

48

Soul's joy, bend not those morning stars° from me,
   Where Virtue is made strong by Beauty's might,
   Where Love is chasteness, Pain doth learn delight,
And Humbleness grows one with Majesty.
Whatever may ensue, O let me be   5
   Copartner of the riches of that sight:
   Let not mine eyes be hell-driv'n from that light:
O look, O shine, O let me die and see.
   For though I oft myself of them bemoan,
   That through my heart their beamy darts be gone: 10
Whose cureless wounds even now most freshly bleed·
   Yet since my death-wound is already got,
   Dear killer, spare not thy sweet cruel shot:
A kind of grace it is to slay with speed.

49

I on my horse, and Love on me doth try
   Our horsemanships, while by strange work I prove
   A horseman to my horse, a horse to Love;
And now man's wrongs in me poor beast descry.
The reins wherewith my rider doth me tie,   5
   Are humbled thoughts, which bit of reverence move,
   Curb'd in with fear, but with gilt boss° above
Of hope, which makes it seem fair to the eye.
   The wand° is will, thou fancy saddle art,
Girt fast by memory, and while I spur   10
My horse, he spurs with sharp desire my heart:
He sits me fast, how ever I do stir:
   And now hath made me to his hand so right,
   That in the manage° myself takes delight.

---

1 **stars** Stella's eyes.
7 **boss** metal stud on the side of a bit. 9 **wand** riding crop. 14 **manage** art of training and handling horses.

50

Stella, the fullness of my thoughts of thee
Cannot be stay'd within my panting breast,
But they do swell and struggle forth of me,
Till that in words thy figure be exprest.
5   And yet as soon as they so formèd be,
According to my lord Love's own behest:
With sad° eyes I their weak proportion see,
To portrait that which in this world is best.
       So that I cannot choose but write my mind,
10   And cannot choose but put out° what I write,
While those° poor babes their death in birth do find:
And now my pen these lines had dashèd quite,
           But that they stopt his fury from the same,
           Because their forefront bare sweet Stella's name.

51

Pardon mine ears, both I and they do pray,
       So may your tongue still fluently proceed,
       To them that do such entertainment need,
So may you still have somewhat new to say.
5   On silly° me do not the burthen lay,
       Of all the grave conceits your brain doth breed;
       But find some Hercules to bear, instead
Of Atlas° tir'd, your wisdom's heav'nly sway.°
       For me, while you discourse of courtly tides,
10   Of cunning'st fishers in most troubled streams,
Of straying ways, when valiant error guides:
Meanwhile my heart confers with Stella's beams,
           And is even irkt that so sweet comedy,
           By such unsuited speech should hind'red be.

7 sad also, serious.   10 put out strike out.   11 those 1598: "these."
(The Quarto reading allows a distinction between the general reference of line 11 and the specific gesture of line 12.)

5 silly simple.   8 Atlas who supported the heavens and was, tem-
porarily, relieved of them by Hercules.   8 sway pressure.

52

A strife is grown between Virtue and Love,
    While each pretends° that Stella must be his:
    Her eyes, her lips, her all, saith Love do° this,
Since they do wear his badge,° most firmly prove.
But Virtue thus that title doth disprove,   5
    That° Stella (O dear name) that Stella is
    That virtuous soul, sure heir of heav'nly bliss:
Not this fair outside, which our hearts doth move.
    And therefore, though her beauty and her grace
Be Love's indeed, in Stella's self he may   10
By no pretense claim any manner place.
Well, Love, since this demur° our suit° doth stay,
    Let Virtue have that Stella's self; yet thus,
    That Virtue but that body grant to us.

53

In martial sports I had my cunning tried,
    And yet to break more staves did me address:
    While with the people's shouts I must confess,
Youth, luck, and praise, even fill'd my veins with pride.
When Cupid having me his slave descried,   5
    In Mars's livery, prancing in the press:°
    What now sir fool, said he, I would no less,°
Look here, I say. I look'd, and Stella spied:
    Who hard by made a window send forth light,
My heart then quak'd, then dazzled were mine eyes,   10
One hand forgot to rule, th'other to fight.
Nor trumpets' sound I heard, nor friendly cries;
    My foe came on, and beat the air for me,
    Till that her blush taught me my shame to see.

2 **pretends** in law, bring a charge or action. 3 **do** auxiliary to
"prove" (line 4). 4 **his badge** Love's livery. 6 **That** i.e., claiming
that. 12 **demur** legal plea, creating delay; it acknowledges facts
stated by opponent, but denies his right to relief. 12 **suit** (1) legal;
(2) courtship of Stella.

6 **press** throng. 7 **I . . . less** Open punctuation allows several readings: (1) Cupid speaking, a peremptory reinforcement of "Look
here . . ."; (2) Cupid speaking—"no less" referring to title of "Sir
Fool"; (3) Astrophel, reflecting ironically on the title.

54

Because I breathe not love to every one,
   Nor do not use set colors for to wear,
   Nor nourish special locks of vowèd hair,
Nor give each speech a full point° of a groan,
5   The courtly nymphs, acquainted with the moan
   Of them, who in their lips Love's standard bear;
   What he? say they of me, now I dare swear,
He cannot love: no, no, let him alone.
   And think° so still, so Stella know my mind,
10   Profess in deed I do not Cupid's art;
But you fair maids, at length this true shall find,
That his right badge is but worn in the heart:
   Dumb swans, not chatt'ring pies,° do lovers prove,
   They love indeed, who quake to say they love.

55°

Muses, I oft invok'd your holy aid,
   With choicest flowers° my speech to engarland so;
   That it despis'd in true but naked show,
Might win some grace in your sweet grace° array'd.°
5   And oft whole troops° of saddest words I stay'd,
   Striving abroad a foraging to go;
   Until by your inspiring I might know,
How their black banner might be best display'd.
   But now I mean no more your help to try,
10   Nor other sug'ring of my speech to prove,
But on her name incessantly to cry:
For let me but name her whom I do love,
   So sweet sounds straight mine ear and heart do hit,
   That I well find no eloquence like it.

---

4 **full point** as punctuation, a full stop or period.   9 **think** has force
of an imperative.   13 **pies** magpies.

0 In Quartos, this sonnet follows 56. 2 **flowers** See sonnet 15, lines
3–4. 4 **grace** Quartos: "skill." 4 **array'd** (1) dressed; (2) ordered,
as in military use (see "troops," line 5). 5 **troops** with pun on
"tropes" (an alternate spelling in sixteenth century).

56

Fie school of Patience, fie, your lesson is
    Far far too long to learn it without book:°
    What, a whole week without one piece of look,
And think I should not your large precepts miss?°
When I might read those letters fair of bliss,   5
    Which in her face teach virtue, I could brook
    Somewhat thy lead'n counsels, which I took,
As of a friend that meant not much amiss:
    But now that I alas do want° her sight,
What, dost thou think that I can ever take   10
In thy cold stuff a phlegmatic° delight?
No Patience, if thou wilt my good, then make
    Her come, and hear with patience my desire,
    And then with patience bid me bear my fire.

57

Woe, having made with many fights° his own
    Each sense of mine, each gift, each power of mind,
    Grown now his slaves, he forc'd them out to find
The thorowest° words, fit for woe's self to groan,
Hoping that when they might find Stella alone,   5
    Before she could prepare to be unkind,
    Her soul arm'd but with such a dainty rind,
Should soon be pierc'd with sharpness of the moan.
    She heard my plaints, and did not only hear,
But them (so sweet is she) most sweetly sing,   10
With that fair breast making woe's darkness clear:
A pretty case° I hopèd her to bring
    To feel my griefs, and she with face and voice,
    So sweets my pains, that my pains me rejoice.

---

2 **without book** by memory. 4 **miss** forget. 9 **want** lack. 11 **phlegmatic** the cold, moist humor (opposed to "fire," line 14).
1 **fights** Quartos: "sighs." 4 **thorowest** most penetrating. 12 **case** modern editions punctuate: "case!" Neither 1598 nor Q2 punctuates at this point.

58

Doubt there hath been when with his golden chain,°
  The orator so far men's hearts doth bind,
  That no pace else their guided steps can find,
But as he them more short or slack doth rein,
5 Whether with words this sovereignty he gain,
  Cloth'd with fine tropes, with strongest reasons°
     lin'd,
  Or else pronouncing grace,° wherewith his mind
Prints his own lively form in rudest brain:
  Now judge by this, in piercing phrases late,
10   Th' anatomy of all my woes I wrate,
Stella's sweet breath the same to me did read.
  O voice, O face, maugre° my speech's might,
  Which wooèd woe, most ravishing delight,
Even those sad words, even in sad me did breed.

59

Dear, why make you more of a dog than me?
  If he do love, I burn, I burn in love:
  If he wait well, I never thence would move:
If he be fair, yet but a dog can be.
5 Little he is, so little worth is he;
  He barks, my songs thine own voice oft doth prove:°
  Bidd'n perhaps he fetcheth thee a glove,
But I unbid, fetch even my soul to thee.
  Yet while I languish, him that bosom clips,°
10 That lap doth lap, nay lets in spite of spite,
This sour-breath'd mate taste of those sug'red lips.
  Alas, if you grant only such delight
  To witless things, then Love, I hope (since wit
Becomes a clog°) will soon ease me of it.

---

1 **golden chain** an emblem of eloquence. Hercules is pictured drawing crowds by a chain leading from his mouth. 6 **tropes . . .
reasons** See sonnet 3. 7 **pronouncing grace** delivery. 12 **maugre** in
spite of.
6 **prove** try. 9 **clips** embraces. 14 **clog** heavy block of wood, at-
tached to leg to impede motion.

60

When my good angel guides me to the place,
    Where all my good I do in Stella see,
    That heav'n of joys throws only down on me
Thund'red disdains and lightnings of disgrace:°
But when the rugged'st step of Fortune's race   5
    Makes me fall from her sight, then sweetly she
    With words, wherein the Muses' treasures be,
Shows love and pity to my absent case.
    Now I wit-beaten long by hardest Fate,
So dull am, that I cannot look into   10
The ground of this fierce love and lovely hate:
Then some good body tell me how I do,
    Whose presence, absence, absence presence is;
    Blist in my curse, and cursèd in my bliss.

61

Oft with true sighs, oft with uncallèd tears,
Now with slow words, now with dumb eloquence
I Stella's eyes assail, invade her ears;
But this at last is her sweet breath'd defense:
    That who indeed infelt affection bears,   5
So captives to his saint both soul and sense,
That wholly hers, all selfness he forbears,
Thence his desires he learns, his live's course thence.
    Now since her chaste mind hates this love in me,
    With chast'ned mind, I straight must show that she   10
Shall quickly me from what she hates remove.
    O Doctor° Cupid, thou for me reply,
    Driv'n else to grant by angel's sophistry,
That I love not, without I leave to love.°

---

4 **disgrace** disfavor.   12 **Doctor** of philosophy or logic.   14 **leave to love** stop loving.

62

Late tir'd with woe, even ready for to pine°
With rage of love, I call'd my love unkind;
She in whose eyes love though unfelt doth shine,
Sweet said that I true love in her should find.
5   I joyed, but straight thus wat'red was my wine,
That love she did, but loved a love not blind,°
Which would not let me, whom she loved, decline
From nobler course, fit for my birth and mind:
    And therefore by her love's authority,
10   Will'd me these tempests of vain love to fly,
And anchor fast myself on virtue's shore.
    Alas, if this the only metal be
    Of love, new coin'd to help my beggary,
Dear, love me not, that you may love me more.

63

O grammar rules, O now your virtues show;
    So children still read you with awful° eyes,
    As my young dove may in your precepts wise
Her grant to me, by her own virtue know.
5 For late with heart most high, with eyes most low,
    I crav'd the thing which ever she denies:
    She light'ning Love, displaying Venus' skies,
Least once should not be heard, twice said, No, No.
    Sing then my Muse, now *Io Pean*° sing,
10   Heav'ns envy not at my high triumphing:
But grammar's force with sweet success° confirm:
    For grammar says (O this dear Stella weigh,)
    For grammar says (to grammar who says nay)
That in one speech two negatives affirm.

---

1 **pine** waste away. 6 **not blind** refers to traditional representation
of Cupid blindfolded.
2 **awful** respectful. 9 **Io Pean** technically a hymn of praise to
Apollo, but, as Ringler suggests, likely to be associated with the
opening of Book II of Ovid's *Ars Amatoria*, a cry of triumph at
having obtained his mistress' favors. 11 **success** also, result.

First Song

Doubt you to whom my Muse these notes intendeth,
Which now my breast o'ercharg'd to music lendeth:
To you, to you, all song of praise is due,
Only in you my song begins and endeth.

Who hath the eyes which marry state with pleasure,   5
Who keeps the key of Nature's chiefest treasure:
To you, to you, all song of praise is due,
Only for you the heav'n forgat all measure.

Who hath the lips, where wit in fairness reigneth,
Who womankind at once both decks and staineth:°   10
To you, to you, all song of praise is due,
Only by you Cupid his crown maintaineth.

Who hath the feet, whose step all sweetness planteth,
Who else for whom Fame worthy trumpets wanteth:
To you, to you, all song of praise is due,   15
Only to you her scepter Venus granteth.

Who hath the breast, whose milk doth passions
        nourish,
Whose grace is such, that when it chides doth cherish,
To you, to you, all song of praise is due,
Only through you the tree of life doth flourish.   20

Who hath the hand which without stroke subdueth,
Who long dead beauty with increase reneweth:
To you, to you, all song of praise is due,
Only at you all envy hopeless rueth.

Who hath the hair which loosest fastest tieth,   25
Who makes a man live then glad when he dieth:
To you, to you, all song of praise is due:
Only of you the flatterer never lieth.

Who hath the voice, which soul from senses sunders,
Whose force but yours the bolts of beauty thunders: 30
To you, to you, all song of praise is due:
Only with you not miracles° are wonders.

10 **staineth** eclipses, deprives of its luster.   32 **not miracles** (1) possibly an inversion: "miracles are not wonders"; (2) things not
miracles, i.e., natural things, made wonders by Stella.

Doubt you to whom my Muse these notes intendeth,
Which now my breast o'ercharg'd to music lendeth:
35 To you, to you, all song of praise is due:
Only in you my song begins and endeth.

64

No more, my dear, no more these counsels try,
    O give my passions leave to run their race:
    Let Fortune lay on me her worst disgrace,
Let folk o'ercharg'd with brain against me cry.
5 Let clouds bedim my face, break in mine eye,°
    Let me no steps but of lost labor trace:
    Let all the earth with scorn recount my case,
But do not will me from my love to fly.
    I do not envy Aristotle's wit,
10 Nor do aspire to Caesar's bleeding fame;
    Nor ought do care, though some above me sit:
    Nor hope, nor wish another course to frame,
        But that which once may win thy cruel heart,
        Thou art my wit, and thou my virtue art.

65

Love by sure proof I may call thee unkind,
That giv'st no better ear to my just cries:
Thou whom to me such my good turns should bind,
As I may well recount, but none can prize:°
5   For when nak'd boy thou couldst no harbor find
In this old world, grown now so too too wise:
I lodg'd thee in my heart, and being blind
By Nature born, I gave to thee mine eyes.
    Mine eyes, my light, my heart, my life, alas,
10 If so great services may scornèd be:
Yet let this thought thy tigrish courage pass:°
That I perhaps am somewhat kin to thee;
        Since in thine arms,° if learn'd fame truth hath
            spread,
        Thou bear'st the arrow, I the arrow head.

---

5 **break . . . eye** i.e., as tears.

---

4 **prize** reckon the value of.   11 **pass** pierce, penetrate.   13 **arms**
the pun refers to heraldry: Sidney's own device includes an arrow-
head.

66

And do I see some cause a hope to feed,
Or doth the tedious burd'n of long woe
In weakened minds, quick apprehending breed,
Of every image, which may comfort show?
    I cannot brag of word, much less of deed,   5
Fortune wheels still with me in one sort slow,°
My wealth no more, and no whit less my need,
Desire still on the stilts° of fear doth go.
    And yet amid all fears a hope there is,
Stol'n to my heart since last fair night, nay day,°   10
Stella's eyes sent to me the beams of bliss,
Looking on me, while I lookt other way:
    But when mine eyes back to their heav'n did move,
    They fled with blush, which guilty seem'd of love.

67

Hope, art thou true, or doest thou flatter me?
    Doth Stella now begin with piteous eye,
    The ruins of her conquest to espy:
Will she take time,° before all wrackèd be?
Her eyes-speech is translated thus by thee: 5
    But fail'st thou not in phrase so heav'nly high?
    Look on again, the fair text better try:
What blushing notes doest thou in margin see?
    What sighs stol'n out, or kill'd before full born?
Hast thou found such and such like arguments?°   10
Or art thou else to comfort me forsworn?°
Well, how so thou interpret the contents,
    I am resolv'd thy error to maintain,
    Rather than by more truth to get more pain.

---

6 **in . . . slow** with unvarying slowness. 8 **stilts** crutches. 10 **last
. . . day** literally night; metaphorically day: transformed by Stella's
glance.

4 **take time** take the opportunity, relent. 10 **arguments** evidence,
proof. 11 **forsworn** falsely sworn.

68

Stella, the only planet of my light,
   Light of my life, and life of my desire,
   Chief good, whereto my hope doth only aspire,
World of my wealth, and heav'n of my delight.
5 Why dost thou spend the treasures of thy sprite,
   With voice more fit to wed Amphion's° lyre,
   Seeking to quench in me the noble fire,
Fed by thy worth, and kindled° by thy sight?
   And all in vain, for while thy breath most sweet,
10 With choicest words, thy words with reasons rare,
Thy reasons firmly set on Virtue's feet,
Labor to kill in me this killing care:
   O think I then, what paradise of joy
   It is, so fair a Virtue to enjoy.

69

O joy, too high for my low style to show:
   O bliss, fit for a nobler state than me:
   Envy, put out thine eyes, lest thou do see
What oceans of delight in me do flow.
5 My friend, that oft saw through all masks my woe,
   Come, come, and let me pour myself on thee;
   Gone is the winter of my misery,
My spring appears, O see what here doth grow.
For Stella hath with words where faith doth shine,
10 Of her high heart giv'n me the monarchy:
I, I, O I may say, that she is mine.
   And though she give but thus condition'ly
   This realm of bliss, while virtuous course I take,
   No kings be crown'd, but they some covenants make.

6 **Amphion's** whose skillful music raised the walls of Thebes.
8 **kindled** 1598: "blinded."

70

My Muse may well grudge at my heav'nly joy,
If still I force her in sad rhymes to creep:
She oft hath drunk my tears, now hopes to enjoy
Nectar of mirth, since I Jove's cup do keep.°
    Sonnets° be not bound prentice to annoy: 5
Trebles sing high, as well as basses deep:
Grief but Love's winter livery is, the boy
Hath cheeks to smile, as well as eyes to weep.
    Come then my Muse, show thou height of delight
In well rais'd notes, my pen the best it may   10
Shall paint out joy, though but in black and white.
Cease eager Muse, peace pen, for my sake stay,
    I give you here my hand for truth of this,
    Wise silence is best music unto bliss.

71

Who will in fairest book of Nature know,
    How Virtue may best lodg'd in beauty be,
    Let him but learn of Love to read in thee
Stella, those fair lines, which true goodness show.
There shall he find all vices' overthrow,   5
    Not by rude force, but sweetest sovereignty
    Of reason, from whose light those night-birds° fly;
That inward sun in thine eyes shineth so.
    And not content to be perfection's heir
Thyself, doest strive all minds that way to move: 10
Who mark in thee what is in thee most fair.
So while thy beauty draws the heart to love,
    As fast thy Virtue bends that love to good:
    But ah, Desire still cries, give me some food.

---

4 **Jove's . . . keep** like Ganymede, a cupbearer to Jove.   5 **Sonnets**
earliest form, "sonet," a song or melody, hence linked to trebles
and basses of line 6.

7 **night-birds** i.e., vices.

72

Desire, though thou my old companion art,
  And oft so clings to my pure love, that I
  One from the other scarcely can descry,
While each doth blow the fire of my heart;
5 Now from thy fellowship I needs must part,
  Venus is taught with Dian's wings to fly:
  I must no more in thy sweet passions lie;
Virtue's gold now must head my Cupid's dart.
  Service and honor, wonder with delight,
10 Fear to offend, will worthy to appear,°
Care shining in mine eyes, faith in my sprite.
  These things are left me by my only dear;
   But thou Desire, because thou wouldst have all,
   Now banisht art, but yet alas how shall?

Second Song

Have I caught my heav'nly jewel,
Teaching sleep most fair to be?
Now will I teach her that she,
When she wakes, is too too cruel.

5 Since sweet sleep her eyes hath charmèd,
The two only darts of Love:
Now will I with that boy prove
Some play, while he is disarmèd.

Her tongue waking still refuseth,
10 Giving frankly niggard No:
Now will I attempt to know,
What No her tongue sleeping useth.

See the hand which waking guardeth,
Sleeping, grants a free resort:
15 Now will I invade the fort;
Cowards Love with loss rewardeth.

---

10 **will . . . appear** (1) wish to appear worthy; (2) will or desire
transformed, hence "worthy to appear."

But O fool, think of the danger,
Of her just and high disdain:
Now will I alas refrain,
Love fears nothing else but anger.   20

Yet those lips so sweetly smelling,
Do invite a stealing kiss:
Now will I but venture this,
Who will read must first learn spelling.

Oh sweet kiss, but ah she is waking,   25
Louring beauty chastens me:
Now will I away hence flee:
Fool, more fool, for no more taking.

73

Love still a boy, and oft a wanton is,
School'd only by his mother's tender eye:
What wonder then if he his lesson miss,°
When for so soft a rod dear play he try?
    And yet my star, because a sug'red kiss   5
In sport I suckt, while she asleep did lie,
Doth lour, nay, chide; nay, threat for only this:
Sweet, it was saucy Love, not humble I.
    But no 'scuse serves, she makes her wrath appear
    In Beauty's throne, see now who dares come near 10
Those scarlet judges, threatning bloody pain?
    O heav'nly fool, thy most kiss-worthy face,
    Anger invests with such a lovely grace,
That Anger' self I needs must kiss again.

74

I never drank of Aganippe well,
Nor ever did in shade of Tempe° sit:
And Muses scorn with vulgar brains to dwell,

3 **miss** See sonnet 46, line 11.

1–2 **Aganippe, Tempe** places sacred to poetry: Aganippe, a fountain
dedicated to the Muses, at the foot of Helicon; Tempe's shade, i.e.,
the laurel, poet's reward, into which Daphne had been transformed
when pursued by Apollo.

Poor layman I, for sacred rites unfit.
5   Some do I hear of poets' fury° tell,
But (God wot) wot not what they mean by it:
And this I swear by blackest brook of hell,
I am no pick-purse of another's wit.
    How falls it then, that with so smooth an ease
10 My thoughts I speak, and what I speak doth flow
In verse, and that my verse best wits doth please?
Guess we the cause, what is it thus? fie no:
    Or so? much less: how then? sure thus it is:
    My lips are sweet, inspired with Stella's kiss.

75

Of all the kings that ever here did reign,
Edward named fourth,° as first in praise I name,
Not for his fair outside, nor well lin'd brain;
Although less gifts imp° feathers oft on Fame.
5   Nor that he could young-wise, wise-valiant frame
His sire's revenge, join'd with a kingdom's gain:
And gain'd by Mars, could yet mad Mars so tame,°
That balance weigh'd what sword did late obtain.
    Nor that he made the Flouredeluce° so 'fraid,
10 Though strongly hedg'd° of bloody lion's° paws,
That witty Lewis to him a tribute paid.
Nor this, nor that, nor any such small cause,
    But only for this worthy knight durst prove
    To lose his crown, rather than fai˙ his love.°

5 **fury** of inspiration.
2 **Edward . . . fourth** who, usurping the claim of Henry VI, seized
the throne, thus avenging his father, Duke of York, who had been
slain in battle against the Lancastrians. The chroniclers presented
him as violent and intemperate; hence Sidney's use of the example
is somewhat tongue-in-cheek. 4 **imp** graft feathers to a falcon's
wing to improve flight. 7 **yet . . . tame** after his violent seizure of
power, succeeded in making peace with both Scotland and France.
9 **Flouredeluce** fleur-de-lys, royal emblem of France, in whose defense Louis XI (line 11) paid tribute for withdrawal of English
troops. 10 **hedg'd** bordered. 10 **bloody lion's** red lion, royal
emblem of Scotland, another traditional enemy with whom Edward
had negotiated a truce. 14 **lose . . . love** Edward was briefly driven
from the throne by Warwick whose marriage negotiations on his
behalf he set aside in order to marry Lady Elizabeth Gray.

76

She comes, and straight therewith her shining twins do
      move
  Their rays to me, who in her tedious absence lay
  Benighted in cold woe, but now appears my day,
The only light of joy, the only warmth of love.
She comes with light and warmth, which like Aurora   5
      prove
  Of gentle force, so that mine eyes dare gladly play
  With such a rosy morn, whose beams most freshly
      gay
Scorch not, but only do dark chilling sprites remove.
  But lo, while I do speak, it groweth noon with me,
Her flamy glist'ring lights increase with time and place;   10
My heart cries ah, it burns, mine eyes now dazzled be:
No wind, no shade can cool, what help then in my case,
  But with short breath, long looks, stay'd feet and
      walking° head,
    Pray that my sun go down with meeker beams to
      bed.

77

Those looks, whose beams be joy, whose motion is
      delight,
That face, whose lecture° shows what perfect beauty is:
That presence, which doth give dark hearts a living
      light:
That grace, which Venus weeps that she herself doth
      miss:
  That hand, which without touch holds more than   5
      Atlas might;
Those lips, which make death's pay a mean price for
      a kiss:
That skin, whose pass-praise hue scorns this poor term
      of white:

---

13 **walking** agitated (opposed to "stay'd").
2 **lecture** act of reading.

Those words, which do sublime the quintessence° of
    bliss:
    That voice, which makes the soul plant himself in
        the ears:
10 That conversation sweet, where such high comforts be,
    As conster'd° in true speech, the name of heav'n it
        bears,
    Makes me in my best thoughts and quietst judgement
        see,
      That in no more but these I might be fully blest:
      Yet ah, my maid'n Muse doth blush to tell the best.

78

O now the pleasant airs of true love be
    Infected by those vapors, which arise
    From out that noisome gulf, which gaping lies
Between the jaws of hellish Jealousy.
5 A monster, other's harm, self-misery,
    Beauty's plague, Virtue's scourge, succour of lies:
    Who his own joy to his own hurt applies,
And only cherish doth with injury.
    Who since he hath, by Nature's special grace,
10   So piercing paws, as spoil when they embrace,
So nimble feet as stir still, though on thorns:
    So many eyes aye seeking their own woe,
    So ample ears as never good news know:
Is it not evil that such a devil wants° horns?°

79

Sweet kiss, thy sweets I fain would sweetly indite,
    Which even of sweetness sweetest sweet'ner art:
    Pleasingst consort,° where each sense holds a part,
Which° coupling doves° guides Venus' chariot right.

---

8 **sublime . . . quintessence** alchemical terms: extract the fifth, or
pure essence of things.   11 **conster'd** construed (so, in Q1 and Q2).
14 **wants** lacks.   14 **horns** the cuckold's horns.
3 **consort** combination of instruments.   4 **Which** antecedent "kiss"
or "consort."   4 **coupling doves** bringing to couple doves, which
traditionally draw Venus' chariot.

Best charge, and bravest retrait° in Cupid's fight,   5
   A double key, which opens to the heart,
   Most rich, when most his riches it impart:
Nest of young joys, schoolmaster of delight,
   Teaching the mean, at once to take and give
The friendly fray, where blows both wound and heal,   10
The pretty death, while each in other live.
Poor hope's first wealth, ostage° of promist weal,
   Breakfast of love, but lo, lo, where she is,
   Cease we to praise, now pray we for a kiss.

80

Sweet swelling lip, well may'st thou swell in pride,
   Since best wits think it wit thee to admire;
   Nature's praise, Virtue's stall,° Cupid's cold fire,
Whence words, not words, but heav'nly graces slide.
The new Parnassus, where the Muses bide,   5
   Sweet'ner of music, wisdom's beautifer:
   Breather of life, and fast'ner° of desire,
Where Beauty's blush in Honor's grain° is dyed.
   Thus much my heart compell'd my mouth to say,
   But now spite of my heart my mouth will stay,   10
Loathing all lies, doubting° this flattery is:
   And no spur can his resty° race renew,
   Without° how far this praise is short of you,
Sweet lip, you teach my mouth with one sweet kiss.

81

O kiss, which doest those ruddy gems° impart,
Or gems, or fruits of new-found Paradise,
Breathing all bliss and sweet'ning to the heart,

---

5 **retrait** (1) in battle; (2) place of refuge.   12 **ostage** hostage or pledge.

3 **stall** seat of dignity.   7 **fast'ner** Q1: "fastness" (stronghold).
8 **grain** (1) originally, scarlet color; (2) to die in grain is to die fast, or thoroughly.   11 **doubting** fearing.   12 **resty** restive.   13 **Without** unless.

1 **gems** also, buds.

Teaching dumb lips a nobler exercise.
5   O kiss, which souls, even souls together ties
By links of Love, and only Nature's art:
How fain would I paint thee to all men's eyes,
Or of thy gifts at least shade out° some part.
    But she forbids, with blushing words, she says,
10   She builds her fame on higher seated praise:
But my heart burns, I cannot silent be.
    Then since (dear life) you fain would have me
        peace,°
And I, mad with delight, want wit to cease,
Stop you my mouth with still still° kissing me.

82

Nymph of the gard'n, where all beauties be:
    Beauties which do in excellency pass,
    His° who till death lookt in a wat'ry glass,
Or hers° whom naked the Trojan boy did see.
5   Sweet gard'n nymph, which keeps the cherry tree,
    Whose fruit doth far th'Esperian taste° surpass:
    Most sweet-fair, most fair-sweet, do not alas,
From coming near those cherries banish me:
    For though full of desire, empty of wit,
10   Admitted late by your best-gracèd grace,
I caught at one of them a hungry bit;°
Pardon that fault, once more grant me the place,
    And I do swear even by the same delight,
    I will but kiss, I never more will bite.

---

8 **shade out** sketch faintly, as in a drawing. 12 **peace** be silent.
14 **still still** with pun on still = silent.

3 **His** Narcissus died gazing at his reflection in a pool. 4 **hers**
Venus, whose appearance before Paris was part of the chain of
events leading to the Trojan war. 6 **th'Esperian taste** the golden
apples of the Hesperides, garden guarded by a dragon which it was
one of Hercules' tasks to slay. 11 **bit** bite.

83

Good brother Philip,° I have borne you long,
   I was content you should in favor creep,
   While craftily you seem'd your cut to keep,°
As though that fair soft hand did you great wrong.
I bare (with envy) yet I bare your song,   5
   When in her neck you did love ditties peep;
   Nay, more fool I, oft suffered you to sleep
In lilies' nest, where Love's self lies along.
   What, doth high place ambitious thoughts augment?
Is sauciness reward of courtesy?   10
Cannot such grace your silly self content,
But you must needs with those lips billing be?
   And through those lips drink nectar from that
      tongue;
   Leave that sir Phip, lest off your neck be wrung.

Third Song

If Orpheus' voice had force to breathe such music's
     love
Through pores of senseless trees, as it could make
     them move;
If stones good measure danc'd, the Theban walls to
     build,
To cadence of the tunes, which Amphion's° lyre did
     yield,
More cause a like effect at leastwise bringeth: 5
O stones, O trees, learn hearing, Stella singeth.

If love might sweet'n so a boy of shepherd brood,
To make a lizard dull to taste love's dainty food:
If eagle fierce could so in Grecian maid° delight,

1 **Philip** name for pet sparrow in love poetry (see Skelton's "Philip
Sparrow"). 3 **cut to keep** keep one's distance; behave decorously.
1–4 **Orpheus' . . . Amphion's** See *Apology*, p. 217. 7–9 **boy . . .
Grecian maid** Referring to stories from Pliny: the boy, Thoas, was
rescued from robbers by a dragon which he had raised; the Grecian
maid tamed an eagle which brought her food and, at her death,
flew into her funeral pyre.

10   As his light was her eyes, her death his endless night:
     Earth gave that love, heaven I trow love refineth:
     O birds, O beasts look, love, lo, Stella shineth.

     The birds, beasts,° stones and trees feel this, and
                 feeling love:
     And if the trees, nor stones stir not the same to prove,
15   Nor beasts, nor birds do come unto this blessèd gaze,
     Know, that small love is quick, and great love doth
                 amaze:
     They are amaz'd, but you with reason armèd,
     O eyes, O ears of men, how are you charmèd!

                         84

     Highway since you my chief Parnassus° be,
         And that my Muse to some ears not unsweet,
         Tempers° her words to trampling horses' feet,
     More oft than to a chamber melody,
5   Now blessèd you, bear onward blessèd me
         To her, where I my heart safel'est° shall meet,
         My Muse and I must you of duty greet
     With thanks and wishes, wishing thankfully.
         Be you still fair, honor'd by public heed,
10   By no encroachment wrong'd, nor time forgot:
     Nor blam'd for blood,° nor sham'd for sinful deed.
         And that you know, I envy you no lot°
             Of highest wish, I wish you so much bliss,
             Hundreds of years you Stella's feet may kiss.

---

13 **birds, beasts** Both 1598 and Q1 reverse the order; Ringler emends
on the basis of the poem's elaborate symmetry.

1 **Highway . . . Parnassus** absence or journeying as source of poetic
inspiration.   3 **Tempers** attunes.   6 **safel'est** with most secrecy and
security.   11 **blood** violence.   12 **lot** fortune.

85

I see the house, my heart thyself contain,
    Beware full sails drown not thy tott'ring° barge:
    Lest joy by nature apt sprites to enlarge,
Thee to thy wrack beyond thy limits strain.
Nor do like lords, whose weak confusèd brain,   5
    Not pointing to fit folks each undercharge,
    While every office themselves will discharge,°
With doing all, leave nothing done but pain.
    But give apt servants their due place, let eyes
See Beauty's total sum summ'd in her face: 10
Let ears hear speech, which wit to wonder ties.
Let breath suck up those sweets, let arms embrace
    The globe of weal, lips Love's indentures° make:
    Thou but of all the kingly tribute take.

Fourth Song

Only joy, now here you are,
Fit to hear and ease my care:
Let my whispering voice obtain,
Sweet reward for sharpest pain:
Take me to thee, and thee to me.   5
No, no, no, no, my dear, let be.°

Night hath clos'd all in her cloak,
Twinkling stars love-thoughts provoke:
Danger hence good care doth keep,
Jealousy itself doth sleep: 10
Take me to thee, and thee to me.
No, no, no, no, my dear, let be.

Better place no wit can find,
Cupid's yoke to loose or bind:
These sweet flowers on fine bed too,   15
Us in their best language woo:
Take me to thee, and thee to me.
No, no, no, no, my dear, let be.

---

2 **tott'ring** pitching and tossing. **7 every . . . discharge** lords do
each job themselves. 13 **indentures** (1) contracts; (2) indentations.

6 **No . . . be** The poem organized as a confrontation with Stella's
reply as refrain.

This small light the moon bestows,
20 Serves thy beams but to disclose,
So to raise my hap more high;
Fear not else, none can us spy:
Take me to thee, and thee to me.
No, no, no, no, my dear, let be.

25 That you heard was but a mouse,
Dumb sleep holdeth all the house:
Yet asleep, methinks they say,
Young folks, take time while you may:
Take me to thee, and thee to me.
30 No, no, no, no, my dear, let be.

Niggard Time threats, if we miss
This large offer of our bliss,
Long stay ere he grant the same:
Sweet then, while each thing doth frame:
35 Take me to thee, and thee to me.
No, no, no, no, my dear, let be.

Your fair mother is abed,
Candles out, and curtains spread:
She thinks you do letters write:
40 Write, but first let me indite:
Take me to thee, and thee to me.
No, no, no, no, my dear, let be.

Sweet alas, why strive you thus?
Concord better fitteth us:
45 Leave to Mars the force of hands,
Your power in your beauty stands:
Take me to thee and thee to me.
No, no, no, no, my dear, let be.

Woe to me, and do you swear
50 Me to hate, but I forbear,
Cursèd by my destines all,
That brought me so high to fall:
Soon with my death I will please thee.
No, no, no, no, my dear, let be.

86

Alas, whence came this change of looks? If I
   Have chang'd desert, let mine own conscience be
   A still felt plague, to self condemning° me:
Let woe gripe on my heart, shame load mine eye.
But if all faith, like spotless ermine lie   5
   Safe in my soul, which only doth to thee
   (As his sole object of felicity)
With wings of Love in air of wonder fly,
   O ease your hand, treat not so hard your slave:
In justice pains come not till faults do call,   10
Or if I needs (sweet judge) must torments have,
Use something else to chast'n me withal,
   Than those blest eyes, where all my hopes do dwell,
   No doom should make one's heav'n become his hell.

Fifth Song

While favor fed my hope, delight with hope was
         brought,
Thought waited on delight, and speech did follow
         thought:
Then grew my tongue and pen records unto thy glory:
I thought all words were lost, that were not spent of
         thee:
I thought each place was dark but where thy lights   5
         would be,
And all ears worse than deaf, that heard not out thy
         story.

I said, thou wert most fair, and so indeed thou art:
I said, thou wert most sweet, sweet poison to my heart:
I said, my soul was thine (O that I then had lièd)
I said, thine eyes were stars, thy breasts the milk'n way,   10
Thy fingers Cupid's shafts, thy voice the angels' lay:
And all I said so well, as no man it denièd.

---

3 **self condemning** (1) as adjective: "self-condemning"; (2) "self"
as object of "to": "condemning" as participial modifier of "conscience."

But now that hope is lost, unkindness kills delight,
Yet thought and speech do live, thou metamorphos'd
  quite:
15 For rage now rules the reins, which guided were by
  pleasure.
I think now of thy faults, who late thought of thy
  praise,
That speech falls now to blame, which did thy honor
  raise,
The same key op'n can, which can lock up a treasure.

Thou then whom partial heavens conspir'd in one to
  frame,
20 The proof of Beauty's worth, th'inheritrix of fame,
The mansion seat of bliss, and just excuse of lovers;
See now those feathers pluckt, wherewith thou flewst
  most high:
See what clouds of reproach shall dark thy honor's sky,
Whose own fault casts him down, hardly high seat
  recovers.

25 And O my Muse, though oft you lull'd her in your lap,
And then a heav'nly child gave her ambrosian pap:
And to that brain of hers you hidd'nest gifts infusèd,
Since she disdaining me, doth you in me disdain:
Suffer not her to laugh, while both we suffer pain:
30 Princes in subjects wrong'd, must deem themselves
  abusèd.

Your client poor myself, shall Stella handle so?
Revenge, revenge, my Muse. Defiance' trumpet blow:
Threat'n what may be done, yet do more than you
  threat'n.
Ah, my suit granted is, I feel my breast doth swell:
35 Now child, a lesson new you shall begin to spell:
Sweet babes must babies° have, but shrewd° girls must
  be beat'n.

36 **babies** dolls. 36 **shrewd** shrewish.

Think now no more to hear of warm fine odor'd snow,
Nor blushing lilies, nor pearls' ruby-hidden row,
Nor of that golden sea, whose waves in curls are
      brok'n:
But of thy soul, so fraught with such ungratefulness,   *40*
As where thou soon mightst help, most faith dost most
      oppress,
Ungrateful who is call'd, the worst of evils is spok'n:

Yet worse than worst, I say thou art a thief, a thief?
Now God forbid. A thief, and of worst thieves the
      chief:
Thieves steal for need, and steal but goods which pain   *45*
      recovers,
But thou rich in all joys, doest rob my joys from me,
Which cannot be restor'd by time nor industry:
Of foes the spoil is evil, far worse of constant lovers.

Yet gentle English thieves do rob, but will not slay;
Thou English murdering thief, wilt have hearts for thy   *50*
      prey:
The name of murd'rer now on thy fair forehead sitteth:
And even while I do speak, my death wounds bleeding
      be:
Which (I protest) proceed from only cruel thee,
Who may and will not save, murder in truth
      committeth.

But murder private fault seems but a toy to thee,   *55*
I lay then to thy charge unjustest tyranny,
If rule by force without all claim a tyran showeth,
For thou doest lord my heart, who am not born thy
      slave,
And which is worse, makes me most guiltless torments
      have,
A rightful prince by unright deeds a tyran groweth.   *60*

Lo you grow proud with this, for tyrans make folk
      bow:
Of foul rebellion then I do appeachᵒ thee now;

62 **appeach** accuse; impeach.

Rebel by nature's law, rebel by law of reason,
Thou sweetest subject wert born in the realm of Love,
65 And yet against thy Prince thy force dost daily prove:
No virtue merits praise, once toucht with blot of
          treason.

But valiant rebels oft in fools' mouths purchase fame:
I now then stain thy white with vagabonding shame,
Both rebel to the son, and vagrant from the mother;
70 For wearing Venus' badge, in every part of thee,
Unto Diana's train thou run away didst fly:
Who faileth one, is false, though trusty to another.

What is not this enough? nay far worse cometh here;
A witch I say thou art, though thou so fair appear;
75 For I protest, my sight never thy face enjoyeth,
But I in me am chang'd, I am alive and dead:
My feet are turn'd to roots, my heart becometh lead,
No witchcraft is so evil, as which man's mind
          destroyeth.

Yet witches may repent, thou art far worse than they,
80 Alas, that I am forc'd such evil of thee to say,
I say thou art a devil though cloth'd in angel's shining:
For thy face tempts my soul to leave the heav'n for
          thee,
And thy words of refuse,° do pour even hell on me:
Who tempt, and tempted plague, are devils in true
          defining.

85 You then ungrateful thief, you murd'ring tyran you,
You rebel run away, to lord and lady untrue,
You witch, you divill (alas) you still of me belovèd,
You see what I can say; mend yet your froward mind,
And such skill in my Muse you reconcil'd shall find,
90 That all these cruel words your praises shall be provèd.

83 **refuse** refusal.

Sixth Song

O you that hear this voice,
O you that see this face,
Say whether° of the choice
Deserves the former place:°
Fear not to judge this bate,°   5
For it is void of hate.

This side doth beauty° take,
For that doth music speak,
Fit orators to make
The strongest judgements weak: 10
The bar to plead their right,
Is only true delight.

Thus doth the voice and face,
These gentle lawyers wage,
Like loving brothers' case,   15
For father's heritage:
That each while each contends,
Itself to other lends.

For beauty beautifies,
With heavenly hue and grace,   20
The heavenly harmonies;
And in this faultless face,
The perfect beauties be
A perfect harmony.

Music more loft'ly swells   25
In speeches nobly placed:
Beauty as far excels,
In action aptly graced:
A friend each party draws,
To countenance his cause: 30

---

3 **whether** which. 4 **former place** precedence. 5 **bate** debate.
7 **This . . . beauty** beauty and music as counsels pleading the respective causes.

Love more affected seems
To beauty's lovely light,
And wonder more esteems
Of music's wondrous might:
35 But both to both so bent,
As both in both are spent.

Music doth witness call
The ear, his truth to try:
Beauty brings to the hall,
40 The judgement of the eye,
Both in their objects such,
As no exceptions° touch.

The common sense, which might
Be arbiter of this,
45 To be forsooth upright,
To both sides partial is:
He lays on this chief praise,
Chief praise on that he lays.

Then reason Princess high,
50 Whose throne is in the mind,
Which music can in sky
And hidden beauties find,
Say whether thou wilt crowne,
With limitless renowne.

Seventh Song

Whose senses in so evil consort, their stepdame Nature
    lays,
That ravishing delight in them most sweet tunes do not
    raise;
Or if they do delight therein, yet are so cloyed with wit,
As with sententious lips to set a title vain on it:
5 O let them hear these sacred tunes, and learn in
    wonder's schools,
To be in things past bounds of wit fools, if they be not
    fools.

42 **exceptions** legal objections.

Who have so leaden eyes, as not to see sweet beauty's
    show,
Or seeing, have so wodden° wits, as not that worth to
    know;
Or knowing, have so muddy minds, as not to be in
    love;
Or loving, have so frothy thoughts, as eas'ly thence to   *10*
    move:
O let them see these heavenly beams, and in fair letters
    read
A lesson fit, both sight and skill, love and firm love to
    breed.

Hear then, but then with wonder hear; see but adoring
    see,
No mortal gifts, no earthly fruits, now here descended
    be:
See, do you see this face? a face? nay image of the   *15*
    skies,
Of which the two life-giving lights are figured in her
    eyes:
Hear you this soul-invading voice, and count it but a
    voice?
The very essence of their tunes, when angels do rejoice.

Eighth Song

In a grove most rich of shade,
Where birds wanton music made,
May then young his pied weeds showing,
New perfumed with flowers fresh growing,

Astrophel with Stella sweet,   *5*
Did for mutual comfort meet,
Both within themselves oppressèd,
But each in the other blessèd.

Him great harms had taught much care,
Her fair neck a foul yoke bare,   *10*
But her sight his cares did banish,
In his sight her yoke did vanish.

8 **wodden** wooden.

Wept they had, alas the while,
But now tears themselves did smile,
15 While their eyes by love directed,
Interchangeably reflected.

Sigh they did, but now betwixt
Sighs of woes were glad sighs mixt,
With arms cross'd, yet testifying
20 Restless rest, and living dying.

Their ears hungry of each word,
Which the dear tongue would afford,
But their tongues restrain'd from walking,
Till their hearts had ended talking.

25 But when their tongues could not speak,
Love itself did silence break;
Love did set his lips asunder,
Thus to speak in love and wonder:

"Stella sovereign of my joy,
30 Fair triumpher of annoy,
Stella star of heavenly fire,
Stella lodestar of desire.

"Stella, in whose shining eyes,
Are the lights of Cupid's skies,
35 Whose beams where they once are darted,
Love therewith is straight imparted.

"Stella, whose voice when it speaks,
Senses all asunder breaks;
Stella, whose voice when it singeth,
40 Angels to acquaintance bringeth.

"Stella, in whose body is
Writ each character of bliss,
Whose face all, all beauty passeth,
Save thy mind which yet surpasseth.

45 "Grant, O grant, but speech alas,
Fails me fearing on to pass,
Grant, O me, what am I saying?
But no fault there is in praying.

"Grant, O dear, on knees I pray,
(Knees on ground he then did stay)
That not I but since I love you,
Time and place for me may move you.   50

"Never season was more fit,
Never room more apt for it;
Smiling air allows my reason,
These birds sing, now use the season.   55

"This small wind which so sweet is,
See how it the leaves doth kiss,
Each tree in his best attiring,
Sense of love to love inspiring.   60

"Love makes earth the water drink,
Love to earth makes water sink;
And if dumb things be so witty,
Shall a heavenly grace want pity?"

There his hands in their speech, fain   65
Would have made tongue's language plain;
But her hands his hands repelling,
Gave repulse all grace excelling.

Then she spake; her speech was such,
As not ears but heart did touch: 70
While such wise she love denièd,
As yet love she signifièd.

"Astrophel," said she, "my love
Cease in these effects to prove:
Now be still, yet still believe me,   75
Thy grief more than death would grieve me.

"If that any thought in me,
Can taste comfort but of thee,
Let me fed with hellish anguish,
Joyless, hopeless, endless languish.   80

"If those eyes you praisèd, be
Half so dear as you to me,
Let me home return, stark blinded
Of those eyes, and blinder minded.

85   "If to secret of my heart,
        I do any wish impart,
        Where thou art not foremost placèd,
        Be both wish and I defacèd.

        "If more may be said, I say,
90   All my bliss in thee I lay;
        If thou love, my love content thee,
        For all love, all faith is meant thee.

        "Trust me while I thee deny,
        In myself the smart I try,
95   Tyran honor doth thus use thee,
        Stella's self might not refuse thee.

        "Therefore, dear, this no more move,
        Lest though I leave not thy love,
        Which too deep in me is framèd,
100   I should blush when thou art namèd."

        Therewithal away she went,
        Leaving him so passion rent,
        With what she had done and spoken,
        That therewith my song is broken.

Ninth Song

        Go my flock, go get you hence,
        Seek a better place of feeding,
        Where you may have some defense
        From the storms in my breast breeding,
5   And showers from mine eyes proceeding.

        Leave a wretch, in whom all woe
        Can abide to keep no measure,
        Merry flock, such one forgo,
        Unto whom mirth is displeasure,
10   Only rich in mischief's treasure.

        Yet alas before you go,
        Hear your woeful master's story,
        Which to stones I else would show:
        Sorrow only then hath glory,
15   When 'tis excellently sorry.

Stella fiercest shepherdess,
Fiercest but yet fairest ever;
Stella whom O heavens do bless,
Tho' against me she persever,
Tho' I bliss inherit never.   20

Stella hath refusèd me,
Stella who more love hath provèd,
In this caitiff heart to be,
Than can in good ewes be movèd
Toward lamkins best belovèd.   25

Stella hath refusèd me,
Astrophel that so well servèd,
In this pleasant spring must see
While in pride flowers be preservèd,
Himself only winter-stervèd.   30

Why alas doth she then swear,
That she loveth me so dearly,
Seeing me so long to bear
Coals of love that burn so clearly;
And yet leave me helpless merely?   35

Is that love? forsooth I trow,
If I saw my good dog grievèd,
And a help for him did know,
My love should not be believèd,
But he were by me relievèd.   40

No, she hates me, wellaway,
Faining love, somewhat to please me:
For she knows, if she display
All her hate, death soon would seize me,
And of hideous torments ease me.   45

Then adieu, dear flock adieu:
But alas, if in your straying
Heavenly Stella meet with you,
Tell her in your piteous blaying,
Her poor slave's unjust decaying.   50

87

When I was forc'd from Stella ever dear,
Stella food of my thoughts, heart of my heart,
Stella whose eyes make all my tempests clear,
By iron laws of duty to depart:
5   Alas I found, that she with me did smart,
I saw that tears did in her eyes appear;
I saw that sighs her sweetest lips did part,
And her sad words my sadded sense did hear.
    For me, I wept to see pearls scattered so,
10   I sigh'd her sighs, and wailèd for her woe,
Yet swam in joy, such love in her was seen.
    Thus while th' effect most bitter was to me,
    And nothing than the cause more sweet could be,
I had been vext, if vext I had not been.

88

Out traitor absence, darest thou counsel me,
From my dear captainness to run away?
Because in brave array° here marcheth she,°
That to win me, oft shows° a present pay?°
5   Is faith so weak? Or is such force in thee?
When sun is hid, can stars such beams display?
Cannot heav'ns food once felt, keep stomachs free,
From base desire on earthly cates° to prey?
    Tush absence while thy mists eclipse that light,
10   My orphan sense flies to the inward sight,
Where memory sets forth the beams of love.
    That where before heart loved and eyes did see,
    In heart both sight and love now coupled be;
United powers make each the stronger prove.

---

3 **array** See sonnet 55, line 4. 3 **she** another woman. 4 **shows**
offers. 4 **pay** also, pleasure. 8 **cates** food.

89

Now that of absence the most irksome night,
   With darkest shade doth overcome my day;
   Since Stella's eyes wont to give me my day,
Leaving my hemisphere, leave me in night,
Each day seems long, and longs for long-stay'd night,   *5*
   The night as tedious, woos th'approach of day;
   Tired with the dusty toils of busy day,
Languisht with horrors of the silent night;
Suffering the evils both of the day and night,
   While no night is more dark than is my day,   *10*
Nor no day hath less quiet than my night:
   With such bad mixture of my night and day,
That living thus in blackest winter night,
   I feel the flames of hottest summer day.

90

Stella think not that I by verse seek fame
   Who seek, who hope, who love, who live but thee;
   Thine eyes my pride, thy lips my history:
If thou praise not, all other praise is shame.
Nor so ambitious am I, as to frame   *5*
   A nest for my young praise in laurel tree:°
   In truth I swear, I wish not there should be
Graved° in mine epitaph a poet's name:
   Ne if I would, could I just title make,
That any laud to me thereof should grow,   *10*
Without° my plumes from others' wings I take.
For nothing from my wit or will doth flow,
   Since all my words thy beauty doth indite,
   And love doth hold my hand, and makes me write.

---

6 **laurel tree** See sonnet 74. 8 **Graved** (1) engraved; (2) buried.
11 **Without** unless.

91

Stella, while now by honor's cruel might,
 I am from you, light of my life mis-led,°
 And that fair you my sun, thus overspread,
With absence' veil, I live in sorrow's night.
5 If this dark place yet show like candle light,
  Some beauty's piece as amber color'd head,
  Milk hands, rose cheeks, or lips more sweet, more red,
 Or seeing jets° black but in blackness bright.
  They please I do confess, they please mine eyes,
10 But why? because of you they models be,
Models such be wood-globes° of glist'ring skies.
 Dear, therefore be not jealous over me,
  If you hear that they seem my heart to move,
  Not them, O no, but you in them I love.

92

Be your words made (good sir) of Indian ware,°
 That you allow me them by so small rate?
 Or do you cutted° Spartans imitate,
Or do you mean my tender ears to spare?
5 That to my questions you so total° are,
  When I demand of Phoenix Stella's state,
  You say forsooth, you left her well of late,
 O God, think you that satisfies my care?
  I would know whether she did sit or walk,
10 How cloth'd, how waited on, sigh'd she or smil'd,
Whereof, with whom, how often did she talk,
 With what pastime, time's journey she beguil'd
  If her lips deign'd to sweeten my poor name,
  Say all, and all, well said, still say the same.

---

2 **mis-led** (1) governing "from you"; (2) possibly modifying "life."
8 **seeing jets** eyes. 11 **wood-globes** models of the heavens and con-
stellations.

1 **Indian ware** i.e., precious or rare. 3 **cutted** laconic. 5 **total** brief.

Tenth Song

O dear life, when shall it be,
　That mine eyes thine eyes may see?
　And in them thy mind discover,
　Whether absence have had force
　Thy remembrance to divorce, 5
　From the image of thy lover?

O if I myself find not,
　After parting ought forgot,
　Nor debarr'd from beauty's treasure,
　Let no tongue aspire to tell, 10
　In what high joys I shall dwell,
　Only thought aims at the pleasure.

Thought therefore I will send thee,
　To take up the place for me;
　Long I will not after tarry, 15
　There unseen thou may'st be bold,
　Those fair wonders to behold,
　Which in them my hopes do carry.

Thought see thou no place forbear,
　Enter bravely everywhere, 20
　Seize on all to her belonging;
　But if thou wouldst guarded be,
　Fearing her beams, take with thee
　Strength of liking, rage of longing.

Think of that most grateful time, 25
　When my leaping heart will climb,
　In my lips to have his biding,
　There those roses for to kiss,
　Which do breath a sug'red bliss,
　Opening rubies, pearls dividing. 30

Think of my most princely power,
　When I blessèd shall devour,
　With my greedy licorous° senses,

---

33 **licorous** fond of delicious fare (possibly lustful).

Beauty, music, sweetness, love
35   While she doth against me prove
Her strong darts, but weak defenses.

Think, think of those dallyings,
When with dovelike murmurings,
With glad moaning passèd anguish,
40   We change eyes, and heart for heart,
Each to other do impart,
Joying till joy make us languish.

O my thought my thoughts surcease,
Thy delights my woes increase,
45   My life melts with too much thinking;
Think no more but die in me,
Til' thou shalt revivèd be,
At her lips my nectar drinking.

93

O fate, O fault, O curse, child of my bliss,
What sobs can give words grace my grief to show?
What ink is black enough to paint my woe?
Through me, wretch me, even Stella vexèd is.
5   Yet truth (if caitiff's breath might call thee) this
Witness with me, that my foul stumbling so,
From carelessness did in no manner grow,
But wit confus'd with too much care did miss.°
And do I then myself this vain 'scuse give?
10   I have (live I and know this) harmèd thee,
Tho' worlds quite° me, shall I myself forgive?
Only with pains my pains thus easèd be,
That all thy hurts in my heart's wrack I read;
I cry thy sighs; my dear, thy tears I bleed.

8 **miss** fail to apprehend.   11 **quite** acquit.

94

Grief find the words, for thou hast made my brain
   So dark with misty vapors, which arise
   From out thy heavy mold, that inbent eyes
Can scarce discern the shape of mine own pain.
Do thou then (for thou canst) do thou complain,   *5*
   For my poor soul, which now that sickness tries,
   Which even to sense, sense of itself denies,
Though harbingers of death lodge there his train.
   Or if thy love of plaint yet mine forbears,
As of a caitiff worthy so to die,   *10*
Yet wail thyself, and wail with causeful tears,
That though in wretchedness thy life doth lie,
Yet growest more wretched than thy nature bears,
By being placed in such a wretch as I.

95

Yet sighs, dear sighs, indeed true friends you are,
   That do not leave your left° friend at the worst,
   But as you with my breast I oft have nurst,
So grateful now you wait upon my care.
Faint coward joy no longer tarry dare,   *5*
   Seeing hope yield when this woe strake him first:
   Delight protests he is not for the accurst,
Thought oft himself my mate-in-arms he sware.
   Nay sorrow comes with such main rage, that he
Kills his own children, tears, finding that they   *10*
By love were made apt to consort with me.
Only true sighs, you do not go away,
   Thank may you have for such a thankful part,
   Thank-worthiest yet when you shall break my heart.

2 left Q1: "best"; Q2: "least."

96

Thought with good cause thou likest so well the night,
   Since kind° or chance gives both one livery,
   Both sadly black, both blackly dark'ned be,
Night barr'd from sun, thou from thy own sun's light;
5 Silence in both displays his sullen might,
   Slow heaviness in both holds one degree,°
   That full of doubts, thou of perplexity;
Thy tears express night's native moisture right.
   In both a mazeful° solitariness:
10 In night of sprites the ghastly powers stir,
In thee or sprites or sprited ghastliness:
But but (alas) night's side the odds hath fur,°
   For that at length yet doth invite some rest,
   Thou though still tired, yet still dost it detest.

97

Dian that fain would cheer her friend the Night,
   Shows her oft at the full her fairest face,
   Bringing with her those starry nymphs, whose chase
From heavenly standing° hits each mortal wight.
5 But ah poor Night in love with Phoebus' light,
   And endlessly despairing of his grace,
   Herself (to show no other joy hath place)
Silent and sad in mourning weeds doth dight:
   Even so (alas) a lady's Dian's peer,
10 With choice delights and rarest company,
Would fain drive clouds from out my heavy cheer.
But woe is me, though joy itself were she,
   She could not show my blind brain ways of joy,
   While I despair my sun's sight to enjoy.

---

2 **kind** nature. 6 **one degree** the same rank. 9 **mazeful** bewildering. 12 **fur** far (hence odds in night's favor).
4 **standing** a hunter's station.

98

Ah bed, the field where joy's peace some do see,
    The field where all my thoughts to war be train'd,
    How is thy grace by my strange fortune stain'd!
How thy lee shores by my sighs stormèd be!
With sweet soft shades thou oft invitest me   5
    To steal some rest, but wretch I am constrain'd,
    (Spurr'd with love's spur, though gall'd° and shortly
        rein'd
With care's hard hand) to turn and toss in thee.
    While the black horrors of the silent night,
    Paint woe's black face so lively to my sight,   10
That tedious leisure marks each wrinkled line:
    But when Aurora leads out Phoebus' dance,
    Mine eyes then only wink,° for spite perchance,
That worms should have their sun, and I want mine.

99

When far spent night persuades each mortal eye,
    To whom not art nor nature granteth light,
    To lay his then mark wanting° shafts of sight,
Clos'd with their quivers in sleep's armory;
With windows ope then most my mind doth lie,   5
    Viewing the shape of darkness and delight,
    Takes in that sad hue, which with th'inward night,
Of his maz'd powers keeps perfit harmony:
    But when birds charm,° and that sweet air, which is
Morn's messenger, with rose enamel'd skies   10
Calls each wight to salute the flower of bliss;
    In tomb of lids then buried are mine eyes,
    Forc'd by their lord, who is asham'd to find
    Such light in sense, with such a dark'ned mind.

---

7 **gall'd** made sore by chafing.   13 **wink** close.

3 **mark wanting** without a target.   9 **charm** also, blended singing
of many birds.

100

O tears, no tears, but rain from beauty's skies,
　　Making those lilies and those roses grow,
　　Which aye most fair, now more than most fair show,
While graceful pity beauty beautifies.
5　O honey'd sighs, which from that breast do rise,
　　Whose pants do make unspilling cream to flow,
　　Wing'd with whose breath, so pleasing Zephyrs blow,
As can refresh the hell where my soul fries.
　　O plaints conserv'd in such a sug'red phrase,
10　　That eloquence itself envies your praise,
While sobb'd out words a perfect music give.
　　Such tears, sighs, plaints, no sorrow is, but joy:
　　Or if such heavenly signs must prove᷄ annoy,
All mirth farewell, let me in sorrow live.

101

Stella is sick, and in that sick bed lies
Sweetness, that breathes and pants as oft as she:
And grace sick too, such fine conclusions tries,
That sickness brags itself best graced to be.
5　Beauty is sick, but sick in so fair guise,
That in that paleness beauty's white we see,
And joy which is inseparate from those eyes,
Stella now learns (strange case) to weep in thee.
　　Love makes thy pain, and like a faithful page
10　As thy looks stir, runs up and down to make
All folks press'd at th‿ will thy pain to 'suage,
Nature with care sweats for her darling's sake,
　　Knowing worlds pass, ere she enough can find
　　Of such heaven stuff, to clothe so heavenly mind.

13 **prove** signify.

102

Where be those roses gone, which sweet'ned so our
    eyes?
  Where those red cheeks, which oft with fair
      increase° did frame
  The neight of honor in the kindly badge of shame?
Who hath the crimson weeds stol'n from my morning
    skies?
How doth the color vade° of those vermilion dies,   *5*
  Which Nature self did make, and self engrain'd° the
    same?
  I would know by what right this paleness overcame
That hue, whose force my heart still unto thralldom
    ties?
  Galen's adoptive sons,° who by a beaten way
Their judgements hackney on, the fault on sickness   *10*
    lay,
But feeling proof makes me say they mistake it fur:°
  It is but love which makes his paper perfit white,
  To write therein more fresh the story of delight,
While beauty's reddest ink Venus for him doth stir.

103

O happy Thames, that did'st my Stella bear,
I saw thyself with many a smiling line
Upon thy cheerful face, joy's livery wear:
While those fair planets on thy streams did shine.
  The boat for joy could not to dance forbear,   *5*
While wanton winds with beauties so divine
Ravisht, stay'd not, till in her golden hair
They did themselves (O sweetest prison) twine.
  And fain those Aeols' youths° there would their stay
Have made, but forc'd by Nature still to fly,   *10*
First did with puffing kiss those locks display:

2 **fair increase** i.e., blushing. 5 **vade** fade. 6 **engrain'd** dyed.
9 **Galen's . . . sons** old-fashioned physicians, followers of Galen.
11 **fur** far.

9 **Aeols' youths** breezes.

She so dishevell'd, blusht; from window I
    With sight thereof cried out; O fair disgrace,
    Let honor self to thee grant highest place.

104

Envious wits what hath been mine offense,
    That with such poisonous care my looks you mark,
    That to each word, nay sigh of mine you hark,
As grudging me my sorrow's eloquence?
5   Ah, is it not enough, that I am thence,
    Thence, so far thence, that scarcely any spark
    Of comfort dare come to this dungeon dark,
Where rigor's exile locks up all my sense?
    But if I by a happy window° pass,
10   If I but stars upon mine armor bear,
Sick, thirsty, glad (though but of empty glass:)
    Your moral notes straight my hid meaning tear,
    From out my ribs, and puffing prove that I
    Do Stella love, fools who doth it deny?

Eleventh Song°

Who is it that this dark night,
Underneath my window plaineth?
It is one who from thy sight,
Being (ah) exil'd, disdaineth
5   Every other vulgar light.

Why alas, and are you he?
Be not yet those fancies changèd?
Dear when you find change in me,
Though from me you be estrangèd,
10   Let my change to ruin be.

9 **happy window** i.e., one in which Stella appears or has appeared.
0 **Eleventh Song** Again a confrontation of Astrophel and Stella, the
last three lines of each stanza given to Astrophel's responses.

Well in absence this will die,
Leave to see, and leave to wonder:
Absence sure will help, if I
Can learn, how myself to sunder
From what in my heart doth lie. 15

But time will these thoughts remove:
Time doth work what no man knoweth.
Time doth as the subject prove,
With time still th'affection groweth
In the faithful turtle dove. 20

What if you new beauties see,
Will not they stir new affection?
I will think they pictures be,
(Image like of saints' perfection)
Poorly counterfeiting thee. 25

But your reason's purest light,
Bids you leave such minds to nourish.
Dear, do reason no such spite,
Never doth thy beauty flourish
More than in my reason's sight. 30

But the wrongs love bears, will make
Love at length leave undertaking;
No, the more fools it do shake,
In a ground of so firm making,
Deeper still they drive the stake. 35

Peace, I think that some give ear:
Come no more, lest I get anger.
Bliss, I will my bliss forbear,
Fearing (sweet) you to endanger,
But my soul shall harbor there. 40

Well, be gone, be gone I say,
Lest that Argus eyes perceive you.
O unjustest fortune's sway,
Which can make me thus to leave you,
And from louts to run away. 45

105

Unhappy sight, and hath she vanisht by
    So near, in so good time so free a place?
    Dead glass° dost thou thy object so embrace,
As what my heart still sees thou canst not spy?
5 I swear by her I love and lack, that I
    Was not in fault, who bent thy dazzling race°
    Only unto the heav'n of Stella's face,
Counting but dust what in the way did lie.
    But cease mine eyes, your tears do witness well,
10 That you guiltless thereof, your nectar missed:
Curst be the page from whom the bad torch fell,
Curst be the night which did your strife resist,
    Curst be the coachman which did drive so fast,
    With no worse curse than absence makes me taste.

106

O absent presence Stella is not here;
    False flattering hope, that with so fair a face,
    Bare me in hand,° that in this orphan place,
Stella, I say my Stella, should appear.
5 What say'st thou now, where is that dainty cheer,
    Thou told'st mine eyes should help their famisht case?
    But thou art gone now that self felt disgrace
Doth make me most to wish thy comfort near.
    But here I do store of fair ladies meet,
10 Who may with charm of conversation sweet,
Make in my heavy mould° new thoughts to grow:
    Sure they prevail as much with me, as he
    That bade his friend but then new maim'd, to be
Merry with him, and not think of his woe.

---

3 **glass** eye. 6 **dazzling race** dazed course of sight.
3 **Bare . . . hand** led to believe, delude. 11 **mould** body, alluding
to its being of "earth."

107

Stella since thou so right a princess art
 Of all the powers which life bestows on me,
  That ere by them ought undertaken be,
They first resort unto that sovereign part;
Sweet for a while give respite to my heart,   5
 Which pants as though it still should leap to thee:
  And on my thoughts give the lieftenancy
To this great cause, which needs both use° and art.
 And as a queen, who from her presence sends
Whom she employs, dismiss from thee my wit,   10
Till it have wrought what thy own will attends.
On servant's shame oft master's blame doth sit;
 O let not fools in me thy works reprove,
  And scorning say, see what it is to love.

108

When sorrow (using mine own fire's might)
 Melts down his lead into my boiling breast,
  Through that dark furnace to my heart opprest,
There shines a joy from thee my only light;
But soon as thought of thee breeds my delight,   5
 And my young soul flutters to thee his nest,
  Most rude despair my daily unbidden guest,
Clips straight my wings, straight wraps me in his night,
 And makes me then bow down my head, and say,
Ah what doth Phoebus' gold that wretch avail,   10
Whom iron doors do keep from use of day?
So strangely (alas) thy works in me prevail,
 That in my woes for thee thou art my joy,
  And in my joys for thee my only annoy.

8 **use** experience.

From

THE PSALMS OF
DAVID

Psalm 1 *Beatus vir*

He blessèd is who neither loosely treads
    The straying steps, as wicked counsel leads
Ne for bad mates in way of sinning waiteth,
    Nor yet himself with idle scorners seateth
But on God's law his heart's delight doth bind   5
    Which night and day he calls to marking mind.

He shall be like a freshly planted tree
    To which sweet springs of waters neighbors be
Whose branches fail not timely fruit to nourish
    Nor withered leaf shall make it fail to flourish.   10
So all the things whereto that man doth bend
    Shall prosper still with well-succeeding end.

Such blessings shall not wicked wretches see:
    But like vile chaff with wind shall scatt'red be.
For neither shall the men in sin delighted   15
    Consist,° when they to highest doom are cited,
Ne yet shall suff'red be a place to take,
    Where godly men do their assembly make.

Psalm 6 *Domine ne in furore*

Lord, let not me, a worm, by thee be shent°
    While thou art in the heat of thy displeasure:
    Ne let thy rage, of my due punishment
        Become the measure.

But mercy, Lord, let mercy thine descend,   5
    For I am weak, and in my weakness languish:
    Lord, help, for ev'n my bones their marrow spend
        With cruel anguish.

Nay, ev'n my soul fell troubles do appall.
    Alas, how long, my God, wilt thou delay me?   10
    Turn thee, sweet Lord, and from this ugly fall
        My dear God, stay me.

16 **Consist** hold together, exist.
1 **shent** shamed.

Mercy, O mercy, Lord, for mercy's sake,
    For death doth kill the witness of thy glory;
15   Can, of thy praise, the tongues entombèd make
        A heav'nly story?

Lo, I am tir'd, while still I sigh and groan:
    My moist'ned bed proofs of my sorrow showeth:
    My bed (while I with black night mourn alone)
20   With my tears floweth.

Woe, like a moth, my face's beauty eats,
    And age, pull'd on with pains, all freshness fretteth;°
    The while a swarm of foes with vexing feats
        My life besetteth.

25 Get hence you evil, who in my ill rejoice,
    In all whose works vainness is ever reigning:
    For God hath heard the weeping sobbing voice
        Of my complaining.

The Lord my suit did hear, and gently hear;
30   They shall be sham'd and vext, that breed my crying:
    And turn their backs, and straight on backs appear
        Their shameful flying.

Psalm 13 *Usque quo Domine?*

How long (O Lord) shall I forgotten be?
        What? ever?
How long wilt thou thy hidden face from me
        Dissever?
5 How long shall I consult with careful sprite
        In anguish?
How long shall I with foes' triumphant might
        Thus languish?
Behold me Lord, let to thy hearing creep
10   My crying.
Nay, give me eyes, and light, lest that I sleep
        In dying:
Lest my foe brag, that in my ruin he
        Prevailèd;

22 **fretteth** wears away.

And at my fall they joy that, troublous, me   *15*
      Assailèd.
No, no, I trust on thee, and joy in thy
      Great pity:
Still therefore of thy graces shall be my
      Song's ditty.   *20*

Psalm 19   *Coeli enarrant*

The heav'nly frame sets forth the fame
  Of him that only thunders;
The firmament so strangely bent
  Shows his hand-working wonders.

Day unto day, it doth display,   *5*
  Their course doth it acknowledge:
And night to night, succeeding right,
  In darkness teach clear knowledge.

There is no speech, nor language, which
  Is so of skill bereavèd,   *10*
But of the skies the teaching cries,
  They have heard and conceivèd.

There be no eyne, but read the line
  From so fair book proceeding:
Their words be set in letters great   *15*
  For ev'ry body's reading.

Is not he blind that doth not find
  The tabernacle builded
There, by his grace, for sun's fair face,
  In beams of beauty gilded?   *20*

Who forth doth come, like a bridegroom
  From out his veiling places:
As glad is he as giants be
  To run their mighty races.

25 His race is ev'n from ends of heav'n;
    About that vault he goeth:
There be no rea'ms hid from his beams,
    His heat to all he throweth.

O law of his, how perfect 'tis
30   The very soul amending;
God's witness sure for aye doth dure
    To simplest, wisdom lending.

God's dooms be right, and cheer the sprite:
    All his commandments being
35 So purely wise, as gives the eyes
    Both light and force of seeing.

Of him the fear doth cleanness bear
    And so endures for ever:
His judgements be self verity
40   They are unrighteous never.

Then what man would so soon seek gold,
    Of glitt'ring golden money?
By them is past, in sweetest taste
    Honey, or comb of honey.

45 By them is made, thy servant's trade
    Most circumspectly guarded:
And who doth frame to keep the same
    Shall fully be rewarded.

Who is the man, that ever can
50   His faults know and acknowledge?
O Lord, cleanse me from faults that be
    Most secret from all knowledge.

Thy servant keep, lest in him creep
    Presumptuous sins' offenses:
55 Let them not have me for their slave,
    Nor reign upon my senses.

So shall my sprite be still upright
   In thought and conversation;
So shall I bide, well purified
   From much abomination.   60

So let words sprung from my weak tongue
   And my heart's meditation,
My saving might, Lord, in thy sight
   Receive good acceptation.

Psalm 23   *Dominus regit me*

The Lord, the Lord my shepherd is,
   And so can never I
      Taste misery.
He rests me in green pasture his:
   By waters still, and sweet   5
      He guides my feet.

He me revives: leads me the way,
   Which righteousness doth take,
      For his name's sake.
Yea though I should through valleys stray,   10
   Of death's dark shade, I will
      No whit fear ill.

For thou, dear Lord, thou me beset'st:
   Thy rod, and thy staff be
      To comfort me;   15
Before me thou a table set'st,
   Even when foe's envious eye
      Doth it espy.

With oil thou dost anoint my head,
   And so my cup dost fill   20
      That it doth spill.
Thus, thus shall all my days be fed,
   This mercy is so sure
      It shall endure,
And long yea long abide I shall,   25
   There where the Lord of all
      Doth hold his hall.

Psalm 43 *Judica me Deus*

Judge of all, judge me
 And protector be
Of my cause, oppressèd
 By most cruel sprites;
5 Save me from bad wights
 In false colors dressèd.

For, my God, thy sight
 Giveth me my might,
Why then hast thou left me?
10 Why walk I in woes?
 While prevailing foes
Have of joys bereft me?

Send thy truth and light;
 Let them guide me right
15 From the paths of folly,
 Bringing me to thy
 Tabernacles high
In thy hill most holy.

To God's altars tho
20 Will I boldly go,
Shaking off all sadness,
 To that God that is
 God of all my bliss,
God of all my gladness.

25 Then, lo, then I will
 With sweet music's skill
Grateful meaning show thee:
 Then, God, yea my God,
 I will sing abroad
30 What great thanks I owe thee.

Why art thou my soul
 Cast down in such dole?
What ails thy discomfort?
 Wait on God, for still
35 Thank my God I will,
 Sure aid, present comfort.

OTHER POEMS

Argalus and Parthenia°

His being was in her alone:
And he not being, she was none.
 They joy'd one joy, one grief they griev'd,
 One love they lov'd, one life they liv'd.
 The hand was one, one was the sword   5
 That did his death, her death afford.
As all the rest, so now the stone
That tombs the two, is justly one.

Two Pastorals, Made by Sir Philip Sidney

*Upon his meeting with his two worthy Friends
and fellow-Poets, Sir Edward Dyer,°
and Master Fulke Greville.°*

Join mates in mirth to me,
Grant pleasure to our meeting:
Let Pan our good god see,
How grateful is our greeting.
 Join hearts and hands, so let it be,   5
 Make but one mind in bodies three.

Ye hymns, and singing skill
Of god Apollo's giving,
Be press'd° our reeds to fill,
With sound of music living.   10
 Join hearts and hands, so let it be,
 Make but one mind in bodies three.

Sweet Orpheus' harp, whose sound
The steadfast mountains movèd,
Let here thy skill abound,   15
To join sweet friends belovèd.
 Join hearts and hands, so let it be,
 Make but one mind in bodies three.

0 **Argalus and Parthenia** Doomed lovers in one of the inset tales of the *Arcadia.* The poem is probably by Sidney, though it does not appear in the earliest edition of the romance.
0 **Dyer** See p. 111.   0 **Greville** schoolboy friend of Sidney; poet; and later, Sidney's biographer and one of his literary executors.
9 **press'd** ready.

My two and I be met,
20 A happy blessed trinity;
As three most jointly set,
In firmest band of unity.
 Join hearts and hands, so let it be,
 Make but one mind in bodies three.

25 Welcome my two to me, E.D. F.G. P.S.
The number best belovèd,
Within my heart you be
In friendship unremovèd.
 Join hearts and hands, so let it be,
30 *Make but one mind in bodies three.*

Give leave your flocks to range,
Let us the while be playing,
Within the elmy grange,
Your flocks will not be straying.
35 *Join hearts and hands, so let it be,*
 Make but one mind in bodies three.

Cause all the mirth you can,
Since I am now come hither,
Who never joy, but when
40 I am with you together.
 Join hearts and hands, so let it be,
 Make but one mind in bodies three.

Like lovers do their love,
So joy I, in your seeing;
45 Let nothing me remove
From always with you being.
 Join hearts and hands, so let it be,
 Make but one mind in bodies three.

And as the turtle-dove
50 To mate with whom he liveth,
Such comfort, fervent love
Of you, to my heart giveth.
 Join hearts and hands, so let it be,
 Make but one mind in bodies three.

Now joinèd by our hands, 55
Let them be ne'r a sunder,
But linkt in binding bands
By metamorphos'd wonder.
  So should our sever'd bodies three
  As one for ever joinèd be. 60

Dispraise of a courtly life

Walking in bright Phoebus' blaze
Where with heat oppress'd I was,
I got to a shady wood,
Where green leaves did newly bud.
And of grass was plenty dwelling, 5
Deckt with pied flowers sweetly smelling.

In this wood a man I met,
On lamenting wholly set:
Rueing change of wonted state,
Whence he was transformèd late, 10
Once to shepherd's god retaining,°
Now in servile court remaining.

There he wand'ring malcontent,
Up and down perplexèd went,
Daring not to tell to me, 15
Spake unto a senseless tree,
One among the rest electing
These same words, or this effecting:

My old mates I grieve to see,
Void of me in field to be, 20
Where we once our lovely sheep,
Lovingly like friends did keep,
Oft each other's friendship proving,
Never striving, but in loving.

But may love abiding be 25
In poor shepherd's base degree?
It belongs to such alone

11 **retaining** serving.

To whom art of love is known:
Seely° shepherds are not witting
80   What in art of love is fitting.

Nay, what need the art to those,
To whom we our love disclose?
It is to be usèd then,
When we do but flatter men:
85   Friendship true in heart assurèd,
Is by nature's gifts procurèd.

Therefore shepherds wanting skill,
Can love's duties best fulfill:
Since they know not how to fain,
40   Nor with love to cloak disdain,
Like the wiser sort, whose learning,
Hides their inward will of harming.

Well was I, while under shade
Oaten reeds me music made,
45   Striving with my mates in song,
Mixing mirth our songs among,
Greater was that shepherd's treasure,
Than this false, fine, courtly pleasure.

Where, how many creatures be,
50   So many pufft in mind I see,
Like to Juno's birds° of pride,
Scarce each other can abide,
Friends like to black swans° appearing,
Sooner these than those in hearing.

55   Therefore Pan, if thou mayst be
Made to listen unto me,
Grant, I say (if seely man
May make treaty to god Pan)
That I, without thy denying,
60   May be still to thee relying.

29 **Seely** simple.   51 **Juno's birds** peacocks.   53 **black swans** cited for their rarity.

Only for my two loves' sake, *Sir E.D. and M.F.G.*°
In whose love I pleasure take,
Only two do me delight
With their ever-pleasing sight,
Of all men to thee retaining,   65
Grant me with those two remaining.

So shall I to thee always,
With my reeds, sound mighty praise;
And first lamb that shall befall,
Yearly deck thine altar shall: 70
If it please thee be reflected,
And I from thee not rejected.

So I left him in that place,
Taking pity on his case,
Learning this among the rest,   75
That the mean estate is best,
Better fillèd with contenting,
Void of wishing and repenting.

61 **Sir E.D. and M.F.G.** see preceding poem, p. 207.

AN APOLOGY FOR POETRY

An Apology for Poetry

When the right virtuous Edward Wotton and I were at the Emperor's[1] court together, we gave ourselves to learn horsemanship of John Pietro Pugliano: one that with great commendation had the place of an esquire in his stable. And he, according to the fertileness of the Italian wit, did not only afford us the demonstration of his practice, but sought to enrich our minds with the contemplations therein, which he thought most precious. But with none I remember mine ears were at any time more loaden, than when (either angered with slow payment, or moved with our learner-like admiration) he exercised his speech in the praise of his faculty. He said, soldiers were the noblest estate of mankind, and horsemen, the noblest of soldiers. He said, they were the masters of war, and ornaments of peace: speedy goers, and strong abiders, triumphers both in camps and courts. Nay, to so unbelieved a point he proceeded, as that no earthly thing bred such wonder to a prince, as to be a good horseman. Skill of government, was but a *pedanteria*[2] in comparison: then would he add certain praises, by telling what a peerless beast a horse was. The only serviceable courtier without flattery, the beast of most beauty, faithfulness, courage, and such more, that, if I had not been a piece of a logician before I came to him, I think he would have persuaded me to have wished myself a horse. But thus much at least with his no few words he drave into me, that self-love is better than any gilding to make that seem gorgeous, wherein ourselves are parties. Wherein, if Pugliano his strong affection and weak arguments will not satisfy you, I will give you a nearer example

[1] **Emperor's** Maximilian II, at whose court Sidney passed the winter 1574–75.   [2] **pedanteria** a matter of pedantry.

of myself, who (I know not by what mischance) in these my not old years and idlest times, having slipped into the title of a poet, am provoked to say something unto you in the defence of that my unelected vocation, which if I handle with more good will than good reasons, bear with me, sith the scholar is to be pardoned that followeth the steps of his master.[3] And yet I must say, that as I have just cause to make a pitiful defense of poor Poetry, which from almost the highest estimation of learning, is fallen to be the laughingstock of children. So have I need to bring some more available[4] proofs: sith the former[5] is by no man barred of his deserved credit, the silly latter[6] hath had even the names of philosophers[7] used to the defacing of it, with great danger of civil war among the Muses. And first, truly to all them that professing learning inveigh against poetry, may justly be objected, that they go very near to ungratefulness, to seek to deface that, which in the noblest nations and languages that are known, hath been the first lightgiver to ignorance, and first nurse, whose milk by little and little enabled them to feed afterwards of tougher knowledges: and will they now play the hedgehog, that being received into the den, drave out his host? or rather the vipers, that with their birth kill their parents? Let learned Greece in any of her manifold sciences, be able to show me one book before Musaeus,[8] Homer, and Hesiodus, all three nothing else but poets. Nay, let any history be brought, that can say any writers were there before them, if they were not men of the same skill, as Orpheus, Linus,[9] and some other are named: who, having been the first of that country, that made pens deliverers of their knowledge to their posterity, may justly challenge to be called their fathers in learning: for not only in time they had this

---

[3] **scholar . . . master** Sidney following Pugliano.   [4] **available** of avail, effective.   [5] **the former** i.e., horsemanship.   [6] **the silly latter** "poor Poetry."   [7] **philosophers** notably Plato, whose banishment of poets from his *Republic*, or ideal state, provided classical authority for those whom Sidney is arguing against.   [8] **Musaeus** legendary pre-Homeric poet, thought in the Renaissance to be author of the Greek "Hero and Leander."   [9] **Orpheus, Linus** invoked here as founders of poetry, believed to be the first kind of writing. Linus was the master of Orpheus, legend claiming each as son of a Muse and either descendant or servant to Apollo.

priority (although in itself antiquity be venerable), but
went before them, as causes to draw with their charming[10]
sweetness, the wild untamed wits to an admiration of
knowledge. So as Amphion was said to move stones with
his poetry, to build Thebes. And Orpheus to be listened to
by beasts, indeed, stony and beastly people. So among the
Romans were Livius Andronicus, and Ennius. So in the
Italian language, the first that made it aspire to be a treas-
urehouse of science,[11] were the poets Dante, Boccace, and
Petrarch. So in our English were Gower and Chaucer.

After whom, encouraged and delighted with their excellent fore-going, others have followed, to beautify our
mother tongue, as well in the same kind as in other arts.
This[12] did so notably show itself, that the philosophers of
Greece, durst not a long time appear to the world but under
the masks of poets. So Thales, Empedocles, and Par-
menides sang their natural[13] philosophy in verses: so did
Pythagoras and Phocylides their moral counsels: so did
Tyrtaeus in war matters, and Solon in matters of policy:[14]
or rather, they being poets, did exercise their delightful
vein in those points of highest knowledge, which before
them lay hid to the world. For that wise Solon was directly
a poet, it is manifest, having written in verse, the notable
fable of the Atlantic Island,[15] which was continued by
Plato.

And truly, even Plato, whosoever well considereth, shall
find, that in the body of his work, though the inside and
strength were philosophy, the skin as it were and beauty,
depended most of poetry: for all standeth upon dialogues,
wherein he feigneth many honest burgesses of Athens to
speak of such matters, that if they had been set on the
rack, they would never have confessed them. Besides, his
poetical describing the circumstances of their meetings, as
the well ordering of a banquet, the delicacy of a walk,[16]

---

10 **charming** from Latin *carmen:* song, incantation.   11 **science** learning.
12 **This** i.e., poetry as "nurse of learning."   13 **natural** of the natural
world; scientific.   14 **policy** government.   15 **Atlantic Island** lost con-
tinent of Atlantis, referred to in Plato's *Timaeus.*   16 **banquet . . . walk**
settings for his *Symposium* and *Phaedrus,* respectively.

with interlacing mere tales, as Gyges' ring,[17] and others,
which who knoweth not to be flowers of poetry did never
walk into Apollo's garden.

And even historiographers, (although their lips sound of
things done, and verity be written in their foreheads,)
have been glad to borrow both fashion, and perchance
weight of poets. So Herodotus entitled his History,[18] by the
name of the nine Muses: and both he and all the rest that
followed him, either stole or usurped of poetry, their passionate describing of passions, the many particularities of
battles, which no man could affirm: or if that be denied
me, long orations put in the mouths of great kings and
captains, which it is certain they never pronounced. So that
truly, neither philosopher nor historiographer, could at the
first have entered into the gates of popular judgements, if
they had not taken a great passport of poetry, which in all
nations at this day where learning flourisheth not, is plain
to be seen: in all which they have some feeling of poetry.
In Turkey, besides their law-giving divines, they have no
other writers but poets. In our neighbor country Ireland,
where truly learning goeth very bare, yet are their poets
held in a devout reverence. Even among the most barbarous and simple Indians where no writing is, yet have
they their poets, who make and sing songs which they call
areytos, both of their ancestors' deeds, and praises of their
gods. A sufficient probability, that if ever learning come
among them, it must be by having their hard dull wits
softened and sharpened with the sweet delights of poetry.
For until they find a pleasure in the exercises of the mind,
great promises of much knowledge, will little persuade them,
that know not the fruits of knowledge. In Wales, the true
remnant of the ancient Britons, as there are good authorities to show the long time they had poets, which they
called *bards:* so through all the conquests of Romans,
Saxons, Danes, and Normans, some of whom did seek to

---

[17] **Gyges' ring** an illustrative legend in the *Republic*, telling of a shepherd who uses a magic ring from the underworld to slay a king and become, himself, a ruler.   [18] **History** the division into nine books, each
bearing the name of a Muse, was in fact the work of Alexandrian
scholars.

ruin all memory of learning from among them, yet do their poets even to this day, last; so as it is not more notable in soon beginning than in long continuing. But since the authors of most of our sciences were the Romans, and before them the Greeks, let us a little stand upon their authorities, but even so far as to see, what names they have given unto this now scorned skill.

Among the Romans a poet was called *vates*, which is as much as a diviner, fore-seer, or prophet, as by his conjoined words *vaticinium* and *vaticinari*,[19] is manifest: so heavenly a title did that excellent people bestow upon this heart-ravishing knowledge. And so far were they carried into the admiration thereof, that they thought in the chanceable hitting upon any such verses, great fore-tokens of their following fortunes were placed. Whereupon grew the word of *sortes Virgilianae*,[20] when by sudden opening Virgil's book, they lighted upon any verse of his making, whereof the histories of the Emperors' lives are full: as of Albinus[21] the governor of our island, who in his childhood met with this verse,

Arma amens capio nec sat rationis in armis.[22]

And in his age performed it, which although it were a very vain, and godless superstition, as also it was to think that spirits were commanded by such verses, where upon this word charms, derived of *carmina* cometh, so yet serveth it to show the great reverence those wits were held in. And altogether not without ground, since both the oracles of Delphos and Sibylla's prophecies, were wholly delivered in verses. For that same exquisite observing of number and measure in words, and that high flying liberty of conceit[23] proper to the poet, did seem to have some divine force in it.

And may not I presume a little further, to show the reasonableness of this word *vates*? And say that the holy

---

[19] **vaticinium, vaticinari** a prophecy, to prophesy. [20] **sortes Virgilianae** accepting as prophecy a line of Virgil chosen by random opening of the *Aeneid*. [21] **Albinus** governor of Britain, whose troops declared him emperor in 193, but who fell before Septimius Severus in 197. [22] **Arma . . . armis** "Frantic, I seize arms; yet there is little purpose in arms" (*Aeneid*, II, 314). [23] **conceit** imaginative conception.

David's Psalms are a divine poem? If I do, I shall not do it without the testimony of great learned men, both ancient and modern: but even the name Psalms will speak for me, which being interpreted, is nothing but songs. Then that it is fully written in meter, as all learned Hebricians agree, although the rules be not yet fully found. Lastly and principally, his handling his prophecy, which is merely[24] poetical. For what else is the awaking his musical instruments? The often and free changing of persons? His notable *prosopopeias*,[25] when he maketh you as it were, see God coming in his majesty. His telling of the beasts' joyfulness, and hills leaping, but a heavenly poesy: wherein almost[26] he showeth himself a passionate lover, of that unspeakable and everlasting beauty to be seen by the eyes of the mind, only cleared by faith. But truly now having named him, I fear me I seem to profane that holy name, applying it to Poetry, which is among us thrown down to so ridiculous an estimation: but they that with quiet judgements will look a little deeper into it, shall find the end and working of it such, as being rightly applied, deserveth not to be scourged out of the Church of God.

But now, let us see how the Greeks named it, and how they deemed of it. The Greeks called him a *poet*, which name, hath as the most excellent, gone through other languages. It cometh of this word *poiein*, which is, to make: wherein I know not, whether by luck or wisdom, we Englishmen have met with[27] the Greeks, in calling him a maker: which name, how high and incomparable a title it is, I had rather were known by marking the scope of other sciences, than by my partial[28] allegation.

There is no art delivered to mankind, that hath not the works of Nature for his principal object, without which they could not consist, and on which they so depend, as they become actors and players as it were, of what Nature will have set forth. So doth the astronomer look upon the stars, and by that he seeth, setteth down what order Nature

---

[24] **merely** entirely. [25] **prosopopeias** personifications (rhetorical term). [26] **almost** indeed. [27] **have met with** agree with. [28] **partial** open to charges of prejudice.

hath taken therein. So do the geometrician, and arithmetician, in their diverse sorts of quantities. So doth the musician in times,[29] tell you which by nature agree, which not. The natural philosopher thereon[30] hath his name, and the moral philosopher standeth upon the natural virtues, vices, and passions of man; and follow Nature (saith he) therein, and thou shalt not err. The lawyer saith what men have determined. The historian what men have done. The grammarian speaketh only of the rules of speech, and the rhetorician, and logician, considering what in Nature will soonest prove and persuade, thereon give artificial rules, which still are compassed within the circle of a question,[31] according to the proposed matter. The physician weigheth the nature of a man's body, and the nature of things helpful, or hurtful unto it. And the metaphysic, though it be in the second and abstract notions, and therefore be counted supernatural:[32] yet doth he indeed build upon the depth of Nature: only the poet, disdaining to be tied to any such subjection, lifted up with the vigor of his own invention, doth grow in effect into another Nature, in making things either better than Nature bringeth forth, or, quite anew forms such as never were in Nature, as the Heros, Demigods, Cyclops, Chimeras, Furies, and such like: so as he goeth hand in hand with Nature, not enclosed within the narrow warrant of her gifts, but freely ranging only within the zodiac of his own wit.

Nature never set forth the earth in so rich tapestry, as divers poets have done, neither with so pleasant rivers, fruitful trees, sweet smelling flowers: nor whatsoever else may make the too much loved earth more lovely. Her world is brazen, the poets only deliver a golden:[33] but let those things alone and go to man, for whom as the other things are, so it seemeth in him her uttermost cunning is employed, and know whether she have brought forth so

---

[29] **times** rhythmical measure.   [30] **thereon** i.e., from nature.   [31] **still . . . question** always bound by the specific proposed issue.   [32] **supernatural** translating the Greek root of "metaphysics"; beyond physical nature. [33] **brazen . . . golden** referring to tradition of the ages of man: silver, brass, and iron successively retreating from the first and perfect golden age.

true a lover as Theagenes,[34] so constant a friend as Pylades,[35] so valiant a man as Orlando,[36] so right a prince as Xenophon's Cyrus,[37] so excellent a man every way as Virgil's Aeneas: neither let this be jestingly conceived, because the works of the one be essential:[38] the other,[39] in imitation or fiction: for any understanding knoweth the skill of the artificer, standeth in that *idea* or fore-conceit of the work, and not in the work itself.[40] And that the poet hath that *idea*, is manifest, by delivering them forth in such excellency as he hath imagined them. Which delivering forth also, is not wholly imaginative,[41] as we are wont to say by them that build castles in the air: but so far substantially it worketh, not only to make a Cyrus, which had been but a particular excellency, as Nature might have done, but to bestow a Cyrus upon the world, to make many Cyrus' if they will learn aright, why, and how that maker[42] made him.

Neither let it be deemed too saucy a comparison to balance the highest point of man's wit with the efficacy of Nature: but rather give right honor to the heavenly Maker of that maker; who having made man to his own likeness, set him beyond and over all the works of that second nature,[43] which in nothing he[44] showeth so much as in poetry: when with the force of a divine breath,[45] he bringeth things forth far surpassing her[46] doings, with no small argument to the incredulous of that first accursed fall of Adam: sith our erected wit, maketh us know what perfection is, and yet our infected will, keepeth us from reaching unto it. But these arguments will by few be understood, and by fewer granted. Thus much (I hope) will be given me, that the

---

[34] **Theagenes** in the *Aethiopica* of Heliodorus, a Greek romance. [35] **Pylades** friend of Orestes, he helped him win revenge on his mother, Clytemnestra, and married Orestes' sister, Electra. [36] **Orlando** the French Roland; hero of Italian epics, including Ariosto's *Orlando Furioso.* [37] **Cyrus** the Persian king, exemplary hero of Xenophon's *Cyropaedia.* [38] **essential** substantial, real. [39] **the one . . . the other** nature . . . poets. [40] **the work itself** the "imitation of nature" which embodies the idea or "fore-conceit." [41] **imaginative** fanciful. [42] **that maker** the poet. [43] **second nature** physical nature. [44] **he** the poet. [45] **divine breath** literally "inspiration." [46] **her** nature's.

Greeks with some probability of reason, gave him the name above all names of learning.

Now let us go to a more ordinary opening of him,[47] that the truth may be more palpable: and so I hope, though we get not so unmatched a praise as the etymology of his names will grant, yet his very description, which no man will deny, shall not justly be barred from a principal commendation.

Poesy therefore is an art of imitation, for so Aristotle termeth it in his word *mimesis*, that is to say, a representing, counterfeiting, or figuring forth: to speak metaphorically, a speaking picture: with this end, to teach and delight; of this have been three several kinds. The chief both in antiquity and excellency, were they that did imitate the inconceivable excellencies of God. Such were, David in his Psalms, Salomon in his Song of Songs, in his Ecclesiastes, and Proverbs: Moses and Debora in their hymns, and the writer of Job; which beside other, the learned Emanuel Tremilius, and Franciscus Junius,[48] do entitle the poetical part of the Scripture. Against these none will speak that hath the Holy Ghost in due holy reverence.

In this kind, though in a full wrong divinity,[49] were Orpheus, Amphion, Homer in his hymns, and many other, both Greeks and Romans: and this poesy must be used, by whosoever will follow S. James his counsel, in singing Psalms when they are merry: and I know is used with the fruit of comfort by some, when in sorrowful pangs of their death-bringing sins, they find the consolation of the never-leaving goodness.

The second kind, is of them that deal with matters philosophical; either moral, as Tyrtaeus, Phocilides, and Cato, or natural, as Lucretius, and Virgil's Georgics:[50] or astronomical, as Manilius, and Pontanus: or historical, as Lucan: which who mislike, the fault is in their judgements quite out of taste, and not in the sweet food of sweetly uttered knowledge. But because this second sort is wrapped

---

[47] **opening of him** in law, the opening presentation by counsel. [48] **Tremilius . . . Junius** produced in the 1570's a Protestant Latin translation of the Bible. [49] **full . . . divinity** not Christian. [50] **Georgics** praised here as an agricultural treatise.

within the fold of the proposed subject,[51] and takes not the course of his own invention, whether they properly be poets or no, let grammarians dispute: and go to the third, indeed right poets, of whom chiefly this question ariseth; betwixt whom, and these second is such a kind of difference, as betwixt the meaner sort of painters (who counterfeit only such faces as are set before them) and the more excellent: who having no law but wit, bestow that in colors upon you which is fittest for the eye to see: as the constant, though lamenting book of Lucretia,[52] when she punished in herself another's fault.

Wherein he painted not Lucretia whom he never saw, but painteth the outward beauty of such a virtue: for these third[53] be they which most properly do imitate to teach and delight, and to imitate, borrow nothing of what is, hath been, or shall be: but range only reined with learned discretion, into the divine consideration of what may be, and should be. These be they, that as the first and most noble sort, may justly be termed *vates*, so these are waited on in the excellentest languages and best understandings, with the fore described name of poets: for these indeed do merely[54] make[55] to imitate: and imitate both to delight and teach: and delight to move men to take that goodness in hand, which without delight they would fly as from a stranger. And teach, to make them know that goodness whereunto they are moved, which being the noblest scope to which ever any learning was directed, yet want there not idle tongues to bark at them. These be subdivided into sundry more special denominations. The most notable be the heroic, lyric, tragic, comic, satiric, iambic, elegiac, pastoral, and certain others. Some of these being termed according to the matter they deal with, some by the sorts of verses they liked best to write in, for indeed the greatest part of poets have apparelled their poetical inventions in that numbrous[56] kind of writing which is called verse: in-

---

[51] **second sort . . . subject** poetry bound by the nature of its subject matter.   [52] **Lucretia** alluding to representations of Lucretia, who, raped by Tarquin, became a suicide in the name of honor.   [53] **these third** sort of poets, i.e., the "right" poets, mentioned above.   [54] **merely** exclusively.   [55] **make** For poet as "maker," see p. 220.   [56] **numbrous** in meter.

deed but apparelled, verse being but an ornament and no cause to poetry: sith there have been many most excellent poets, that never versified, and now swarm many versifiers that need never answer to the name of poets. For Xenophon,[57] who did imitate so excellently, as to give us *effigiem iusti imperii*, the portraiture of a just empire, under the name of Cyrus (as Cicero saith of him), made therein an absolute heroical poem.

So did Heliodorus[58] in his sugared[59] invention of that picture of love in Theagenes and Cariclea, and yet both these writ in prose: which I speak to show, that it is not rhyming and versing that maketh a poet, no more than a long gown maketh an advocate: who though he pleaded in armor should be an advocate and no soldier. But it is that feigning notable images of virtues, vices, or what else, with that delightful teaching which must be the right describing note to know a poet by: although indeed the senate of poets hath chosen verse as their fittest raiment, meaning, as in matter they passed all in all,[60] so in manner to go beyond them: not speaking (table talk fashion, or like men in a dream,) words as they chanceably fall from the mouth, but peizing[61] each syllable of each word by just proportion according to the dignity of the subject.

Now therefore it shall not be amiss first to weigh this latter sort[62] of poetry by his works, and then by his parts; and if in neither of these anatomies he be condemnable, I hope we shall obtain a more favorable sentence.[63] This purifying of wit, this enriching of memory, enabling of judgement, and enlarging of conceit, which commonly we call learning, under what name soever it come forth, or to what immediate end soever it be directed, the final end is, to lead and draw us to as high a perfection, as our degenerate souls made worse by their clayey lodgings, can be capable of. This according to the inclination of the man, bred many formed impressions, for some that thought this

---

[57] **Xenophon** See note, p. 222.   [58] **Helidorus** See note, p. 222.   [59] **sugared** sweetened, refined (see *Astrophel and Stella,* sonnet 25).   [60] **all in all** all others in all respects.   [61] **peizing** weighing.   [62] **latter sort** the third sort (p. 224).   [63] **sentence** judgment.

felicity principally to be gotten by knowledge, and no knowledge to be so high and heavenly, as acquaintance with the stars, gave themselves to astronomy, others, persuading themselves to be demigods if they knew the causes of things, became natural and supernatural philosophers, some an admirable delight drew to music: and some the certainty of demonstration, to the mathematics. But all, one, and other, having this scope[64] to know, and by knowledge to lift up the mind from the dungeon of the body, to the enjoying his own divine essence. But when by the balance of experience it was found, that the astronomer looking to the stars might fall into a ditch, that the enquiring philosopher might be blind in himself, and the mathematician might draw forth a straight line with a crooked heart: then lo, did proof, the overruler of opinions, make manifest, that all these are but serving[65] sciences, which as they have each a private end in themselves, so yet are they all directed to the highest end of the mistress knowledge, by the Greeks called *architectonike*, which stands (as I think) in the knowledge of a man's self, in the ethic and politic consideration, with the end of well doing and not of well knowing only; even as the saddler's next[66] end is to make a good saddle: but his farther end, to serve a nobler faculty, which is horsemanship, so the horseman's to soldiery, and the soldier not only to have the skill, but to perform the practice of a soldier: so that the ending end of all earthly learning, being virtuous action, those skills that most serve to bring forth that, have a most just title to be princes over all the rest: wherein if we can, show we the poet's nobleness, by setting him before his other competitors, among whom as principal challengers step forth the moral philosophers, whom me thinketh, I see coming towards me with a sullen gravity, as though they could not abide vice by day light, rudely clothed for to witness outwardly their contempt of outward things, with books in their hands against glory, whereto they set their names, sophistically speaking against subtlety, and angry with any man in whom they see the foul fault of anger; these men

[64] scope mark for aiming at.   [65] serving subordinate.   [66] next nearest.

casting larges[67] as they go, of definitions, divisions, and distinctions,[68] with a scornful interrogative do soberly ask, whether it be possible to find any path, so ready to lead a man to virtue, as that which teacheth what virtue is? and teacheth it not only by delivering forth his very being, his causes, and effects; but also, by making known his enemy vice, which must be destroyed, and his cumbersome servant passion, which must be mastered, by showing the generalities that containeth it, and the specialities that are derived from it. Lastly, by plain setting down, how it extendeth itself out of the limits of a man's own little world, to the government of families, and maintaining of public societies.

The historian, scarcely giveth leisure to the moralist to say so much, but that he loaden with old mouse-eaten records, authorizing himself (for the most part) upon other histories, whose greatest authorities, are built upon the notable foundation of hearsay, having much ado to accord differing writers, and to pick truth out of partiality, better acquainted with a thousand years ago, than with the present age: and yet better knowing how this world goeth, than how his own wit runneth; curious for antiquities, and inquisitive of novelties, a wonder to young folks, and a tyrant in table talk, denieth in a great chafe, that any man for teaching of virtue, and virtuous actions, is comparable to him. I am *lux vitae, temporum magistra, vita memoriae, nuncia vetustatis.* &c. The philosopher (saith he) teacheth a disputative virtue, but I do an active: his virtue is excellent in the dangerless Academy of Plato, but mine showeth forth her honorable face, in the battles of Marathon, Pharsalia, Poitiers, and Agincourt. He teacheth virtue by certain abstract considerations, but I only bid you to follow the footing of them that have gone before you. Old-aged experience, goeth beyond the fine-witted philosopher, but I give the experience of many ages. Lastly, if he make the song-book, I put the learner's hand to the lute: and if he be the guide, I am the light.

Then would he allege you innumerable examples, con-

[67] **larges** bounty, largess.   [68] **definitions . . . distinctions** terms of scholastic logic, marking the progressive refinements of an argument.

ferring story by story, how much the wisest senators and princes, have been directed by the credit of history, as Brutus, Alphonsus of Aragon, and who not, if need be? At length, the long line of their disputation maketh a point[69] in this, that the one giveth the precept, and the other[70] the example.

Now, whom shall we find (sith the question standeth for the highest form in the school of learning) to be moderator? Truly, as me seemeth, the poet; and if not a moderator, even the man that ought to carry the title from them both, and much more from all other serving sciences.[71] Therefore compare we the poet with the historian, and with the moral philosopher; and, if he go beyond them both, no other human skill can match him. For as for the divine, with all reverence it is ever to be excepted, not only for having his scope as far beyond any of these, as eternity exceedeth a moment, but even for passing each of these in themselves.

And for the lawyer, though *Ius*[72] be the daughter of justice, and justice the chief of virtues, yet because he seeketh to make men good, rather *formidine poenae*, than *virtutis amore*,[73] or to say righter, doth not endeavor to make men good, but that their evil hurt not others: having no care so he be a good citizen, how bad a man he be. Therefore, as our wickedness maketh him necessary, and necessity maketh him honorable, so is he not in the deepest truth to stand in rank with these;[74] who all endeavor to take the naughtiness away, and plant goodness even in the secretest cabinet of our souls. And these four[75] are all, that any way deal in that consideration of men's manners, which being the supreme knowledge, they that best breed it, deserve the best commendation.

The philosopher therefore and the historian are they which would win the goal: the one by precept, the other

---

[69] **point** full stop, or period.   [70] **the one . . . the other** the philosopher . . . the historian.   [71] **serving sciences** see p. 226.   [72] **Ius** law.   [73] **formidine . . . amore** "rather through fear of punishment than through love of virtue" (phrases from Horace, Epistles, I).   [74] **these** the philosopher, the historian, the poet.   [75] **these four** philosopher, historian, poet, and lawyer.

by example. But both not having both,[76] do both halt. For the philosopher, setting down with thorny argument the bare rule, is so hard of utterance, and so misty to be conceived, that one that hath no other guide but him, shall wade in him till he be old, before he shall find sufficient cause to be honest: for his knowledge standeth so upon the abstract and general, that happy is that man who may understand him, and more happy, that can apply what he doth understand.

On the other side, the historian, wanting[77] the precept, is so tied, not to what should be, but to what is, to the particular truth of things, and not to the general reason of things, that his example draweth no necessary consequence, and therefore a less fruitful doctrine.

Now doth the peerless poet perform both: for whatsoever the philosopher saith should be done, he giveth a perfect picture of it in some one, by whom he presupposeth it was done. So as he coupleth the general notion with the particular example. A perfect picture I say, for he yieldeth to the powers of the mind, an image of that whereof the philosopher bestoweth but a wordish description: which doth neither strike, pierce, nor possess the sight of the soul, so much as that other doth.

For as in outward things, to a man that had never seen an elephant or a rhinoceros, who[78] should tell him most exquisitely all their shapes, color, bigness, and particular marks: or of a gorgeous palace, the architecture, with declaring the full beauties, might well make the hearer able to repeat as it were by rote, all he had heard, yet should never satisfy his inward conceits with being witness to itself of a true lively knowledge: but the same man, as soon as he might see those beasts well painted, or the house well in model, should straightways grow without need of any description, to a judicial comprehending of them, so no doubt the philosopher with his learned definition, be it of virtue, vices, matters of public policy, or private government, replenisheth the memory with many infallible grounds of wis-

---

[76] **both . . . both** neither philosopher nor historian, having both precept and example.   [77] **wanting** lacking.   [78] **who** the man who.

dom: which notwithstanding, lie dark before the imaginative and judging power, if they be not illuminated or figured forth by the speaking picture of poesy.

Tully[79] taketh much pains and many times not without poetical helps, to make us know the force love of our country hath in us. Let us but hear old Anchises[80] speaking in the middest of Troy's flames, or see Ulysses[81] in the fullness of all Calypso's delights, bewail his absence from barren and beggarly Ithaca. Anger the Stoics say, was a short madness, let but Sophocles bring you Ajax on a stage, killing and whipping sheep and oxen, thinking them the army of Greeks, with their chieftains Agamemnon and Menelaus, and tell me if you have not a more familiar insight into anger, than finding in the schoolmen his *genus* and *difference*. See whether wisdom and temperance in Ulysses and Diomedes, valor in Achilles, friendship in Nisus, and Euryalus,[82] even to an ignorant man, carry not an apparent shining: and contrarily, the remorse of conscience in Oedipus, the soon repenting pride in Agamemnon, the self-devouring cruelty in his father Atreus, the violence of ambition in the two Theban brothers,[83] the sour-sweetness of revenge in Medea, and, to fall lower, the Terentian Gnatho,[84] and our Chaucer's Pandar, so expressed, that we now use their names to signify their trades. And finally, all virtues, vices, and passions, so in their own natural seats laid to the view, that we seem not to hear of them, but clearly to see through them. But even in the most excellent determination of goodness, what philosopher's counsel can so readily direct a prince, as the feigned Cyrus in Xenophon? or a virtuous man in all fortunes, as Aeneas in Virgil? or a whole commonwealth, as the way of Sir Thomas More's Utopia? I say the way, because where Sir Thomas More erred, it was the fault of the man and not of the poet, for that way of patterning a commonwealth

---

[79] **Tully** Cicero. [80] **Anchises** *Aeneid*, II. [81] **Ulysses** *Odyssey*, V. [82] **Nisus . . . Euryalus** *Aeneid*, IX. [83] **two Theban brothers** in plays of Aeschylus and Seneca, Polynices and Eteocles, sons of Oedipus, brought civil discord to the government of Thebes. [84] **Gnatho** character in Terence's *Eunuch;* gave its name to the type of parasite, as did Chaucer's Pandar to the go-between.

was most absolute,[85] though he perchance hath not so absolutely performed it: for the question is, whether the feigned image of poesy, or the regular instruction of philosophy, hath the more force in teaching: wherein if the philosophers have more rightly showed themselves philosophers, than the poets have attained to the high top of their profession, as in truth,

> *Mediocribus esse poetis,*
> *Non dii, non homines, non concessere columnae:*[86]

it is I say again, not the fault of the art, but that by few men that art can be accomplished.

Certainly, even our Savior Christ could as well have given, the moral commonplaces of uncharitableness and humbleness, as the divine narration of Dives and Lazarus:[87] or of disobedience and mercy, as that heavenly discourse of the lost child[88] and the gracious father; but that his through-searching wisdom, knew the estate of Dives burning in hell, and of Lazarus being in Abraham's bosom, would more constantly (as it were) inhabit both the memory and judgement. Truly, for myself, meseems I see before my eyes the lost child's disdainful prodigality, turned to envy a swine's dinner: which by the learned divines, are thought not historical acts, but instructing parables. For conclusion, I say the philosopher teacheth, but he teacheth obscurely, so as the learned only can understand him: that is to say, he teacheth them that are already taught, but the poet is the food for the tenderest stomachs, the poet is indeed the right popular philosopher, whereof Aesop's tales give good proof: whose pretty allegories, stealing under the formal tales of beasts, make many, more beastly than beasts, begin to hear the sound of virtue from these dumb speakers.

But now may it be alleged, that if this imagining of matters be so fit for the imagination, then must the historian needs surpass, who bringeth you images of true matters,

---

[85] **absolute** perfect. [86] **Mediocribus . . . columnae** "Neither gods nor men nor booksellers ever brooked poets of middling rank" Horace, *De Arte Poetica*, 372–373. [87] **Dives and Lazarus** Luke 16: 19–31. [88] **lost child** Luke 15: 11–32.

such as indeed were done, and not such as fantastically or
falsely may be suggested to have been done. Truly Aristotle
himself in his discourse of poesy, plainly determineth this
question, saying, that poetry is *philosophoteron* and *spou-
daioteron*, that is to say, it is more philosophical, and more
studiously serious, than history. His reason is, because
poesy dealeth with *katholou*, that is to say, with the universal consideration; and the history with *kathekaston*, the
particular; now saith he, the universal weighs what is fit to
be said or done, either in likelihood or necessity, (which
the poesy considereth in his imposed names), and the particular, only marks, whether Alcibiades did, or suffered,
this or that. Thus far Aristotle: which reason of his (as all
his) is most full of reason. For indeed, if the question were
whether it were better to have a particular act truly or
falsely set down: there is no doubt which is to be chosen,
no more than whether you had rather have Vespasian's
picture right as he was, or at the painter's pleasure nothing resembling. But if the question be for your own use and
learning, whether it be better to have it set down as it
should be, or as it was: then certainly is more doctrinable[89]
the feigned Cyrus of Xenophon than the true Cyrus in
Justin:[90] and the feigned Aeneas in Virgil, than the right
Aeneas in Dares Phrygius.[91]

As to a lady that desired to fashion her countenance to
the best grace, a painter should more benefit her to portrait a most sweet face, writing Canidia[92] upon it, than to
paint Canidia as she was, who Horace sweareth, was foul
and ill favored.

If the poet do his part aright, he will show you in Tantalus,[93] Atreus, and such like, nothing that is not to be
shunned; in Cyrus, Aeneas, Ulysses, each thing to be followed; where[94] the historian, bound to tell things as things

---

[89] **doctrinable** instructive.   [90] **Justin** whose *Histories* include a brief account of Cyrus.   [91] **Dares Phrygius** thought in the Middle Ages to have
provided an eyewitness account of the Trojan War.   [92] **Canidia** the
witch who makes frantic efforts to become beautiful again.   [93] **Tantalus**
punished for greed, by being set in hell in waters which he could not
drink, with an apple hanging before him which he could not eat.
[94] **where** whereas.

were, cannot be liberal (without he will be poetical) of a perfect pattern:[95] but, as in Alexander or Scipio himself, show doings, some to be liked, some to be misliked. And then how will you discern what to follow but by your own discretion, which you had without reading Quintus Curtius?[96] And whereas a man may say, though in universal consideration of doctrine the poet prevaileth; yet that the history, in his saying such a thing was done, doth warrant a man more in that he shall follow. The answer is manifest, that if he stand upon that *was;* as if he should argue, because it rained yesterday, therefore it should rain today, then indeed it hath some advantage to a gross conceit:[97] but if he know an example only informs a conjectured likelihood, and so go by reason,[98] the poet doth so far exceed him,[99] as he is to frame his example to that which is most reasonable: be it in warlike, politic, or private matters; where the historian in his bare *was,* hath many times that which we call fortune, to over-rule the best wisdom. Many times, he must tell events, whereof he can yield no cause: or if he do, it must be poetical; for that a feigned example, hath as much force to teach, as a true example: (for as for to move, it is clear, sith the feigned may be tuned to the highest key of passion) let us take one example, wherein a poet and a historian do concur.

Herodotus and Justin do both testify, that Zopyrus, King Darius' faithful servant, seeing his master long resisted by the rebellious Babylonians, feigned himself in extreme disgrace of his king: for verifying of which, he caused his own nose and ears to be cut off: and so flying to the Babylonians, was received: and for his known valor, so far credited, that he did find means to deliver them over to Darius. Much like matter doth Livy record of Tarquinius and his son. Xenophon excellently feigneth such another stratagem, performed by Abradatas in Cyrus' behalf. Now would I fain know, if occasion be presented unto you, to

---

[95] **liberal . . . pattern** freely present the ideal.   [96] **Quintus Curtius** author of a life of Alexander the Great (first century A.D.).   [97] **gross conceit** coarse understanding.   [98] **reason** here opposed to "conjectured likelihood."   [99] **him** the historian.

serve your prince by such an honest dissimulation, why you
do not as well learn it of Xenophon's fiction, as of the
others' verity: and truly so much the better, as you shall
save your nose[100] by the bargain; for Abradatas did not
counterfeit so far. So then the best of the historian is subject to the poet; for whatsoever action, or faction,[101] whatsoever counsel, policy, or war stratagem, the historian is
bound to recite, that may the poet (if he list) with his
imitation make his own; beautifying it both for further
teaching, and more delighting, as it pleaseth him: having
all, from Dante his heaven, to his hell, under the authority
of his pen. Which if I be asked what poets have done so, as
I might well name some, yet say I, and say again, I speak
of the art, and not of the artificer.

Now, to that which commonly is attributed to the praise
of histories, in respect of the notable learning[102] is gotten
by marking the success,[103] as though therein a man should
see virtue exalted, and vice punished. Truly that commendation is peculiar to poetry, and far off from history. For
indeed poetry ever setteth virtue so out in her[104] best
colors, making Fortune her well-waiting hand-maid, that
one must needs be enamored of her. Well may you see
Ulysses in a storm, and in other hard plights; but they are
but exercises of patience and magnanimity, to make them
shine the more in the near-following prosperity. And of the
contrary part, if evil men come to the stage, they ever go
out (as the tragedy writer[105] answered, to one that misliked the show of such persons) so manacled, as they little
animate folks to follow them. But the historian, being
captived to the truth of a foolish world, is many times a
terror from[106] well doing, and an encouragement to unbridled wickedness.

For, see we not valiant Miltiades[107] rot in his fetters?
The just Phocion,[108] and the accomplished Socrates, put to

---

[100] **save your nose** unlike Zopyrus, above.   [101] **faction** course of con-
duct.   [102] **learning** "which" understood before "is."   [103] **success** out-
come.   [104] **her** virtue's.   [105] **tragedy writer** Euripides, as reported by
Plutarch, replying to a criticism of unpleasant characters in his plays.
[106] **terror from** discourages by terror.   [107] **Miltiades** victor at battle of
Marathon.   [108] **Phocion** Athenian general, opponent of Demosthenes,
who, when condemned, took poison.

death like traitors? The cruel Severus live prosperously? The excellent Severus miserably murthered? Sylla and Marius[109] dying in their beds? Pompey and Cicero[110] slain then, when they would have thought exile a happiness?

See we not virtuous Cato driven to kill himself? and rebel Caesar so advanced, that his name yet after 1600 years, lasteth in the highest honor? And mark but even Caesar's own words of the fore-named Sylla, (who[111] in that only did honestly, to put down his dishonest tyranny,) *literas nescivit,*[112] as if want of learning[113] caused him to do well. He meant it not by poetry, which not content with earthly plagues, deviseth new punishments in hell for tyrants: nor yet by philosophy, which teacheth *occidendos esse,*[114] but no doubt by skill in history: for that indeed can afford you Cypselus, Periander, Phalaris, Dionysius, and I know not how many more of the same kennel,[115] that speed well enough in their abominable unjustice or usurpation. I conclude therefore, that he excelleth history, not only in furnishing the mind with knowledge, but in setting it forward, to that which deserveth to be called and accounted good: which setting forward, and moving to well doing, indeed setteth the laurel crown upon the poet as victorious, not only of the historian, but over the philosopher: howsoever in teaching it may be questionable.[116]

For suppose it be granted (that which I suppose with great reason may be denied) that the philosopher in respect of his methodical proceeding, doth teach more perfectly than the poet: yet do I think, that no man is so much *philophilosophos,*[117] as to compare the philosopher in moving, with the poet.

And that moving is of a higher degree than teaching, it

109 **Sylla and Marius** whose political rivalries ca. 100 B.C. caused unrest and destruction for twenty years. Both died of natural causes. 110 **Pompey and Cicero** both left public life after the battle of Pharsalia (48 B.C.). Pompey fled to Egypt, where he was killed. Cicero, five years later, was sentenced to death by the triumvirate. 111 **who** Caesar **his** Sylla's: after Sylla's death the young Caesar opposed the heirs of Sylla's policies. 112 **literas nescivit** did not know his alphabet. 113 **want of learning** Sylla's. **him** Caesar. **it** Caesar's learning. 114 **occidendos esse** [Tyrants] must be killed. 115 **kennel** pack of dogs. 116 **questionable** arguable. 117 **philophilosophos** lover of philosophers.

may by this appear: that it is well nigh the cause and the effect of teaching. For who will be taught, if he be not moved with desire to be taught? and what so much good doth that teaching bring forth (I speak still of moral doctrine), as that it moveth one to do that which it doth teach? for as Aristotle saith, it is not *gnosis*, but *praxis*[118] must be the fruit. And how *praxis* cannot be, without being moved to practice, it is no hard matter to consider.

The philosopher showeth you the way, he informeth you of the particularities, as well of the tediousness of the way, as of the pleasant lodging you shall have when your journey is ended, as of the many by-turnings that may divert you from your way. But this is to no man but to him that will read him, and read him with attentive studious painfulness.[119] Which constant desire, whosoever hath in him, hath already past half the hardness of the way, and therefore is beholding to the philosopher but for the other half. Nay truly, learned men have learnedly thought, that where once reason hath so much over-mastered passion, as that the mind hath a free desire to do well, the inward light each mind hath in itself, is as good as a philosopher's book; seeing in nature[120] we know it is well, to do well, and what is well, and what is evil, although not in the words of art, which philosophers bestow upon us. For out of natural conceit,[121] the philosophers drew it; but to be moved to do that which we know, or to be moved with desire to know, *hoc opus: hic labor est.*[122]

Now therein of all sciences (I speak still of human, and according to the human conceits) is our poet the monarch. For he doth not only show the way, but giveth so sweet a prospect into the way, as will entice any man to enter into it. Nay, he doth, as if your journey should lie through a fair vineyard, at the first give you a cluster of grapes: that full of that taste, you may long to pass further. He beginneth not with obscure definitions, which must blur the mar-

---

[118] **gnosis . . . praxis** knowing . . . doing.   [119] **with . . . painfulness** painstakingly.   [120] **seeing in nature** considering that by nature.   [121] **conceit** natural understanding (opposed to "words of art").   [122] **hoc . . . est** *Aeneid*, VI, 129: "This is the task, this is the toil."

gent with interpretations, and load the memory with doubt-fulness: but he cometh to you with words set in delightful proportion, either accompanied with, or prepared for the well enchanting skill of music; and with a tale forsooth he cometh unto you: with a tale which holdeth children from play, and old men from the chimney corner. And pretend-ing no more, doth intend the winning of the mind from wickedness to virtue: even as the child is often brought to take most wholesome things, by hiding them in such other as have a pleasant taste: which if one should begin to tell them, the nature of aloes, or rhubarb they should receive, would sooner take their physic at their ears, than at their mouth. So is it in men (most of which are childish in the best things, till they be cradled in their graves,) glad they will be to hear the tales of Hercules, Achilles, Cyrus, and Aeneas: and hearing them, must needs hear the right de-scription of wisdom, valor, and justice; which, if they had been barely, that is to say, philosophically set out, they would swear they be brought to school again.

That imitation whereof poetry is, hath the most con-veniency[123] to Nature of all other, insomuch, that as Aris-totle saith, those things which in themselves are horrible, as cruel battles, unnatural monsters, are made in poetical imitation delightful. Truly, I have known men, that even with reading *Amadis de Gaule*,[124] (which God knoweth wanteth much of a perfect poesy) have found their hearts moved to the exercise of courtesy, liberality, and especially courage.

Who readeth Aeneas carrying old Anchises on his back, that wisheth not it were his fortune to perform so excellent an act? Whom do not the words of Turnus[125] move? (the tale of Turnus, having planted his image in the imagi-nation,)

Fugientem haec terra videbit?
Usque adeone mori miserum est?

---

[123] **conveniency** fitness. [124] **Amadis de Gaule** late medieval romance. [125] **Turnus** *Aeneid*, XII, 645–646, forseeing his own death and defeat: "Shall this land see Turnus in flight? Is death indeed so sad?"

Where the philosophers, as they scorn to delight, so must
they be content little to move: saving wrangling, whether
Virtue be the chief, or the only good: whether the contemplative, or the active life do excell: which Plato and
Boethius well knew, and therefore made mistress philosophy, very often borrow the masking raiment of poesy. For
even those hard hearted evil men, who think virtue a school
name, and know no other good, but *indulgere genio*,[126] and
therefore despise the austere admonitions of the philosopher, and feel not the inward reason they stand upon; yet
will be content to be delighted: which is all, the good fellow[127] poet seemeth to promise: and so steal to see the
form of goodness (which seen they cannot but love) ere
themselves be aware, as if they took a medicine of cherries.
Infinite proofs of the strange effects of this poetical invention might be alleged, only two shall serve, which are so
often remembered, as I think all men know them.

The one of Menenius Agrippa, who when the whole
people of Rome had resolutely divided themselves from the
Senate, with apparent show of utter ruin: though he were
(for that time) an excellent orator, came not among them,
upon trust of figurative speeches[128] or cunning insinuations: and much less, with far-fet maxims of philosophy,
which (especially if they were Platonic) they must have
learned geometry before they could well have conceived:
but forsooth he behaves himself, like a homely, and familiar
poet. He telleth them a tale, that there was a time, when all
the parts of the body made a mutinous conspiracy against
the belly, which they thought devoured the fruits of each
other's labor: they concluded they would let so unprofitable
a spender starve. In the end, to be short, (for the tale is
notorious, and as notorious that it was a tale,) with punish-
ing the belly, they plagued themselves. This applied by him,
wrought such effect in the people, as I never read, that ever
words brought forth but then, so sudden and so good an
alteration: for upon reasonable conditions, a perfect recon-

---

[126] **indulgere genio** to follow one's own devices.   [127] **good fellow** also,
thief.   [128] **figurative speeches** i.e., rhetorical figures.

cilement ensued. The other is of Nathan the prophet, who when the holy David had so far forsaken God, as to confirm adultery with murther: when he was to do the tenderest office of a friend, in laying his own shame before his eyes, sent by God to call again so chosen a servant: how doth he it? but by telling of a man, whose beloved lamb was ungratefully taken from his bosom: the application most divinely true, but the discourse itself, feigned: which made David, (I speak of the second and instrumental cause) as in a glass, to see his own filthiness, as that heavenly psalm of mercy[129] well testifieth.

By these therefore examples and reasons, I think it may be manifest, that the poet with that same hand of delight, doth draw the mind more effectually than any other art doth, and so a conclusion not unfitly ensueth: that as virtue is the most excellent resting place for all worldly learning to make his end of: so poetry, being the most familiar to teach it, and most princely to move towards it, in the most excellent work, is the most excellent workman. But I am content, not only to decipher him by his works, (although works, in commendation or dispraise, must ever hold an high authority) but more narrowly will examine his parts: so that (as in a man) though all together may carry a presence full of majesty and beauty, perchance in some one defectious piece, we may find a blemish: now in his parts, kinds, or species (as you list to term them) it is to be noted, that some poesies have coupled together two or three kinds, as tragical and comical, whereupon is risen, the tragi-comical. Some in the like manner have mingled prose and verse, as Sanazzar[130] and Boethius. Some have mingled matters heroical and pastoral. But that cometh all to one in this question, for if severed they be good, the conjunction cannot be hurtful. Therefore perchance forgetting some, and leaving some as needless to be remembered, it shall not be amiss in a word to cite the special

---

[129] **psalm of mercy** Psalm 51.   [130] **Sanazzar** Jacopo Sannazaro (1455–1530), who mingled prose and verse in his *Arcadia,* one of the models for Sidney's pastoral romance.

kinds, to see what faults may be found in the right use of them.

Is it then the pastoral poem which is misliked? (for perchance, where the hedge is lowest,[131] they will soonest leap over.) Is the poor pipe disdained, which sometime out of Meliboeus' mouth, can show the misery of people, under hard lords, or ravening soldiers? And again, by Tityrus,[132] what blessedness is derived to them that lie lowest from the goodness of them that sit highest? Sometimes, under the pretty tales of wolves and sheep, can include the whole considerations of wrong doing and patience. Sometimes show, that contention for trifles, can get but a trifling victory. Where perchance a man may see, that even Alexander and Darius, when they strave who should be cock of this world's dunghill, the benefit they got, was, that the afterlivers may say,

> *Haec memini et victum frustra contendere Thirsin:*
> *Ex illo Coridon, Coridon est tempore nobis.*[133]

Or is it the lamenting elegiac, which in a kind heart would move rather pity than blame, who bewails with the great philosopher Heraclitus, the weakness of mankind, and the wretchedness of the world: who[134] surely is to be praised, either for compassionate accompanying just causes of lamentation, or for rightly painting out how weak be the passions of woefulness. Is it the bitter, but wholesome iambic,[135] which rubs the galled mind, in making shame the trumpet of villany, with bold and open crying out against naughtiness? Or the satiric, who

> *omne vafer vitium ridenti tangit amico?*

Who sportingly never leaveth, until he make a man laugh

---

[131] **lowest** pastoral considered as having the humblest or lowest style. [132] **Meliboeus' . . . Tityrus** in Virgil's first eclogue. Meliboeus laments the seizure of his land and cattle, while Tityrus is grateful for having his land protected by the emperor. [133] **Haec . . . nobis** Virgil, *Ecl.* VII, after a singing contest between Thyrsis and Corydon: "This I remember, and how Thyrsis, vanquished, strove in vain. From that day it is Corydon, Corydon with us." [134] **who** the elegiac. [135] **iambic** a variety of satiric poem which makes direct attacks.

at folly, and at length ashamed, to laugh at himself: which he cannot avoid, without avoiding the folly. Who while

circum praecordia ludit,[136]

giveth us to feel, how many headaches a passionate life bringeth us to. How, when all is done,

Est Ulubris, animus si nos non deficit aequus.[137]

No, perchance it is the comic, whom naughty play-makers and stage-keepers, have justly made odious. To the argument of abuse, I will answer after. Only thus much now is to be said, that the comedy is an imitation of the common errors of our life, which he representeth, in the most ridiculous and scornful sort that may be. So as it is impossible, that any beholder can be content to be such a one.

Now, as in geometry, the oblique must be known as well as the right: and in arithmetic, the odd as well as the even, so in the actions of our life, who seeth not the filthiness of evil, wanteth a great foil to perceive the beauty of virtue. This doth the comedy handle so in our private and domestical matters, as with hearing it, we get as it were an experience, what is to be looked for of a niggardly Demea: of a crafty Davus: of a flattering Gnatho: of a vainglorious Thraso:[138] and not only to know what effects are to be expected, but to know who be such, by the signifying badge given them by the comedian.[139] And little reason hath any man to say, that men learn evil by seeing it so set out: sith as I said before, there is no man living, but by the force truth hath in nature, no sooner seeth these men play their parts, but wisheth them in *pistrinum*:[140] although perchance the sack of his own faults, lie so behind his back, that he seeth not himself dance the same measure: whereto, yet nothing can more open his eyes, than to find his own actions contemptibly set forth. So that the right use of

---

[136] omne . . . ludit Persius on Horatian satire: "The subtle [Horace] probes every fault of his smiling friend, and once inside, plays around his heart." [137] Est . . . aequus Horace, *Epistles*, I, xi: "Even in Ulubrae [happiness is to be found] if an equiable mind doesn't fail us." [138] Demea . . . Thraso from Terence's comedies. [139] comedian author of comedy. [140] pistrinum a mill where Roman slaves were sent for punishment.

comedy will (I think) by no body be blamed, and much less of the high and excellent tragedy, that openeth the greatest wounds, and showeth forth the ulcers, that are covered with tissue: that maketh kings fear to be tyrants, and tyrants manifest their tyrannical humors; that with stirring the affects[141] of admiration and commiseration, teacheth the uncertainty of this world, and upon how weak foundations gilden roofs are builded. That maketh us know,

> *Qui sceptra saevus duro imperio regit,*
> *Timet timentes, metus in auctorem redit.*[142]

But how much it can move, Plutarch yieldeth a notable testimony, of the abominable tyrant, Alexander Pheraeus; from whose eyes, a tragedy well made, and represented, drew abundance of tears: who without all pity, had murthered infinite numbers, and some of his own blood. So as he, that was not ashamed to make matters for tragedies, yet could not resist the sweet violence of a tragedy.

And if it wrought no further good in him, it was, that he in despite of himself, withdrew himself from hearkening to that, which might mollify his hardened heart. But it is not the tragedy they do mislike: for it were too absurd to cast out so excellent a representation of whatsoever is most worthy to be learned. Is it the lyric that most displeaseth, who with his tuned lyre, and well accorded[143] voice, giveth praise, the reward of virtue, to virtuous acts? who gives moral precepts, and natural problems,[144] who sometimes raiseth up his voice to the height of the heavens, in singing the lauds of the immortal God. Certainly I must confess my own barbarousness, I never heard the old song[145] of Percy and Douglas, that I found not my heart moved more than with a trumpet: and yet is it sung but by some blind crowder,[146] with no rougher voice, than rude style: which

---

[141] **affects** feelings.   [142] **Qui . . . redit** Seneca, *Oedipus*, III, 705–706: "The fierce ruler who governs his dominions harshly fears those who fear him; fear returns to the author."   [143] **accorded** harmonized.   [144] **problems** for logical analysis (as contrasted with "precepts").   [145] **old song** probably the ballad of Chevy Chase.   [146] **crowder** player of the "crowd," an ancient Celtic fiddle.

being so evil apparelled in the dust and cobwebs of that uncivil age, what would it work trimmed in the gorgeous eloquence of Pindar? In Hungary I have seen it the manner at all feasts, and other such meetings, to have songs of their ancestors' valor; which that right soldier-like nation think the chiefest kindlers of brave courage. The incomparable Lacedemonians, did not only carry that kind of music ever with them to the field, but even at home, as such songs were made, so were they all content to be the singers of them, when the lusty men were to tell what they did, the old men, what they had done, and the young men what they would do. And where a man may say, that Pindar many times praiseth highly victories of small moment, matters rather of sport[147] than virtue: as it may be answered, it was the fault of the poet, and not of the poetry; so indeed the chief fault was in the time and custom of the Greeks, who set those toys at so high a price, that Phillip of Macedon reckoned a horserace won at Olympus, among his three fearful felicities.[148] But as the unimitable Pindar often did, so is that kind[149] most capable and most fit, to awake the thoughts from the sleep of idleness, to embrace honorable enterprises.

There rests the heroical, whose very name (I think) should daunt all back-biters; for by what conceit can a tongue be directed to speak evil of that, which draweth with it, no less champions than Achilles, Cyrus, Aeneas, Turnus, Tydeus,[150] and Rinaldo?[151] who doth not only teach and move to a truth, but teacheth and moveth to the most high and excellent truth. Who maketh magnanimity and justice shine, throughout all misty fearfulness and foggy desires. Who, if the saying of Plato and Tully be true, that who could see Virtue, would be wonderfully ravished with the love of her beauty: this man sets her out to make her more lovely in her holiday apparel, to the eye of any that will deign, not to disdain, until they understand. But if

---

[147] **sport** i.e., in the Olympic games.   [148] **three . . . felicities** along with news of the birth of his son Alexander and of a military victory.   [149] **that kind** the lyric.   [150] **Tydeus** in Statius' *Thebais*.   [151] **Rinaldo** in Ariosto's *Orlando Furioso* and *Tasso's Gerusalemme Liberata*.

anything be already said in the defense of sweet poetry, all
concurreth to the maintaining the heroical, which is not
only a kind, but the best, and most accomplished kind of
poetry. For as the image of each action stirreth and in-
structeth the mind, so the lofty image of such worthies,
most inflameth the mind with desire to be worthy, and informs with counsel how to be worthy. Only let Aeneas be
worn in the tablet of your memory, how he governeth himself in the ruin of his country, in the preserving his old
father, and carrying away his religious ceremonies;[152] in
obeying the god's commandment to leave Dido, though not
only all passionate kindness, but even the human consideration of virtuous gratefulness, would have craved other of
him. How in storms, how in sports, how in war, how in
peace, how a fugitive, how victorious, how besieged, how
besieging, how to strangers, how to allies, how to enemies,
how to his own: lastly, how in his inward self, and how in
his outward government. And I think, in a mind not preju-
diced with a prejudicating humor, he will be found in
excellency fruitful: yea, even as Horace saith

melius Chrisippo et Crantore.[153]

But truly I imagine, it falleth out with these poetwhip-
pers, as with some good women, who often are sick, but
in faith they cannot tell where. So the name of poetry is
odious to them, but neither his cause nor effects, neither
the sum that contains him, nor the particularities descend-
ing from him, give any fast[154] handle to their carping
dispraise.

Sith then poetry is of all human learning the most ancient, and of most fatherly antiquity, as from whence other
learnings have taken their beginnings: sith it is so universal,
that no learned nation doth despise it, nor no barbarous
nation is without it: sith both Roman and Greek gave divine names unto it: the one of prophesying, the other of

---

[152] **ceremonies** ceremonial objects.   [153] **melius . . . Crantore** praising
Homer as a better teacher than Chrysippus, early Stoic philosopher, and
Crantor, early commentator on Plato.   [154] **fast** firm.

making. And that indeed, that name of making is fit for
him; considering, that whereas other arts retain themselves
within their subject, and receive as it were, their being from
it: the poet only, bringeth his own stuff, and doth not learn
a conceit out of a matter, but maketh matter for a conceit:
Sith neither his description, nor his end, containeth any
evil, the thing described cannot be evil: Sith his effects be
so good as to teach goodness and to delight the learners:
Sith therein (namely in moral doctrine, the chief of all
knowledges) he doth not only far pass the historian, but
for instructing, is well nigh comparable to the philosopher:
and for moving, leaves him behind him: Sith the holy scripture (wherein there is no uncleanness) hath whole parts in
it poetical. And that even our Savior Christ, vouchsafed
to use the flowers of it: Sith all his kinds are not only in
their united forms, but in their severed dissections fully
commendable, I think (and think I think rightly) the laurel
crown, appointed for triumphing captains, doth worthily
(of all other learnings) honor the poet's triumph. But because we have ears as well as tongues, and that the lightest
reasons that may be, will seem to weigh greatly, if nothing
be put in the counterbalance: let us hear, and as well as we
can, ponder what objections may be made against this art,
which may be worthy, either of yielding, or answering.

First truly I note, not only in these *mysomousoi*[155] poet-
haters, but in all that kind of people, who seek a praise by
dispraising others, that they do prodigally spend a great
many wandering words, in quips, and scoffs; carping and
taunting at each thing, which by stirring the spleen, may
stay the brain from a through[156]-beholding the worthiness
of the subject.

Those kind of objections, as they are full of very idle
easiness, sith there is nothing of so sacred a majesty, but
that an itching tongue may rub itself upon it: so deserve
they no other answer, but instead of laughing at the jest,
to laugh at the jester. We know a playing wit, can praise
the discretion of an ass; the comfortableness of being in

[155] **mysomousoi** those who hate the Muses (Sidney's coinage).
[156] **through** thorough.

debt, and the jolly commodity[157] of being sick of the plague. So of the contrary side, if we will turn Ovid's verse,

Ut lateat virtus proximitate mali,[158]

that good lie hid in nearness of the evil: Agrippa will be as merry in showing the vanity of science, as Erasmus[159] was in commending of folly. Neither shall any man or matter escape some touch of these smiling railers. But for Erasmus and Agrippa, they had another foundation than the superficial part would promise. Marry, these other pleasant fault-finders, who will correct the verb, before they understand the noun, and confute others' knowledge before they confirm their own: I would have them only remember, that scoffing cometh not of wisdom. So as the best title in true English they get with their merriments, is to be called good fools: for so have our grave fore-fathers ever termed that humorous kind of jesters: but that which giveth greatest scope to their scorning humors, is rhyming and versing. It is already said (and as I think, truly said) it is not rhyming and versing, that maketh poesy. One may be a poet without versing, and a versifier without poetry. But yet, presuppose it were inseparable (as indeed it seemeth Scaliger judgeth) truly it were an inseparable commendation. For if *oratio,* next to *ratio,* speech next to reason, be the greatest gift bestowed upon mortality: that can not be praiseless, which doth most polish that blessing of speech, which considers each word, not only (as a man may say) by his forcible quality, but by his best measured quantity, carrying even in themselves, a harmony: (without[160] perchance number, measure, order, proportion, be in our time grown odious). But lay aside the just praise it hath, by being the only fit speech for music (music, I say, the most divine striker of the senses), thus much is undoubtedly true, that if reading be foolish, without remembering, memory being the only treasurer of knowledge,

---

[157] **commodity** advantage. [158] Ut . . . **mali** so that any virtue may be concealed by connecting it to evil things. [159] **Agrippa . . . Erasmus** who both might be wrongly construed by enemies of knowledge as satirizing true learning rather than its abuses (Cornelius Agrippa in his *Vanity of the Arts,* Erasmus in *In Praise of Folly*). [160] **without** unless.

those words which are fittest for memory, are likewise most convenient for knowledge.

Now, that verse far exceedeth prose in the knitting up of the memory, the reason is manifest. The words (besides their delight which hath a great affinity to memory), being so set, as one word cannot be lost, but the whole work fails: which accuseth itself,[161] calleth the remembrance back to itself, and so most strongly confirmeth it; besides, one word so as it were begetting another, as be it in rhyme or measured verse, by the former a man shall have a near guess to the follower: lastly, even they that have taught the art of memory, have showed nothing so apt for it, as a certain room divided into many places well and throughly known. Now, that hath the verse in effect perfectly: every word having his natural seat, which seat, must needs make the words remembered. But what needeth more in a thing so known to all men? who is it that ever was a scholar, that doth not carry away some verses of Virgil, Horace, or Cato, which in his youth he learned, and even to his old age serve him for hourly lessons? as

Percontatorem fugito, nam garrulus idem est.[162]

Dum sibi quisque placet, credula turba sumus.[163]

But the fitness it hath for memory, is notably proved by all delivery of arts: wherein for the most part, from grammar, to logic, mathematic, physic, and the rest, the rules chiefly necessary to be borne away, are compiled in verses. So that, verse being in itself sweet and orderly, and being best for memory, the only handle of knowledge, it must be in jest that any man can speak against it. Now then go we to the most important imputations laid to the poor poets, for ought I can yet learn, they are these, first, that there being many other more fruitful knowledges, a man might better spend his time in them, than in this. Secondly, that it is the mother of lies. Thirdly, that it is the nurse of abuse,

---

[161] **accuseth itself** i.e., by breaking meter. [162] **Percontatorem . . . est** Horace, *Epistles*, I, xviii, 69: "Flee the inquisitive man; for he is a prattler." [163] **Dum . . . sumus** Ovid, *Remedium Amoris*, 686: "While each man pleases himself we are a gullible crowd."

infecting us with many pestilent desires: with a siren's sweetness, drawing the mind to the serpent's tail of sinful fancy. And herein especially, comedies give the largest field to ear,[164] as Chaucer saith: how both in other nations and in ours, before poets did soften us, we were full of courage, given to martial exercises; the pillars of manlike liberty, and not lulled asleep in shady idleness with poets' pastimes. And lastly, and chiefly, they cry out with an open mouth, as if they outshot Robin Hood, that Plato banished them out of his commonwealth. Truly, this is much, if there be much truth in it. First to the first:[165] that a man might better spend his time, is a reason indeed: but it doth (as they say) but *petere principium*:[166] for if it be as I affirm, that no learning is so good, as that which teacheth and moveth to virtue; and that none can both teach and move thereto so much as poetry: then is the conclusion manifest, that ink and paper cannot be to a more profitable purpose employed. And certainly, though a man should grant their first assumption, it should follow (methinks) very unwillingly, that good is not good, because better is better. But I still and utterly deny, that there is sprung out of earth a more fruitful knowledge. To the second therefore, that they should be the principal liars; I answer paradoxically, but truly, I think truly; that of all writers under the sun, the poet is the least liar: and though he would, as a poet can scarcely be a liar, the astronomer, with his cousin the geometrician, can hardly escape, when they take upon them to measure the height of the stars.

How often, think you, do the physicians lie, when they aver things, good for sicknesses, which afterwards send Charon[167] a great number of souls drowned in a potion before they come to his ferry. And no less of the rest, which take upon them to affirm. Now, for the poet, he nothing affirms, and therefore never lieth. For, as I take it, to lie, is to affirm that to be true which is false. So as the other artists,[168] and especially the historian, affirming many things, can in the cloudy knowledge of mankind, hardly

---

[164] **ear** plough.   [165] **first** i.e., the first objection.   [166] **petere principium** beg the question.   [167] **Charon** ferryman of the river Styx.   [168] **artists** i.e., the liberal arts.

escape from many lies. But the poet (as I said before) never affirmeth. The poet never maketh any circles[169] about your imagination, to conjure you to believe for true what he writes. He citeth not authorities of other histories, but even for his entry,[170] calleth the sweet Muses to inspire into him a good invention: in troth, not laboring to tell you what is, or is not, but what should or should not be: and therefore, though he recount things not true, yet because he telleth them not for true, he lieth not, without we will say, that Nathan[171] lied in his speech, before alleged to David. Which as a wicked man durst scarce say, so think I, none so simple would say, that Aesop lied in the tales of his beasts: for who thinks that Aesop writ it for actually true, were well worthy to have his name chronicled among the beasts he writeth of.

What child is there, that coming to a play, and seeing Thebes written in great letters upon an old door, doth believe that it is Thebes? If then, a man can arrive, at that child's age, to know that the poet's persons and doings, are but pictures what should be, and not stories what have been, they will never give the lie, to things not affirmatively, but allegorically, and figuratively written. And therefore, as in history, looking for truth, they go away full fraught with falsehood: so in poesy, looking for fiction, they shall use the narration, but as an imaginative groundplot of a profitable invention.

But hereto is replied, that the poets give names to men they write of, which argueth a conceit of an actual truth, and so, not being true, proves a falsehood. And doth the lawyer lie then, when under the names of *John a stile* and *John a noakes,* he puts his case? But that is easily answered. Their naming of men, is but to make their picture the more lively, and not to build any history: painting men, they cannot leave men nameless. We see we cannot play at chess, but that we must give names to our chessmen; and yet methinks, he were a very partial champion of truth, that would say we lied, for giving a piece of wood, the

---

[169] **circles** that mark the bounds of a magician's power. [170] **entry** opening. [171] **Nathan** See p. 239.

reverend title of a bishop. The poet nameth Cyrus or Aeneas, no other way, than to show what men of their fames, fortunes, and estates, should do.

Their third is, how much it abuseth men's wit, training it to wanton sinfulness, and lustful love: for indeed that is the principal, if not the only abuse I can hear alleged. They say, the comedies rather teach, than reprehend, amorous conceits. They say, the lyric is larded with passionate sonnets. The elegiac, weeps the want of his mistress. And that even to the heroical, Cupid hath ambitiously climbed. Alas Love, I would, thou couldest as well defend thyself, as thou canst offend others. I would those, on whom thou dost attend, could either put thee away, or yield good reason, why they keep thee. But grant love of beauty, to be a beastly fault, (although it be very hard, sith only man, and no beast, hath that gift, to discern beauty). Grant, that lovely name of Love, to deserve all hateful reproaches: (although even some of my masters the philosophers, spent a good deal of their lamp-oil, in setting forth the excellency of it.) Grant, I say, whatsoever they will have granted; that not only love, but lust, but vanity, but (if they list) scurrility, possesseth many leaves of the poets' books: yet think I, when this is granted, they will find, their sentence may with good manners, put the last words foremost: and not say, that poetry abuseth man's wit, but that, man's wit abuseth poetry.

For I will not deny, but that man's wit may make poesy, which should be *eikastike* (which some learned have defined, figuring forth good things,) to be *phantastike*:[172] which doth contrariwise, infect the fancy with unworthy objects. As the painter, that should give to the eye, either some excellent perspective, or some fine picture, fit for building or fortification: or containing in it some notable example, as Abraham, sacrificing his son Isaac, Judith killing Holofernes, David fighting with Goliath, may leave those, and please an ill-pleased[173] eye, with wanton shows of better hidden matters. But what, shall the abuse of a

---

[172] **eikastike . . . phantastike** imitative . . . fanciful or fantastic. [173] **ill-pleased** pleased by evil.

thing, make the right use odious? Nay truly, though I yield, that poesy may not only be abused, but that being abused, by the reason of his sweet charming force, it can do more hurt than any other army of words: yet shall it be so far from concluding, that the abuse, should give reproach to the abused, that contrariwise it is a good reason, that whatsoever being abused, doth most harm, being rightly used (and upon the right use each thing conceiveth his title) doth most good.

Do we not see the skill of physic (the best rampire[174] to our often-assaulted bodies), being abused, teach poison the most violent destroyer? Doth not knowledge of law, whose end is, to even and right all things, being abused, grow the crooked fosterer of horrible injuries? Doth not (to go to the highest) God's word abused, breed heresy? and his Name abused, become blasphemy? Truly, a needle cannot do much hurt, and as truly (with leave of ladies be it spoken) it cannot do much good. With a sword, thou mayst kill thy father, and with a sword thou mayst defend thy prince and country. So that, as in their calling poets the fathers of lies, they say nothing: so in this their argument of abuse, they prove the commendation.

They allege herewith, that before poets began to be in price,[175] our nation hath set their hearts' delight upon action, and not upon imagination: rather doing things worthy to be written, than writing things fit to be done. What that before time was, I think scarcely Sphinx can tell: sith no memory is so ancient, that hath the precedence of poetry. And certain it is, that in our plainest homeliness, yet never was the Albion Nation without poetry. Marry, this argument, though it be levelled against poetry, yet is it indeed, a chain-shot[176] against all learning, or bookishness, as they commonly term it. Of such mind were certain Goths, of whom it is written, that having in the spoil of a famous city,[177] taken a fair library; one hangman[178] (belike fit to execute the fruits of their wits) who had murthered a great

---

[174] **rampire** rampart.   [175] **in price** esteemed.   [176] **chain-shot** discharge of two cannonballs linked by a chain.   [177] **famous city** Athens, sacked in 267 A.D.   [178] **hangman** villain.

number of bodies, would have set fire on it: no said another, very gravely, take heed what you do, for while they are busy about these toys, we shall with more leisure conquer their countries.

This indeed is the ordinary doctrine of ignorance, and many words sometimes I have heard spent in it; but because this reason is generally against all learning, as well as poetry; or rather, all learning but poetry: because it were too large a digression, to handle, or at least, too superfluous: (sith it is manifest, that all government of action, is to be gotten by knowledge, and knowledge best, by gathering many knowledges, which is, reading,) I only with Horace, to him that is of that opinion,

Jubeo stultum esse libenter:[179]

for as for poetry itself, it is the freest from this objection. For poetry is the companion of camps.

I dare undertake, *Orlando Furioso,* or honest King Arthur, will never displease a soldier: but the quiddity[180] of *ens* and *prima materia,*[181] will hardly agree with a corslet:[182] and therefore, as I said in the beginning, even Turks and Tartars are delighted with poets. Homer a Greek, flourished, before Greece flourished. And if to a slight conjecture, a conjecture may be opposed: truly it may seem, that as by him, their learned men, took almost their first light of knowledge, so their active men, received their first motions of courage. Only Alexander's example[183] may serve, who by Plutarch is accounted of such virtue, that Fortune was not his guide, but his footstool: whose acts speak for him, though Plutarch did not:[184] indeed, the phoenix of warlike princes. This Alexander left his schoolmaster, living Aristotle, behind him, but took dead Homer with him: he put the philosopher Calisthenes to death, for his seeming philosophical, indeed mutinous stubbornness.

---

[179] **Iubeo . . . libenter** bid him be a fool if he wishes.   [180] **quiddity** essential nature.   [181] **ens . . . prima materia** in scholastic philosophy, "pure being" and "first matter."   [182] **corslet** armor covering the body.   [183] **Only . . . example** Alexander's example alone.   [184] **though . . . not** even if Plutarch had not.

But the chief thing he ever was heard to wish for, was, that Homer had been alive. He well found, he received more bravery of mind, by the pattern of Achilles, than by hearing the definition of fortitude: and therefore, if Cato misliked Fulvius, for carrying Ennius[185] with him to the field, it may be answered, that if Cato misliked it, the noble Fulvius liked it, or else he had not done it: for it was not the excellent Cato Uticensis, (whose authority I would much more have reverenced), but it was the former:[186] in truth, a bitter punisher of faults, but else, a man that had never well sacrificed to the Graces. He misliked and cried out upon all Greek learning, and yet being eighty years old, began to learn it. Belike, fearing that Pluto[187] understood not Latin. Indeed, the Roman laws allowed, no person to be carried to the wars, but he that was in the soldier's role: and therefore, though Cato misliked his unmustered person,[188] he misliked not his work. And if he had, Scipio Nasica, judged by common consent the best Roman, loved him. Both the other Scipio brothers, who had by their virtues[189] no less surnames, than of Asia and Africa, so loved him,[190] that they caused his body to be buried in their sepulcher. So as Cato, his authority being but against his person, and that answered, with so far greater than himself, is herein of no validity. But now indeed my burthen is great; now Plato[191] his name is laid upon me, whom I must confess, of all philosophers, I have ever esteemed most worthy of reverence, and with great reason: sith of all philosophers, he is the most poetical. Yet if he will defile the fountain, out of which his flowing streams have proceeded, let us boldly examine with what reasons he did it. First truly, a man might maliciously object, that Plato, being a philosopher, was a natural enemy of poets: for indeed, after the philosophers, had picked out of the sweet mysteries of poetry, the right discerning true points of knowledge, they forth-

---

[185] **Ennius** earliest of the Roman poets, accompanied the consul M. Fulvius Nobilior to battle in Greece. [186] **the former** Cato the Censor, as distinguished from his great-grandson Cato of Utica. [187] **Pluto** god of the underworld. [188] **his . . . person** i.e., Ennius, not enlisted in the army. [189] **by their virtues** victories over Hannibal in Africa and Antiochus in Asia. [190] **him** Ennius. [191] **Plato** see p. 217.

with putting it in method,[192] and making a school art of
that which the poets did only teach, by a divine delightfulness, beginning to spurn at their guides, like ungrateful
prentices, were not content to set up shops for themselves,
but sought by all means to discredit their masters. Which
by the force of delight being barred them, the less they
could overthrow them, the more they hated them. For
indeed, they found for Homer, seven cities strove who
should have him for their citizen: where many cities banished philosophers, as not fit members to live among them.
For only repeating certain of Euripides' verses, many Athenians had their lives saved of the Syracusians: when the
Athenians themselves thought many philosophers unworthy
to live.

Certain poets, as Simonides, and Pindarus, had so pre-
vailed with Hiero the first, that of a tyrant they made him
a just king, where Plato could do so little with Dionysius,[193]
that he himself, of a philosopher, was made a slave. But
who should do thus,[194] I confess, should requite the objections made against poets, with like cavillation against philosophers, as likewise one should do, that should bid one
read *Phaedrus,* or *Symposium* in Plato, or the discourse
of love in Plutarch, and see whether any poet do authorize
abominable filthiness, as they do. Again, a man might ask
out of what common-wealth Plato did banish them? in-
sooth, thence where he himself alloweth community of
women:[195] so as belike, this banishment grew not for
effeminate wantonness, sith little should poetical sonnets
be hurtful, when a man might have what woman he listed.
But I honor philosophical instructions, and bless the wits
which bred them: so as they be not abused, which is likewise stretched to poetry.

S. Paul himself (who yet for the credit of poets allegeth[196] twice two poets,[197] and one of them by the name

[192] **method** systematic procedure for arranging philosophical topics.
[193] **Dionysius** Syracusan tyrant, said to have been instrumental in giving
Plato into slavery. [194] **thus** i.e., "maliciously object," p. 253. [195] **community of women** in *Republic,* V. [196] **allegeth** quotes. [197] **twice two
poets** St. Paul is said to have drawn upon four Greek poets: Aratus,
Cleanthes, Epimenides, and Menander.

of a prophet) setteth a watch-word[198] upon philosophy, indeed upon the abuse. So doth Plato, upon the abuse, not upon poetry. Plato found fault, that the poets of his time, filled the world, with wrong opinions of the gods, making light tales of that unspotted essence; and therefore, would not have the youth depraved with such opinions. Herein may much be said, let this suffice: the poets did not induce[199] such opinions, but did imitate those opinions already induced. For all the Greek stories can well testify, that the very[200] religion of that time, stood upon many, and many-fashioned gods, not taught so by the poets, but followed, according to their nature of imitation. Who list, may read in Plutarch the discourses of Isis, and Osiris, of the cause why oracles ceased, of the divine providence: and see, whether the theology of that nation, stood not upon such dreams, which the poets indeed superstitiously observed: and truly (sith they had not the light of Christ) did much better in it than the philosophers, who, shaking off superstition, brought in atheism. Plato therefore, (whose authority I had much rather justly conster,[201] than unjustly resist) meant not in general of poets, in those words of which Julius Scaliger saith, *Qua authoritate barbari quidam atque hispidi abuti velint ad poetas e republica exigendos:*[202] but only meant, to drive out those wrong opinions of the Deity (whereof now, without further law, Christianity hath taken away all the hurtful belief) perchance, (as he thought) nourished by the then esteemed poets. And a man need go no further than to Plato himself, to know his meaning: who in his dialogue called *Ion,* giveth high and rightly divine commendation to poetry. So as Plato, banishing the abuse, not the thing, not banishing it, but giving due honor unto it, shall be our patron, and not our adversary. For indeed I had much rather (sith truly I may do it) show their mistaking of Plato (under whose lion's skin they would make an ass-like braying against poesy) than go about to overthrow his authority, whom the wiser a man is,

---

[198] **watch-word** warning (Colossians 2:8). [199] **induce** introduce. [200] **very** true. [201] **conster** construe. [202] **Qua . . . exigendos** whose authority certain barbarous and crude men wish to use to banish poets from the Republic.

the more just cause he shall find to have in admiration: especially, sith he attributeth unto poesy more than myself do; namely, to be a very inspiring of a divine force, far above man's wit; as in the afore-named dialogue[203] is apparent.

Of the other side, who would show the honors, have[204] been by the best sort of judgements granted them, a whole sea of examples would present themselves. Alexanders, Caesars, Scipios, all favorers of poets. Laelius, called the Roman Socrates, himself a poet: so as part of *Heautontimorumenos* in Terence, was supposed to be made by him. And even the Greek Socrates, whom Apollo confirmed[205] to be the only wise man, is said to have spent part of his old time, in putting Aesop's fables into verses. And therefore, full evil should it become his scholar Plato, to put such words in his master's mouth against poets. But what need more? Aristotle writes the Art of Poesy: and why if it should not be written? Plutarch teacheth the use to be gathered of them, and how if they should not be read? And who reads Plutarch's either history of philosophy, shall find, he trimmeth both their garments with guards[206] of poesy. But I list not to defend poesy, with the help of her underling, historiography. Let it suffice, that it is a fit soil for praise to dwell upon: and what dispraise may set upon it, is either easily overcome, or transformed into just commendation. So that, sith the excellencies of it, may be so easily, and so justly confirmed, and the low-creeping objections so soon trodden down: it not being an art of lies, but of true doctrine: not of effeminateness, but of notable stirring of courage: not of abusing man's wit, but of strengthening man's wit: not banished, but honored by Plato: let us rather plant more laurels, for to engarland our poets' heads, (which honor of being laureate, as besides them, only triumphant captains wear, is a sufficient authority, to show the price they ought to be had in,) than suffer the illfavoring breath of such wrong-speakers, once to blow upon the clear springs of poesy.

[203] **afore-named dialogue** *Ion.* [204] **honors, have** honors which have. [205] **whom ... confirmed** see *Astrophel and Stella*, sonnet 25. [206] **guards** ornamental borders.

But sith I have run so long a career[207] in this matter, methinks, before I give my pen a full stop, it shall be but a little more lost time, to inquire, why England (the mother of excellent minds) should be grown so hard a step-mother to poets, who certainly in wit ought to pass all other: sith all only proceedeth from their wit, being indeed makers of themselves, not takers of others. How can I but exclaim,

Musa, mihi causas memora, quo numine laeso.[208]

Sweet poesy, that hath anciently had kings, emperors, senators, great captains, such, as besides a thousand others, David, Adrian,[209] Sophocles, Germanicus, not only to favor poets, but to be poets. And of our nearer times, can present for her patrons, a Robert,[210] king of Sicil, the great king Francis[211] of France, King James of Scotland. Such cardinals as Bembus, and Bibiena. Such famous preachers and teachers, as Beza and Melancthon. So learned philosophers, as Fracastorius and Scaliger. So great orators, as Pontanus and Muretus. So piercing wits, as George Buchanan. So grave counsellors, as besides many, but before all, that Hospital of France:[212] than whom (I think) that realm never brought forth a more accomplished judgement: more firmly builded upon virtue. I say these, with numbers of others, not only to read others' poesies, but to poetise for others' reading, that poesy thus embraced in all other places, should only find in our time, a hard welcome in England, I think the very earth lamenteth it, and therefore decketh our soil with fewer laurels than it was accustomed. For heretofore, poets have in England also flourished. And which is to be noted, even in those times, when the trumpet of Mars did sound loudest. And now, that an over-faint quietness should seem to strew the house for poets, they are almost in as good reputation, as the mountebanks at

---

[207] **career** course. [208] **Musa . . . laeso** Virgil, *Aeneid*, I, 8: "Muse, tell me the cause, through what offended power . . . ." [209] **Adrian** the Roman emperor Hadrian (117–138 A.D.), himself a writer of verse. [210] **Robert** Robert II of Anjou, patron of Petrarch. [211] **Francis** Francis I (1494–1547), patron of Renaissance literature and art in France. [212] **Hospital of France** Michel de l'Hôpital, chancellor of France from 1560 to 1568.

Venice. Truly even that, as of the one side, it giveth great
praise to poesy, which like Venus (but to better purpose)
had rather be troubled in the net with Mars, than enjoy
the homely quiet of Vulcan: so serves it for a piece of a
reason, why they are less grateful[213] to idle England, which
now can scarce endure the pain of a pen. Upon this, neces-
sarily followeth, that base men, with servile wits undertake
it: who think it enough, if they can be rewarded of the
printer. And so as Epaminondas[214] is said, with the honor
of his virtue, to have made an office, by his exercising it,
which before was contemptible, to become highly re-
spected: so these, no more but setting their names to it,
by their own disgracefulness, disgrace the most graceful
poesy. For now, as if all the Muses were got with child,
to bring forth bastard poets, without any commission, they
do post over the banks of Helicon, till they make the readers more weary than post-horses: while in the meantime,
they

Queis meliore luto finxit praecordia Titan,[215]

are better content, to suppress the out-flowing of their wit,
than by publishing them, to be accounted knights of the
same order. But I, that before ever I durst aspire unto the
dignity, am admitted into the company of the paperblurrers,
do find the very true cause of our wanting estimation, is
want of desert: taking upon us to be poets, in despite of
Pallas.[216] Now wherein we want desert, were a thank-
worthy labor to express: but if I knew, I should have
mended myself. But I, as I never desired the title, so have
I neglected the means to come by it. Only, over-mastered
by some thoughts, I yielded an inky tribute unto them.
Marry, they that delight in poesy itself, should seek to
know what they do, and how they do; and, especially, look
themselves in an unflattering glass of reason, if they be
inclinable unto it. For poesy, must not be drawn by the

---

[213] **grateful** pleasing.   [214] **Epaminondas** Theban general, who, given the
office of *telearch* or sanitation official, transformed it into one command-
ing great respect.   [215] **Queis . . . Titan** adapted from Juvenal, *Satires,*
XIV: "Whose hearts Titan has shaped of better clay."   [216] **in . . . Pallas**
scorning wisdom.

ears, it must be gently led; or, rather, it must lead. Which was partly the cause that made the ancient-learned affirm, it was a divine gift, and no human skill: sith all other knowledges, lie ready for any that hath strength of wit; a poet, no industry can make, if his own genius be not carried unto it: and therefore is it an old proverb, *orator fit, poeta nascitur*.[217] Yet confess I always, that as the fertilest ground must be manured,[218] so must the highest flying wit, have a Daedalus[219] to guide him. That Daedalus, they say, both in this, and in other, hath three wings, to bear itself up into the air of due commendation: that is, art, imitation,[220] and exercise. But these, neither artificial rules, nor imitative patterns, we much cumber ourselves withal. Exercise indeed we do, but that, very fore-backwardly: for where we should exercise to know, we exercise as having known: and so is our brain delivered of much matter, which never was begotten by knowledge. For, there being two principal parts, matter to be expressed by words, and words to express the matter, in neither, we use art or imitation rightly. Our matter is *quodlibet*[221] indeed, though wrongly performing Ovid's verse:

> *Quicquid conabor dicere versus erit:*[222]

never marshalling it into an assured rank, that almost the readers cannot tell where to find themselves.

Chaucer undoubtedly did excellently in his *Troilus and Criseyde;* of whom, truly I know not, whether to marvel more either that he in that misty time, could see so clearly, or that we in this clear age, walk so stumblingly after him. Yet had he great wants, fit to be forgiven, in so reverent antiquity. I account the *Mirror of Magistrates*,[223] meetly

---

[217] **orator . . . nascitur** an orator is made; a poet is born. [218] **manured** cultivated. [219] **Daedalus** traditionally the founder of the arts. Ignoring his advice, Icarus flew too close to the sun; his wax wings melted and he fell. [220] **imitation** following models of earlier writers. [221] **quodlibet** a question proposed for the sake of exercise or argument; here used to characterize random choice of poetic material. [222] **Quicquid . . . erit** whatever I try to say will turn to verse. [223] **Mirror of Magistrates** a collection of tales by several hands dealing with the fall of princes; first published 1559.

furnished of beautiful parts; and in the Earl of Surrey's[224] *Lyrics*, many things tasting of a noble birth, and worthy of a noble mind. The *Shepherds' Calendar*[225] hath much poetry in his eglogues: indeed worthy the reading if I be not deceived. That same framing of his style, to an old rustic language, I dare not allow,[226] sith neither Theocritus in Greek, Virgil in Latin, nor Sanazar[227] in Italian, did affect it. Besides these, do I not remember to have seen but few (to speak boldly) printed, that have poetical sinews in them: for proof whereof, let but most of the verses be put in prose, and then ask the meaning; and it will be found, that one verse did but beget another, without ordering at the first, what should be at the last: which becomes a confused mass of words, with a tingling[228] sound of rhyme, barely accompanied with reason.

Our tragedies, and comedies (not without cause cried out against) observing rules, neither of honest civility, nor of skillful poetry, excepting *Gorboduc*[229] (again, I say, of those that I have seen,) which notwithstanding, as it is full of stately speeches, and well sounding phrases, climbing to the height of Seneca[230] his style, and as full of notable morality, which it doth most delightfully teach; and so obtain the very end of poesy: yet in troth it is very defectious in the circumstances;[231] which grieveth me, because it might not remain as an exact model of all tragedies. For it is faulty both in place, and time, the two necessary companions of all corporal actions. For where the stage should always represent but one place, and the uttermost time presupposed in it, should be, both by Aristotle's precept,

---

[224] **Surrey** whose lyrics and translation of parts of the *Aeneid* were printed in the mid-sixteenth century. [225] **Shepherds' Calendar**, 1569, pastoral poems which Spenser dedicated to Sidney. Criticized for its archaisms and use of dialect. [226] **allow** commend. [227] **Theocritus . . . Sanazar** considered to be the masters of pastoral. [228] **tingling** tinkling. [229] **Gorboduc** by Sackville and Norton, presented first in 1561, dealing with dynastic rivalries and civil war. [230] **Seneca** the Roman dramatist whose ten tragedies were regarded as the models of high tragic style in the Renaissance. [231] **circumstances** the facts connected to an action (time, place, setting); the term is from the vocabulary of logic and rhetoric.

and common reason, but one day: there is both many days, and many places, inartificially[232] imagined.

But if it be so in *Gorboduc,* how much more in all the rest? where you shall have *Asia* of the one side, and *Afric* of the other, and so many other under-kingdoms, that the player, when he cometh in, must ever begin with telling where he is: or else, the tale will not be conceived. Now ye shall have three ladies, walk to gather flowers, and then we must believe the stage to be a garden. By and by, we hear news of shipwrack in the same place, and then we are to blame, if we accept it not for a rock.

Upon the back of that, comes out a hideous monster, with fire and smoke, and then the miserable beholders are bound to take it for a cave. While in the meantime, two armies fly in, represented with four swords and bucklers, and then what hard heart will not receive it for a pitched field? Now, of time they are much more liberal, for ordinary it is that two young princes fall in love. After many traverses,[233] she is got with child, delivered of a fair boy, he is lost, groweth a man, falls in love, and is ready to get another child, and all this in two hours space: which how absurd it is in sense, even sense may imagine, and art hath taught, and all ancient examples justified: and at this day, the ordinary players in Italy, will not err in. Yet will some bring in an example of *Eunuchus* in Terence, that containeth matter of two days, yet far short of twenty years. True it is, and so was it to be played in two days, and so fitted to the time it set forth. And though Plautus hath in one place[234] done amiss, let us hit with him, and not miss with him. But they will say, how then shall we set forth a story, which containeth both many places, and many times? And do they not know, that a tragedy is tied to the laws of poesy, and not of history? not bound to follow the story, but having liberty, either to feign a quite new matter, or to frame the history to the most tragical conveniency. Again, many things may be told which cannot be showed, if they know the difference betwixt reporting and repre-

232 **inartificially** unskillfully. 233 **traverses** passages; also, obstacles. 234 **in one place** Plautus' *Captives,* criticized by Scaliger for violating the unities of time.

senting. As for example, I may speak (though I am here)
of Peru, and in speech, digress from that, to the description of Calicut: but in action, I cannot represent it without
Pacolet's horse:[235] and so was the manner the ancients
took, by some *nuncius*,[236] to recount things done in former
time, or other place. Lastly, if they will represent an history, they must not (as Horace saith) begin *ab ovo*:[237] but
they must come to the principal point of that one action,
which they will represent. By example this will be best
expressed. I have a story of young Polydorus,[238] delivered
for safety's sake, with great riches, by his father Priamus,
to Polimnestor king of Thrace, in the Troyan war time.
He after some years, hearing the overthrow of Priamus,
for to make the treasure his own, murthereth the child:
the body of the child is taken up by Hecuba, she the same
day findeth a slight to be revenged most cruelly of the
tyrant: where now would one of our tragedy writers begin,
but with the delivery of the child? Then should he sail over
into Thrace, and so spend I know not how many years,
and travel numbers of places. But where doth Euripides?
Even with the finding of the body, leaving the rest to be
told by the spirit of Polydorus. This need no further to be
enlarged, the dullest wit may conceive it. But besides
these gross absurdities, how all their[239] plays be neither
right tragedies, nor right comedies: mingling kings and
clowns, not because the matter so carrieth it: but thrust
in clowns by head and shoulders, to play a part in majes-
tical matters, with neither decency, nor discretion. So as
neither the admiration and commiseration,[240] nor the right
sportfulness,[241] is by their mongrel tragi-comedy obtained.
I know Apuleius[242] did somewhat so, but that is a thing
recounted with space of time, not represented in one moment: and I know, the ancients have one or two examples
of tragi-comedies, as Plautus hath *Amphitrio*. But if we

---

[235] **Pacolet's horse** a flying horse, appearing in the romance *Valentine
and Orson* (1489).   [236] **nuncius** messenger.   [237] **ab ovo** from the egg;
from the beginning.   [238] **Polydorus** from Euripides' *Hecuba*.   [239] **their**
modern writers'.   [240] **admiration and commiseration** proper to tragedy.
[241] **right sportfulness** of comedy.   [242] **Apuleius** in the *Golden Ass*.

mark them well, we shall find, that they never, or very daintily, match horn-pipes and funerals. So falleth it out, that having indeed no right comedy, in that comical part of our tragedy, we have nothing but scurrility, unworthy of any chaste ears: or some extreme show of doltishness, indeed fit to lift up a loud laughter, and nothing else: where the whole tract[243] of a comedy should be full of delight, as the tragedy should be still maintained, in a well raised admiration. But our comedians, think there is no delight without laughter, which is very wrong, for though laughter may come with delight, yet cometh it not of delight, as though delight should be the cause of laughter, but well may one thing breed both together: nay, rather in themselves, they have as it were, a kind of contrariety: for delight we scarcely do, but in things that have a conveniency to ourselves, or to the general nature: laughter almost ever cometh, of things disproportioned to ourselves, and nature. Delight hath a joy in it, either permanent, or present. Laugher, hath only a scornful tickling.

For example, we are ravished with delight to see a fair woman, and yet are far from being moved to laughter. We laugh at deformed creatures, wherein certainly we cannot delight. We delight in good chances, we laugh at mischances; we delight to hear the happiness of our friends, or country; at which he were worthy to be laughed at, that would laugh; we shall contrarily laugh sometimes, to find a matter quite mistaken, and go down the hill against the bias, in the mouth of some such men, as for the respect of them, one shall be heartily sorry, yet he cannot choose but laugh; and so is rather pained, than delighted with laughter. Yet deny I not, but that they may go well together, for as in Alexander's picture well set out, we delight without laughter, and in twenty mad antics[244] we laugh without delight: so in Hercules, painted with his great beard and furious countenance, in woman's attire, spinning at Omphale's commandment, it breedeth both delight and laughter. For the representing of so strange a power in love, procureth delight: and the scornfulness of the action, stirreth

243 **tract** extent; also, treatment.   244 **mad antics** insane dances.

laughter. But I speak to this purpose, that all the end of
the comical part, be not upon such scornful matters, as
stirreth laughter only: but mixed with it, that delightful
teaching which is the end of poesy. And the great fault
even in that point of laughter, and forbidden plainly by
Aristotle, is, that they stir laughter in sinful things; which
are rather execrable than ridiculous: or in miserable, which
are rather to be pitied than scorned. For what is it to make
folks gape at a wretched beggar, or a beggarly clown? or
against law of hospitality, to jest at strangers, because they
speak not English so well as we do? What do we learn,
sith it is certain

> *Nil habet infelix paupertas durius in se,*
> *Quam quod ridiculos homines facit.*[245]

But rather a busy loving courtier: a heartless threatening
Thraso.[246] A self-wise-seeming schoolmaster. An awry-
transformed[247] traveller. These, if we saw walk in stage
names, which we play naturally,[248] therein were delightful
laughter, and teaching delightfulness: as in the other,[249]
the tragedies of Buchanan,[250] do justly bring forth a divine
admiration. But I have lavished out too many words of this
play matter. I do it because as they are excelling parts of
poesy, so is there none so much used in England, and none
can be more pitifully abused. Which like an unmannerly
daughter, showing a bad education, causeth her mother
Poesy's honesty to be called in question.

Other sorts of poetry almost have we none, but that
lyrical kind of songs and sonnets: which, Lord, if he gave
us so good minds, how well it might be employed, and with
how heavenly fruit, both private and public, in singing the
praises of the immortal beauty: the immortal goodness of
that God, who giveth us hands to write, and wits to conceive, of which we might well want words, but never matter, of which, we could turn our eyes to nothing, but we

---

[245] **Nil . . . facit** Juvenal, *Satires*, III, 152–153: "Poverty contains no
harsher misery than that it makes men ridiculous." [246] **Thraso** see p.
241. [247] **awry-transformed** affected. [248] **naturally** i.e., offstage. [249] **the
other** tragedy. [250] **Buchanan** see p. 257.

should ever have new budding occasions. But truly many of such writings, as come under the banner of unresistible love, if I were a mistress, would never persuade me they were in love: so coldly they apply fiery speeches, as men that had rather read lovers' writings, and so caught up certain swelling phrases, which hang together, like a man which once told me, the wind was at northwest, and by south, because he would be sure to name winds enow: than that in truth they feel those passions, which easily (as I think) may be bewrayed, by that same forcibleness, or *energia* (as the Greeks call it) of the writer. But let this be a sufficient, though short note, that we miss the right use of the material point of poesy.

Now, for the outside of it, which is words, or (as I may term it) diction,[251] it is even well worse. So is that honey-flowing matron Eloquence, apparelled, or rather disguised, in a courtesan-like painted affectation: one time with so far-fet words, they may seem monsters: but must seem strangers, to any poor English man. Another time, with coursing of a letter,[252] as if they were bound to follow the method of a dictionary: another time, with figures and flowers,[253] extremely winter-starved. But I would this fault were only peculiar to versifiers, and had not as large possession among prose-printers; and (which is to be marveled) among many scholars; and (which is to be pitied) among some preachers. Truly I could wish, if at least I might be so bold, to wish in a thing beyond the reach of my capacity, the diligent imitators of Tully, and Demosthenes (most worthy to be imitated) did not so much keep Nizolian[254] paperbooks of their figures and phrases, as by attentive translation[255] (as it were) devour them whole, and make them wholly theirs. For now they cast sugar and spice, upon every dish that is served to the table; like those Indians, not content to wear ear-rings at the fit and natural place of the

---

[251] **diction** choice of words.   [252] **coursing . . . letter** "hunting the letter," alliteration.   [253] **figures and flowers** see *Astrophel and Stella*, sonnet 15. [254] **Nizolian** the *Thesaurus Ciceronianus* of Nizolius, a handbook of Ciceronian phrases, abused by Cicero's slavish imitators.   [255] **translation** (1) transformation; (2) transfer (legal term, used of property).

ears, but they will thrust jewels through their nose, and lips because they will be sure to be fine.

Tully, when he was to drive out Catiline, as it were with a thunder-bolt of eloquence, often used that figure of repetition,[256] *Vivit, vivit? imo in Senatun: venit &c.* Indeed, inflamed with a well-grounded rage, he would have his words (as it were) double out of his mouth: and so do that artificially, which we see men do in choler naturally And we, having noted the grace of those words, hale them in sometime to a familiar epistle, when it were too too much choler to be choleric. How well store of *similiter cadences*[257] doth sound with the gravity of the pulpit, I would but invoke Demosthenes' soul to tell, who with a rare daintiness useth them. Truly they have made me think of the sophister,[258] that with too much subtlety would prove two eggs three; and though he might be counted a sophister, had none for his labor. So these men bringing in such a kind of eloquence, well may they obtain an opinion of a seeming fineness, but persuade few, which should be the end of their fineness.

Now for similitudes,[259] in certain printed discourses, I think all herbarists, all stories of beasts, fowls, and fishes are rifled up, that they come in multitudes, to wait upon any of our conceits; which certainly is as absurd a surfeit to the ears, as is possible: for the force of a similitude, not being to prove anything to a contrary disputer, but only to explain to a willing hearer, when that is done, the rest is a most tedious prattling: rather over-swaying the memory from the purpose whereto they were applied, than any whit informing the judgement, already either satisfied, or by similitudes not to be satisfied. For my part, I do not doubt, when Antonius and Crassus, the great forefathers of Cicero in eloquence, the one (as Cicero testifieth of them) pretended not to know art, the other, not to set by it: because with a plain sensibleness, they might win credit of popular

---

[256] **that . . . repetition** doubling a word.   [257] **similiter cadences** similar endings of sentences, whether in rhyming syllables or in similar rhythms. [258] **sophister** logician.   [259] **similitudes** similes, see *Astrophel and Stella*, sonnet 3.

ears: which credit, is the nearest step to persuasion: which persuasion, is the chief mark of oratory; I do not doubt (I say) but that they used these tracks[260] very sparingly, which who doth generally use, any man may see doth dance to his own music: and so be noted by the audience, more careful to speak curiously,[261] than to speak truly.

Undoubtedly (at least to my opinion undoubtedly) I have found in divers smally learned courtiers, a more sound style, than in some professors of learning: of which I can guess no other cause, but that the courtier following that which by practice he findeth fittest to nature, therein, (though he know it not) doth according to art, though not by art: where the other, using art to show art, and not to hide art (as in these cases he should do), flieth from nature, and indeed abuseth art.

But what? methinks I deserve to be pounded,[262] for straying from poetry to oratory: but both have such an affinity in this wordish consideration,[263] that I think this digression, will make my meaning receive the fuller understanding: which is not to take upon me to teach poets how they should do, but only finding myself sick among the rest, to show some one or two spots of the common infection, grown among the most part of writers: that acknowledging ourselves somewhat awry, we may bend to the right use both of matter and manner; whereto our language giveth us great occasion, being indeed capable of any excellent exercising of it. I know, some will say it is a mingled language.[264] And why not so much the better, taking the best of both[265] the other? Another will say it wanteth grammar. Nay truly, it hath that praise, that it wanteth not grammar: for grammar it might have, but it needs it not; being so easy of itself, and so void of those cumbersome differences of cases, genders, moods, and tenses, which I think was a piece of the Tower of Babylon's[266] curse, that a man should be put to school to learn

---

[260] **tracks** features. Alt. reading: "knacks." [261] **curiously** strangely; also, elaborately. [262] **pounded** impounded. [263] **wordish consideration** his subject matter: "diction." [264] **mingled language** drawing upon the roots of several languages. [265] **both** Latin and Greek. [266] **Babylon** believed to have been built over the spot where the tower of Babel stood.

his mother-tongue. But for the uttering sweetly, and properly the conceits of the mind, which is the end of speech, that hath it equally with any other tongue in the world: and is particularly happy in compositions[267] of two or three words together, near the Greek, far beyond the Latin: which is one of the greatest beauties can be in a language.

Now, of versifying there are two sorts, the one ancient, the other modern: the ancient marked the quantity of each syllable, and according to that, framed his verse: the modern, observing only number[268] (with some regard of the accent), the chief life of it, standeth in that like sounding of the words, which we call rhyme. Whether of these be the most excellent, would bear many speeches. The ancient (no doubt) more fit for music, both words and time observing quantity, and more fit lively to express divers passions, by the low or lofty sound of the well-weighed syllable. The latter[269] likewise, with his rhyme, striketh a certain music to the ear: and in fine, sith it doth delight, though by another way, it obtains the same purpose: there being in either sweetness, and wanting in neither majesty. Truly the English, before any other vulgar language I know, is fit for both sorts: for for the ancient, the Italian is so full of vowels, that it must ever be cumbered with elisions.[270] The Dutch,[271] so of the other side with consonants, that they cannot yield the sweet sliding, fit for a verse. The French, in his whole language, hath not one word, that hath his accent in the last syllable, saving two, called *antepenultima*, and little more hath the Spanish: and therefore, very gracelessly may they use *dactyls*. The English is subject to none of these defects.

Now, for the rhyme,[272] though we do not observe quantity, yet we observe the accent very precisely: which other languages, either cannot do, or will not do so absolutely. That *caesura,* or breathing place in the middest of the verse,

---

[267] **compositions** compound words (many of which were coined by Sidney himself). [268] **quantity . . . number** opposing stress accent (number) to assigned length (quantity) for vowels, according to rules and their position. [269] **latter** i.e., the modern. [270] **elisions** contractions of sound when two vowels stand together. [271] **Dutch** German. [272] **rhyme** i.e., modern accentual verse.

neither Italian nor Spanish have, the French and we, never almost fail of. Lastly, even the very rhyme itself, the Italian cannot put in the last syllable, by the French named the masculine rhyme, but still in the next to the last, which the French call the female; or the next before that, which the Italians term *sdrucciola*. The example of the former, is *buono, suono,* of the *sdrucciola, femina, semina.* The French, of the other side, hath both the male, as *bon, son,* and the female, as *plaise, taise.* But the *sdrucciola* he hath not: where the English hath all three, as *due, true, father, rather, motion, potion;*[273] with much more which might be said, but that I find already the triflingness of this discourse, is much too much enlarged. So that sith the ever-praise-worthy poesy, is full of virtue-breeding delightfulness, and void of no gift, that ought to be in the noble name of learning: sith the blames laid against it are either false, or feeble: sith the cause why it is not esteemed in England, is the fault of poet-apes, not poets: sith, lastly, our tongue is most fit to honor poesy, and to be honored by poesy, I conjure you all, that have had the evil luck to read this ink-wasting toy of mine, even in the name of the nine Muses, no more to scorn the sacred mysteries of poesy: no more to laugh at the name of poets, as though they were next inheritors to fools: no more to jest at the reverent title of a rhymer: but to believe with Aristotle, that they were the ancient treasurers, of the Graecians' divinity. To believe with Bembus, that they were first bringers in of all civility. To believe with Scaliger, that no philosopher's precepts can sooner make you an honest man, than the reading of Virgil. To believe with Clauserus, the translator of Cornutus, that it pleased the heavenly Deity, by Hesiod and Homer, under the veil of fables, to give us all knowledge, logic, rhetoric, philosophy, natural and moral: and *quid non*? To believe with me, that there are many mysteries contained in poetry, which of purpose were written darkly, least by profane wits, it should be abused. To believe with Landin, that they are so beloved of the Gods, that whatsoever they write, proceeds of a divine fury. Lastly, to believe themselves,

[273] **motion, potion** in three syllables, with accent on the first.

when they tell you they will make you immortal, by their verses.

Thus doing, your name shall flourish in the printers' shops; thus doing, you shall be of kin to many a poetical preface; thus doing, you shall be most fair, most rich, most wise, most all: you shall dwell upon superlatives. Thus doing, though you be *libertino patre natus*,[274] you shall suddenly grow *Herculea proles*.[275]

> *Si quid mea carmina possunt.*[276]

Thus doing, your soul shall be placed with Dante's Beatrix, or Virgil's Anchises. But if (fie of such a but) you be born so near the dull making cataract of Nilus, that you cannot hear the planet-like music of poetry, if you have so earth-creeping a mind, that it cannot lift itself up, to look to the sky of poetry; or rather, by a certain rustical disdain, will become such a Mome,[277] as to be a Momus of Poetry: then, though I will not wish unto you, the ass's ears of Midas,[278] nor to be driven by a poet's verses (as Bubonax was) to hang himself, nor to be rhymed to death, as it is said to be done in Ireland: yet thus much curse I must send you, in the behalf of all poets, that while you live, you live in love, and never get favor, for lacking skill of a sonnet: and when you die, your memory die from the earth, for want of an epitaph.

FINIS

---

[274] **libertino . . . natus** son of a freedman. [275] **Herculea proles** offspring of Hercules. [276] **Si . . . possunt** Virgil, *Aeneid*, IX, 446, "If my songs can do it." Virgil's context is conferring fame. [277] **Mome** blockhead; from Momus, the son of night. [278] **Midas** given ass's ears for preferring the music of Pan to that of Apollo.

☐ **THE SELECTED POETRY OF BROWNING edited by George Ridenour.** Includes *Pauline*, selections from *The Ring and the Book*, *St. Martin's Summer*, *Fra Lippo Lippi*, *Childe Roland* to the *Dark Tower Came*, and longer works often omitted in standard anthologies. Introduction, Chronology, Bibliography. (#CQ313—95¢)

☐ **THE SELECTED POETRY AND PROSE OF BYRON edited by W. H. Auden.** A comprehensive collection which includes *Beppo*, *Epistle to Augusta*, selections from *Don Juan*, *Childe Harold*, *English Bards* and *Scotch Reviewers*, and extracts from the journals and letters. Introduction, Chronology, Bibliography. (#CQ346—95¢)

☐ **THE SELECTED POETRY OF KEATS edited by Paul de Man.** The major long poems, all the "Odes," many sonnets, and several letters. Introduction, Chronology, Bibliography. (#CQ325—95¢)

☐ **THE SELECTED POETRY AND PROSE OF SHELLEY edited by Harold Bloom, Yale University.** All the major and most of the minor poems. Sixty selections including *Mutability*, *Prometheus Unbound*, *Ode to the West Wind*, selections from *Hellas*, and *A Defense of Poetry*. (#CQ342—95¢)

☐ **THE SELECTED POETRY OF MARVELL edited and with an introduction by Frank Kermode, University of Bristol.** Representative selections from the poet's political, pastoral, satirical, lyric and philosophical work, including *The Garden*, *Upon Appleton House*, *To His Coy Mistress*, *An Horation Ode upon Cromwell's Return from Ireland*. Chronology, Bibliography, Index of First Lines. (#CQ363—95¢)

𝒪